CHEPSTOW
THROUGH TIME
Keith E. Morgan

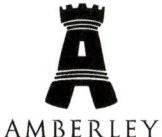

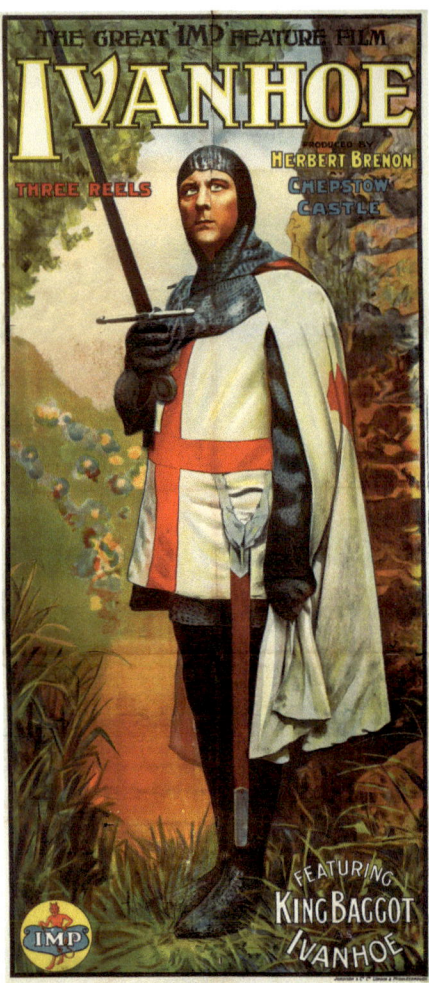

Ivanhoe

In 1913, Chepstow Castle was the location for the first feature silent film version of Sir Walter Scott's classic novel *Ivanhoe*. The studio spent a record amount of money on the film, which was the first example of a studio sending a cast and crew to a remote venue to shoot on location. Completed on 15 July 1913, *Ivanhoe* was described as the biggest venture of its kind attempted before on British soil. To celebrate the 100th anniversary of the making of the film, it was shown to a capacity audience of over 400 at Chepstow Castle in July 2013.

This book is dedicated in memory of Malvina, 'My Special Angell'.

First published 2016

Amberley Publishing
The Hill, Stroud, Gloucestershire, GL5 4EP
www.amberley-books.com

Copyright © Keith E. Morgan, 2016

The right of Keith E. Morgan to be identified as the Author of this work has been asserted in accordance with the Copyrights, Designs and Patents Act 1988.

ISBN 978 1 4456 5506 2 (print)
ISBN 978 1 4456 5507 9 (ebook)

All rights reserved. No part of this book may be reprinted or reproduced or utilised in any form or by any electronic, mechanical or other means, now known or hereafter invented, including photocopying and recording, or in any information storage or retrieval system, without the permission in writing from the Publishers.

British Library Cataloguing in Publication Data.
A catalogue record for this book is available from the British Library.

Origination by Amberley Publishing.
Printed in Great Britain.

Appointed GPSR EU Representative: Easy Access System Europe Oü, 16879218
Address: Mustamäe tee 50, 10621, Tallinn, Estonia
Contact Details: gpsr.requests@easproject.com, +358 40 500 3575

Introduction

Chepstow (Welsh: *Cas-gwent*) is a town in Monmouthshire, Wales, adjoining the border with Gloucestershire, England. It is located on a bend of the River Wye (Welsh: *Afon Gwy*) about 2 miles above its confluence with the River Severn. The region has been continually occupied since the Neolithic period. It has always been considered as the focal point for crossings of the estuary, a physical feature that has been exploited from Roman times to the present day. A Roman civitas was built at Caerwent, 5 miles west of the present town, in about AD 78 when the native Silures tribe was finally subjected to Roman rule. Even though it is known that a Roman fort existed at Chepstow, its remains have not been located and the town itself can be considered to have been founded by the Normans who built a castle in 1067 on the clifftop above the River Wye. This castle, the oldest surviving post-Roman stone fortification in Britain, was extended many times over later centuries until it became a ruin following the Civil War.

The town still has its Norman Port Wall and the remains of a Benedictine priory, now the Parish Priory Church of St Mary. Chepstow received its first charter in 1524 and developed as a port which, in the 1790s, handled a greater tonnage of goods than Swansea, Cardiff and Newport combined. The late eighteenth century saw the town become a focus of early tourism as part of the 'Wye Tour', an industry that still plays a major part in the economy of Chepstow. In the past, fishing and small scale shipbuilding had been carried on for centuries, but during the First World War, the latter received a boost when a National Shipyard was built in the town to make the first prefabricated ships. Other heavy engineering works followed, which included bridge and wind turbine construction.

Chepstow Through Time offers the reader a real insight into the life and times of the town and of the many changes that have taken place over the years to enable it to grow to the prominence it enjoys today. Both the Romans and Normans recognised Chepstow for its commanding position covering the crossings of the Wye and Severn rivers. The Romans crossed at this point in AD 48. Since then, two ferries plied the River Severn for many years, a railway bridge once crossed the Wye about 8 miles upstream and today there are two major arterial motorway suspension bridges that span the waters to connect Wales with England. Brunel brought the South Wales Railway to Chepstow in 1850 and the famous railway tunnel under the River Severn was opened by the Great Western Railway in 1886. If we count the Aust Severn Powerline, this gives a total of eight crossings in the Chepstow area.

Keith E. Morgan

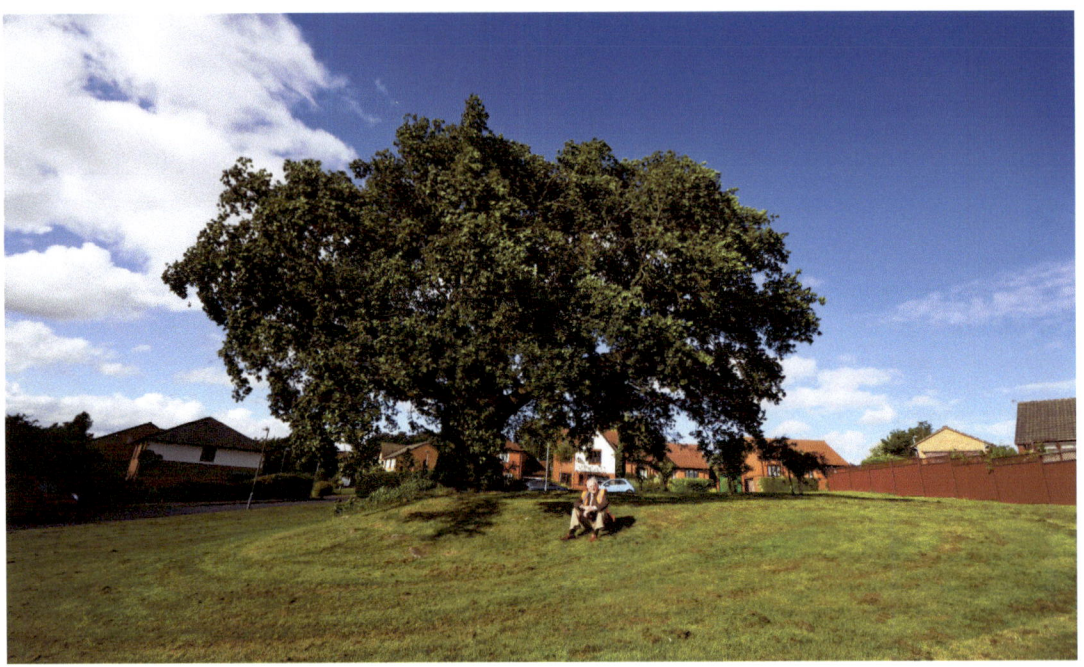

Neolithic Remains

On the Thornwell housing estate to the south of Chepstow are to be found the sad remains of a once-major Neolithic chambered tomb. They are situated under a very large old oak tree at Fountains Way where the remains of a large mound and protruding stones can be seen. Further to the east and a short distance away, the equally sad remains of a Bronze Age Barrow can also be seen. These two archaeological remains form the evidence of the oldest inhabitants of the Chepstow area.

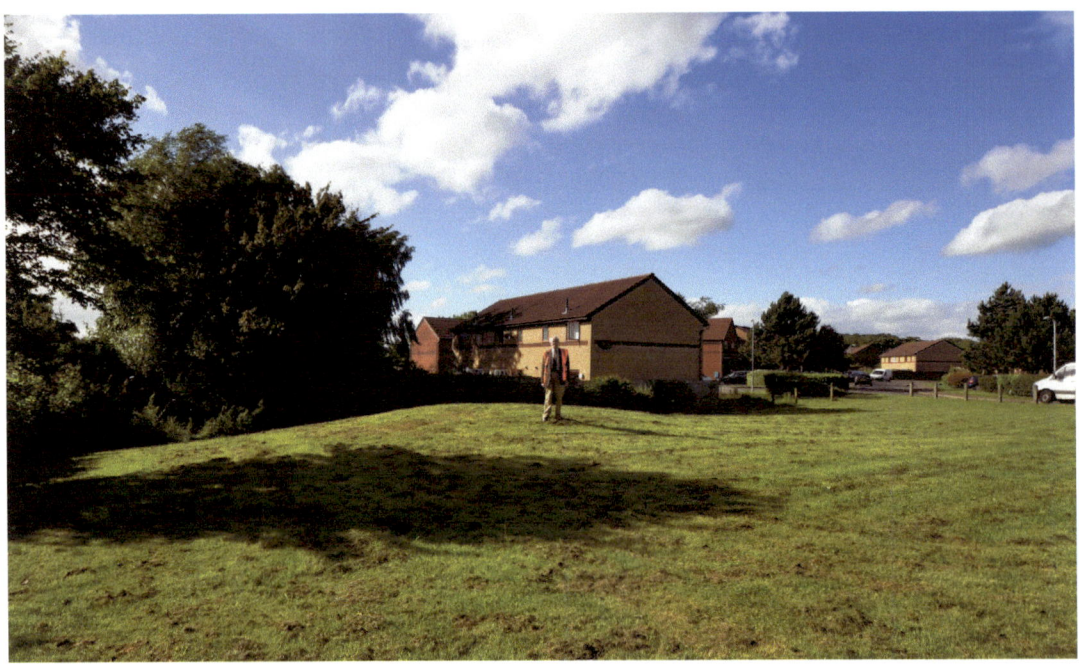

Bulwark(s) Camp

The Bulwark(s) Camp is a small promontory fort of the pre-Roman Iron Age to the south of Chepstow overlooking the Wye near its confluence with the Severn. The 2.5 acre camp was built by the Silures Tribe and is protected on the east side by cliffs, to the south by a steep sided ravine and on the remaining sides by a substantial double-earthen rampart. From the lower photograph, the camp's size can be visualised in comparison to the figure of fellow photographer Patrick Hogan, standing to the right of centre.

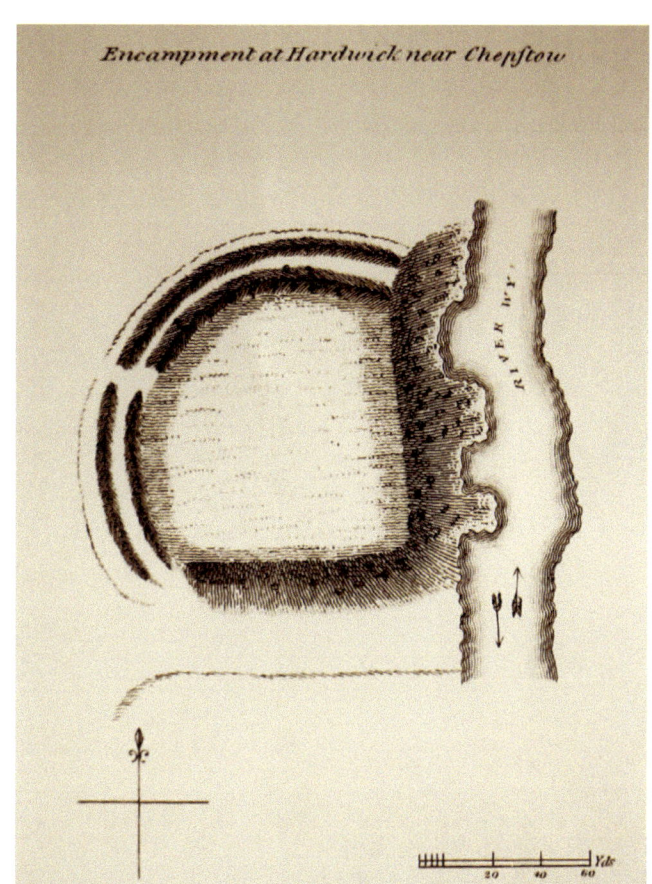

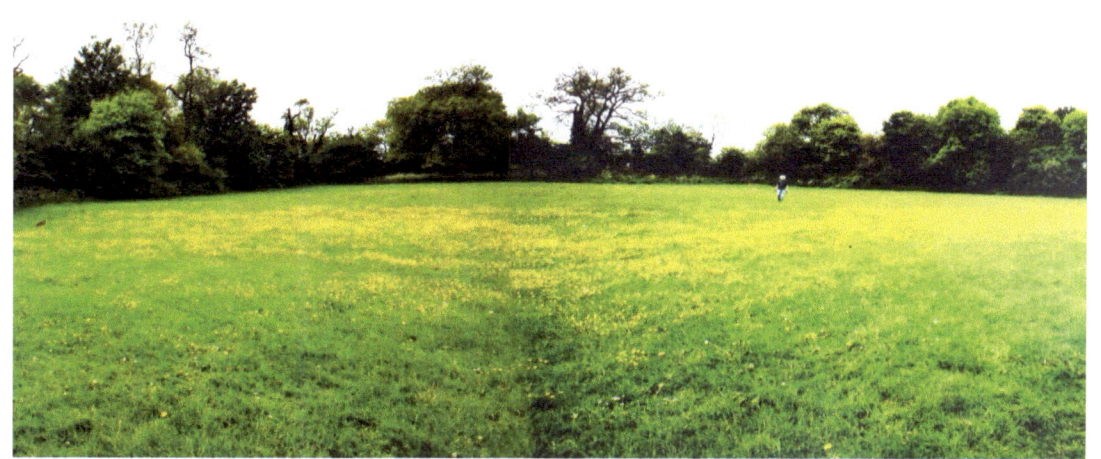

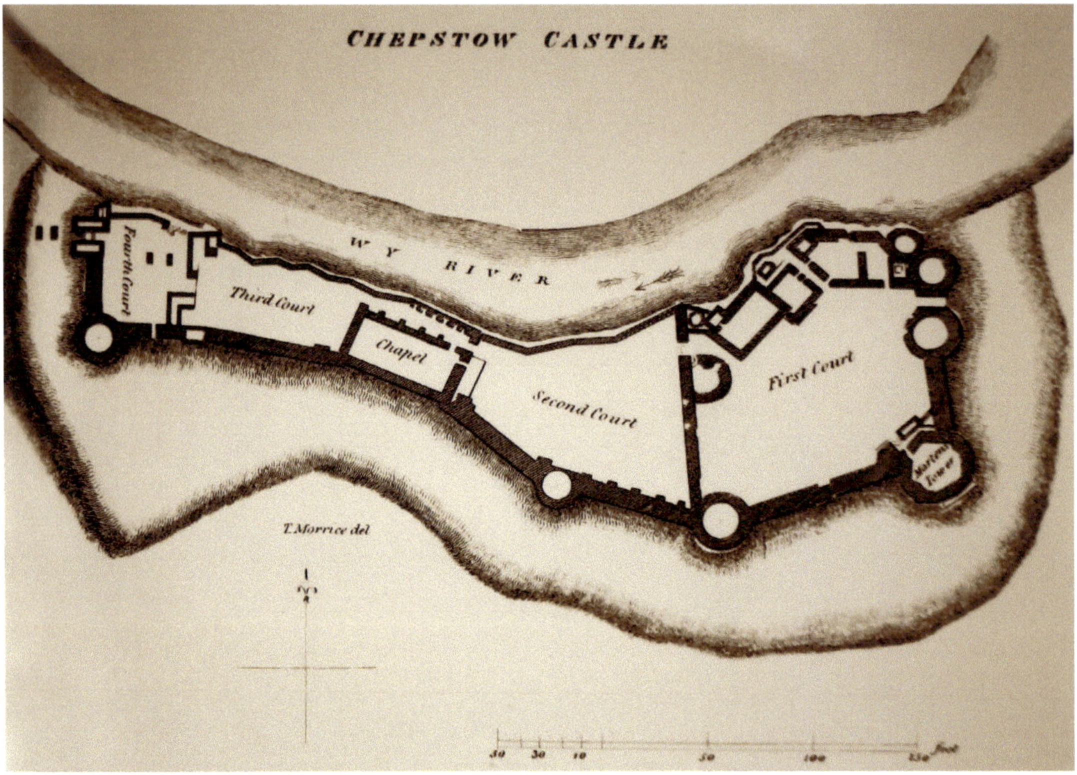

Chepstow Castle

It is to the Normans, who invaded Wales in the early years of the twelfth century, that we are indebted to for the origin of the castle and town of Chepstow on the banks of the River Wye. Possibly the site of a Roman or even earlier fortification, the building of the initial phase of Chepstow Castle, the Great Tower, was begun in 1067. The plan above of Chepstow Castle is dated 1801 and comes from William Coxe's *An Historical Tour in Monmouthshire*, though it incorrectly shows the central building as the 'Chapel' and not the 'Great Tower'.

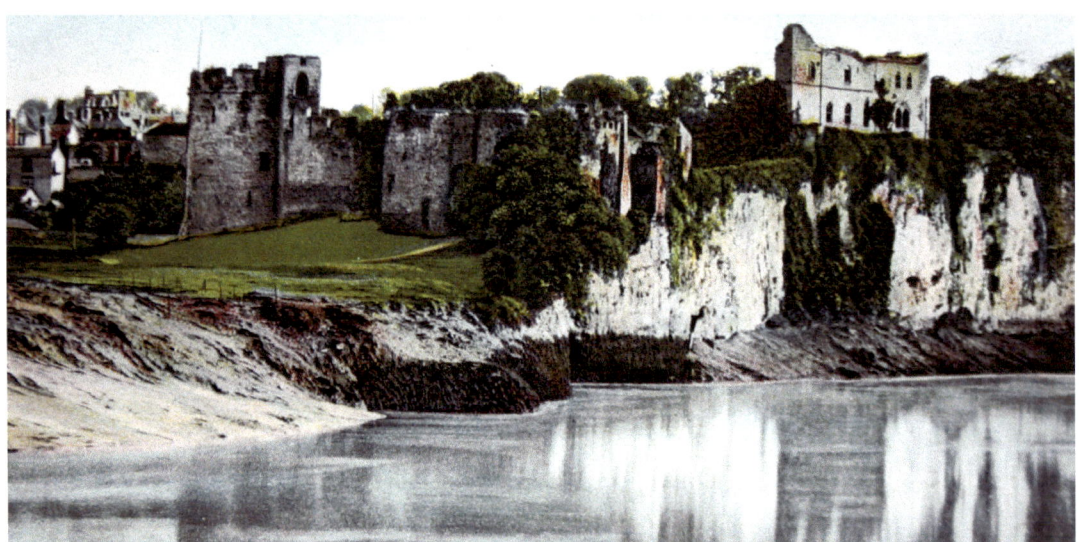

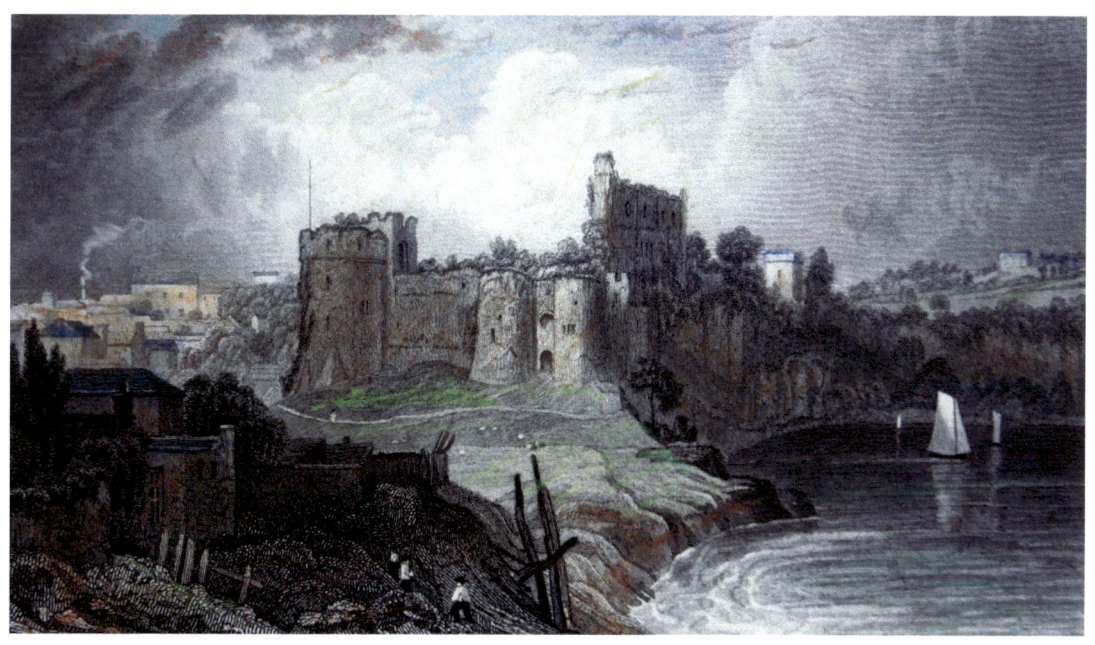

Chepstow Castle
Initially thought to have been constructed under the instructions of the Norman Lord William fitz Osbern, later thinking has come down in favour of perhaps William the Conqueror as the builder of Chepstow Castle's Great Tower, who wanted it as a great audience chamber. The two prints of the castle are from the 1850s period and show the Great Tower rising predominantly above the rest of the castle.

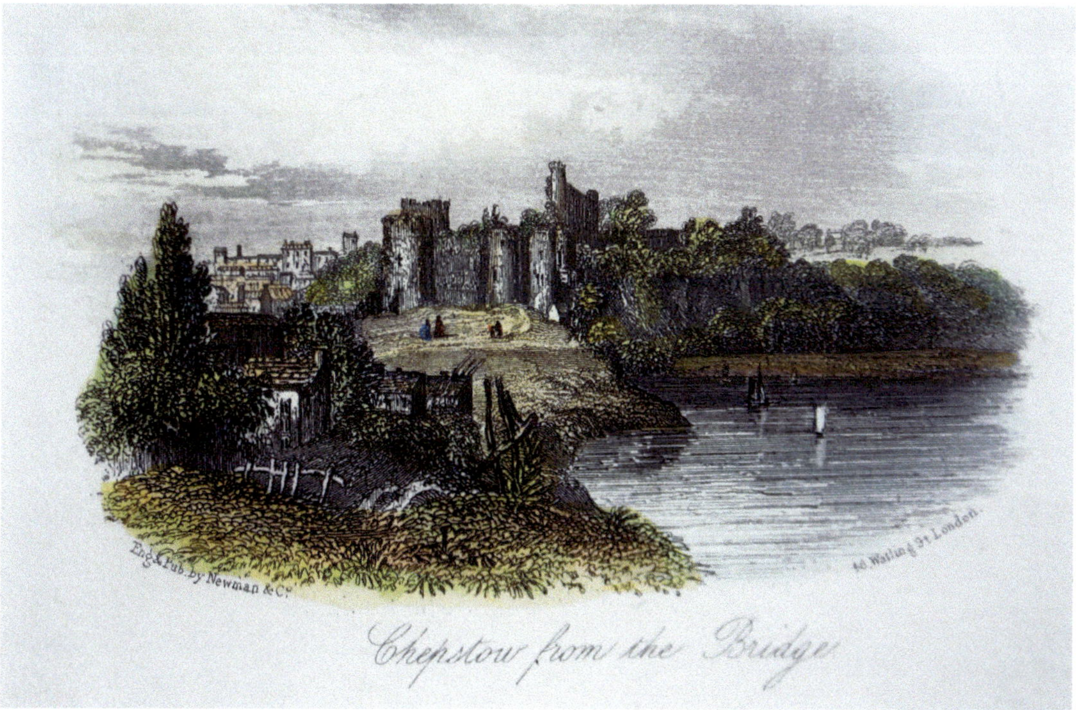

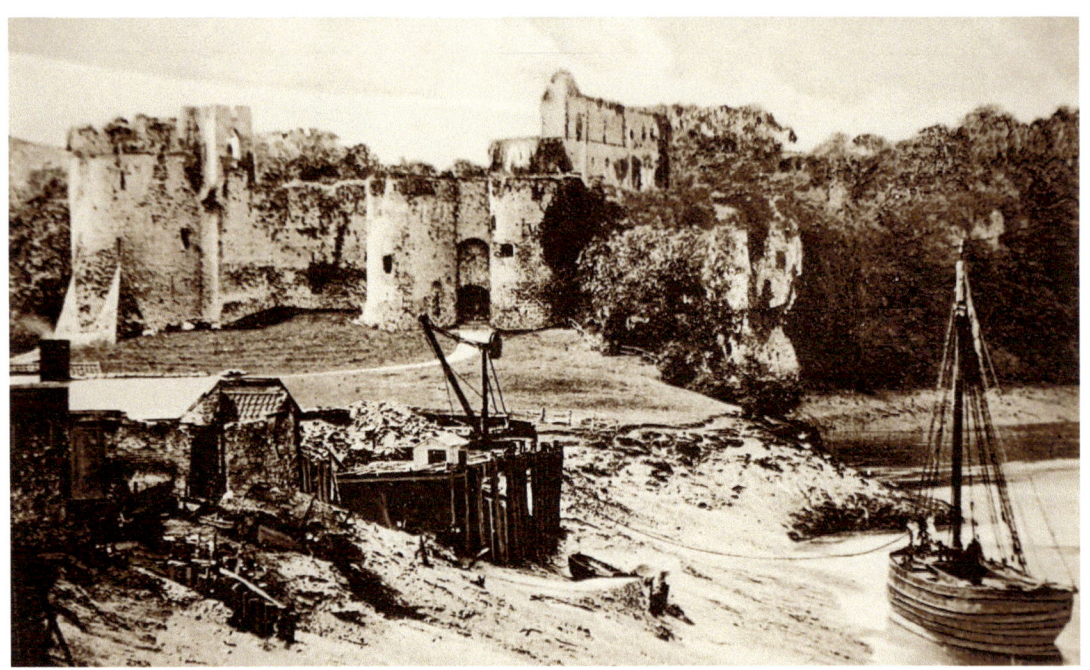

Chepstow Castle
The top photograph, taken from an early 1900s postcard, shows Chepstow Castle fronted by a small shipbuilding yard. The yard has long gone and the area known as The Gables is now occupied by the castle car park, toilets and information centre building.

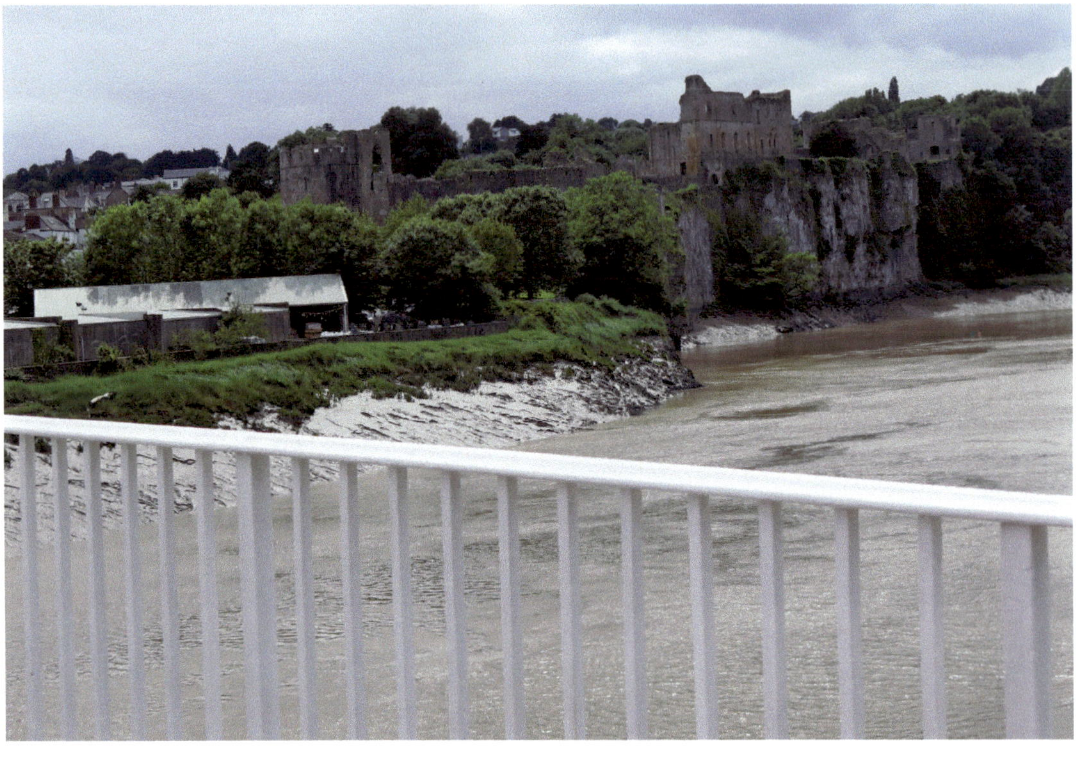

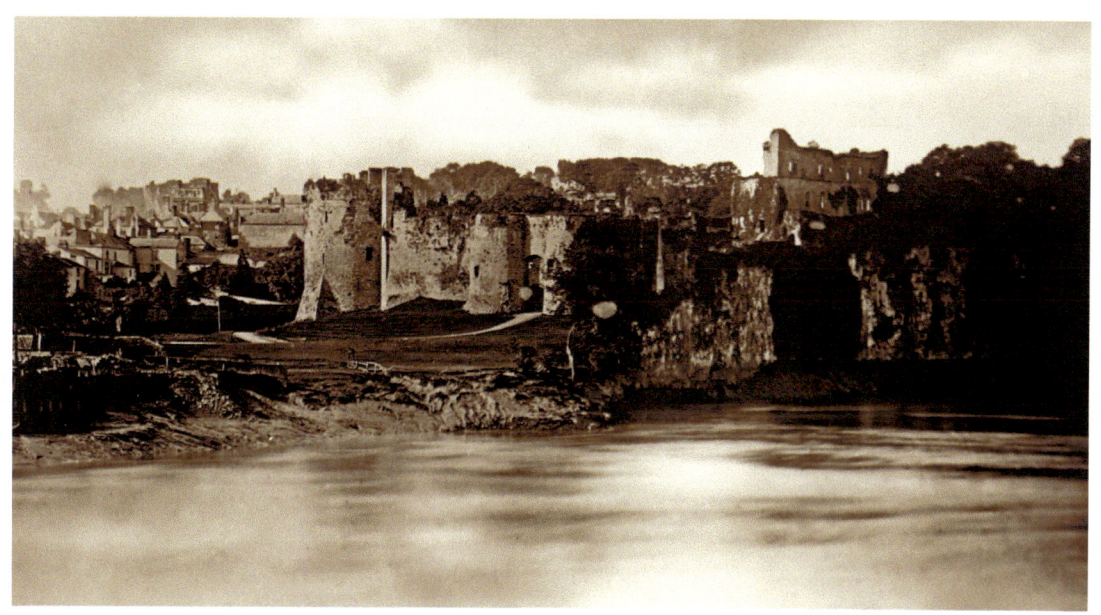

Chepstow Castle
The two photographs clearly show the strategic and commanding position of the Great Tower, together with that of the remainder of Chepstow Castle on the clifftop heights above the River Wye. In the lower photograph, Wye boatman Richard Dutson is dwarfed by the magnitude of both the cliffs and the Great Tower as he leisurely wends his way down the River Wye.

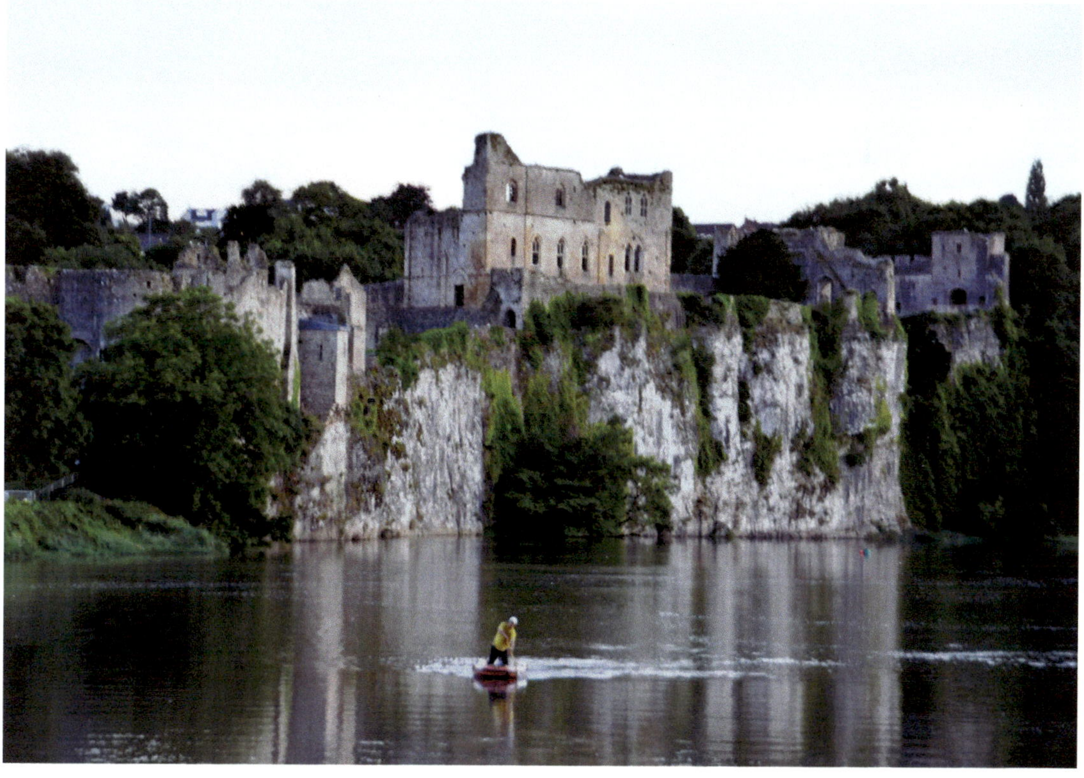

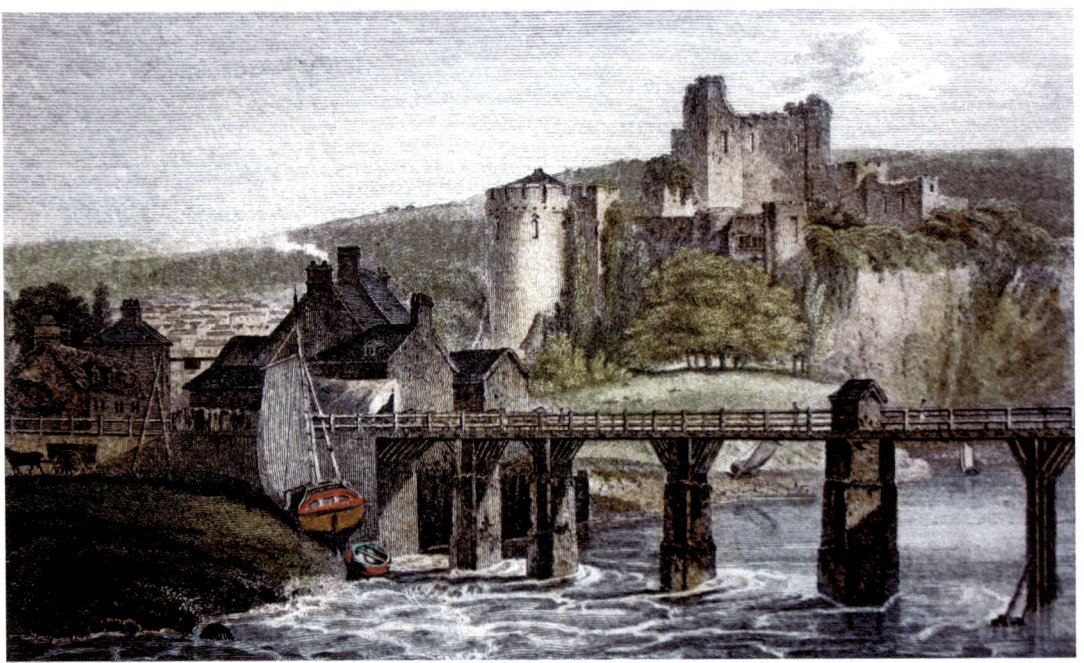

Chepstow Bridge

The Normans built a wooden bridge to span the Wye, which was first mentioned in 1228. There have been a succession of similar wooden trestle bridges crossing the Wye at this point up until 1815–16, when the present iron bridge was built. The top print shows the last of these wooden trestle bridges in what looks like a very good copy of Turner's 1793 watercolour of Chepstow Castle. In the lower image, photographer Patrick Hogan has captured a reflective Chepstow Bridge shrouded with a canopy of early morning 'will o' the wisp'.

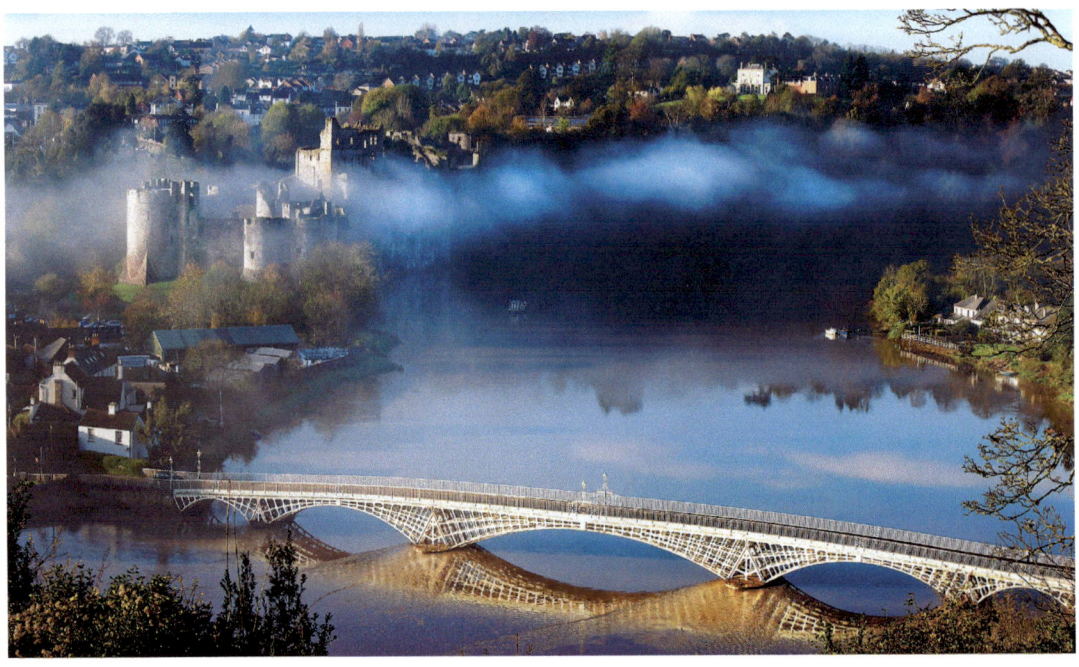

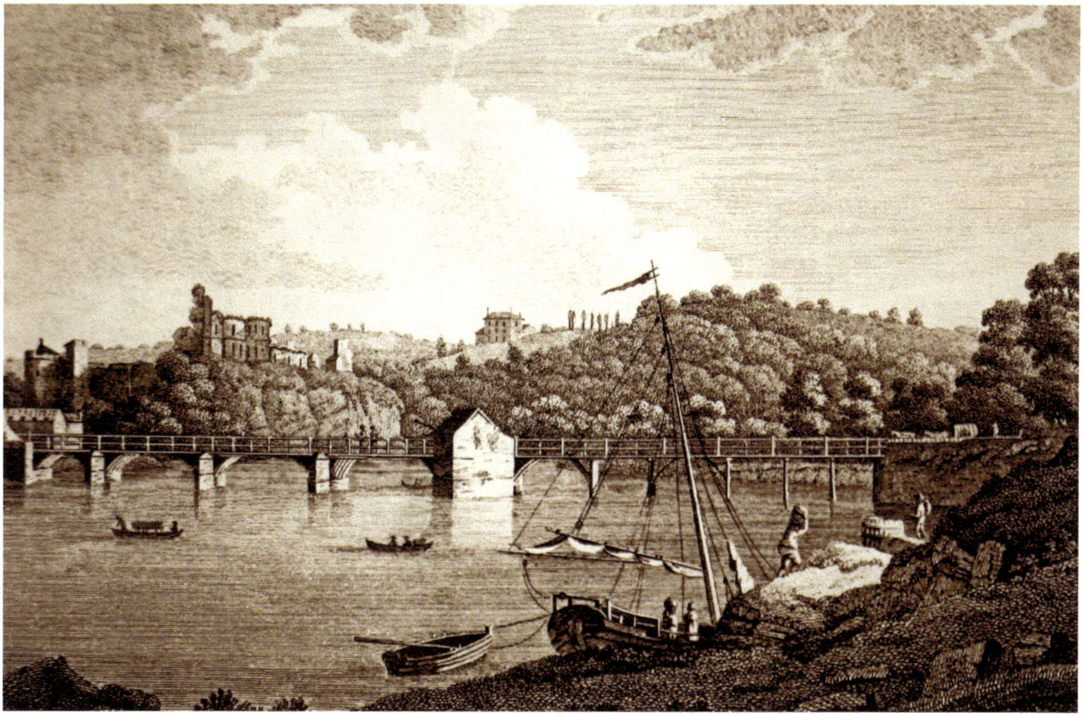

Chepstow Bridge

The top print, taken from William Coxe's 1801 edition of *An Historical Tour in Monmouthshire*, clearly shows the construction of the last wooden bridge to span the Wye at Chepstow. By 1810 this bridge was 'in decay' and estimates were sought to patch it up. However, a bold decision was taken and it was decided to have a new bridge built in iron and not traditional wood and stone.

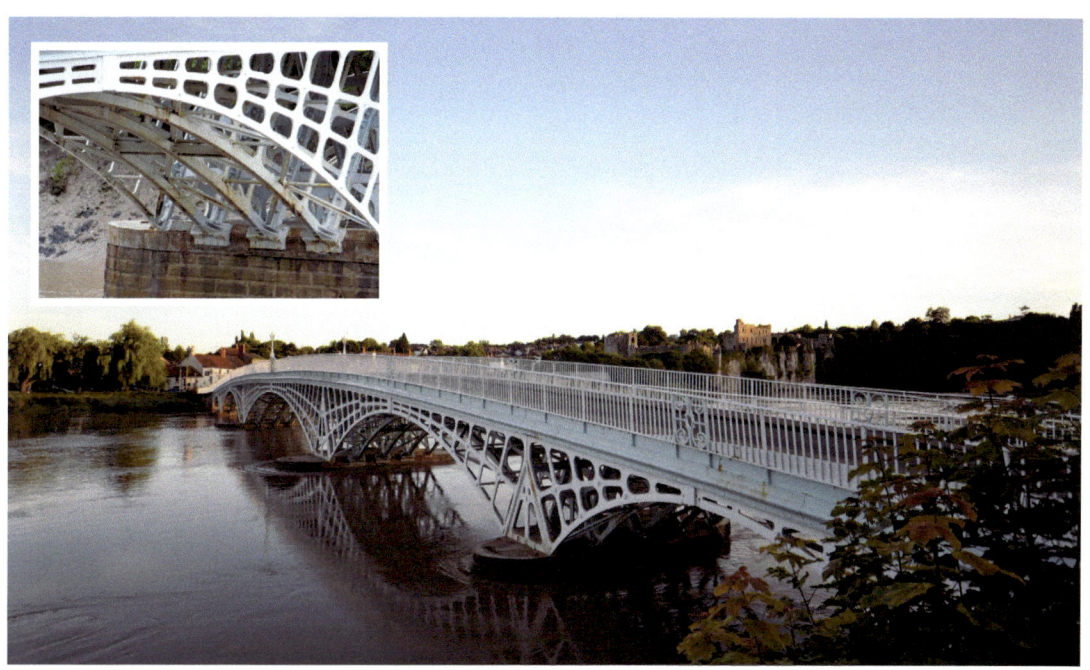

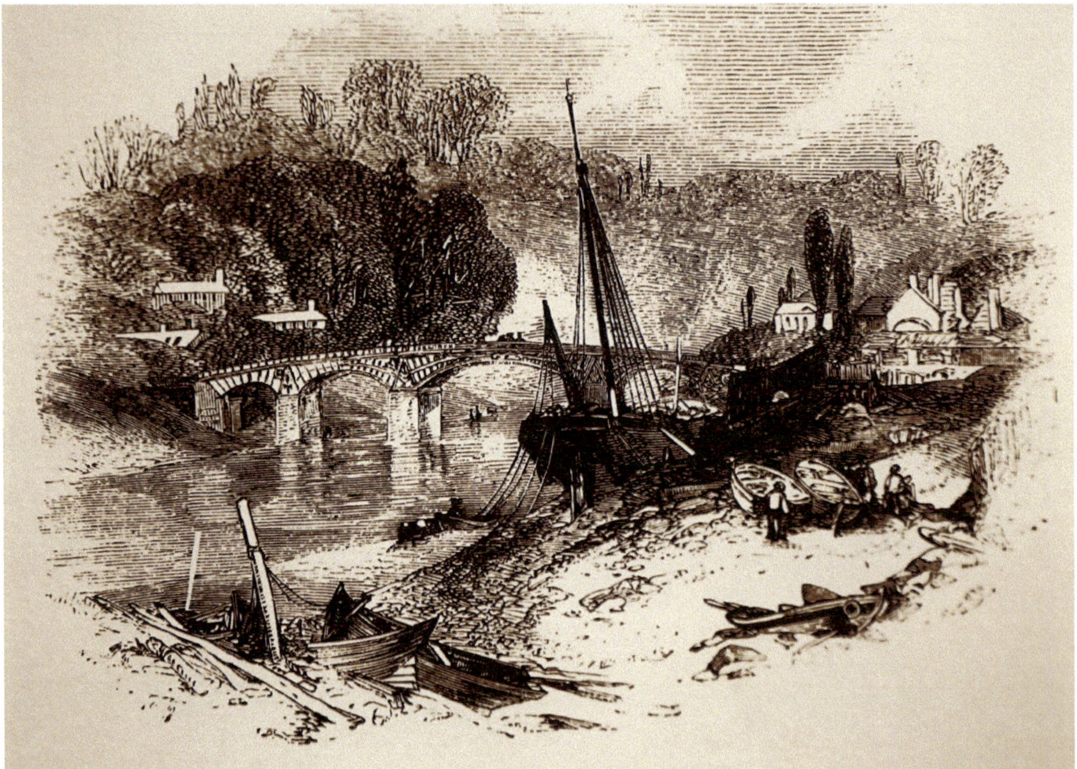

THE WYE BRIDGE, AT CHEPSTOW.

Chepstow Bridge

When Chepstow Bridge was opened on 24 July 1816 it was the third-largest iron arch bridge in the world and a pioneering achievement in its day. The top image is of an 1861 sketch of the bridge and shipyard drawn from a point in front of Chepstow Castle. The print has been taken from Mr and Mrs S. C. Hall's *The Book of the Wye* and shows the new iron Wye Bridge and shipyard. The bridge has long outlived the shipyard, as illustrated in the lower photograph.

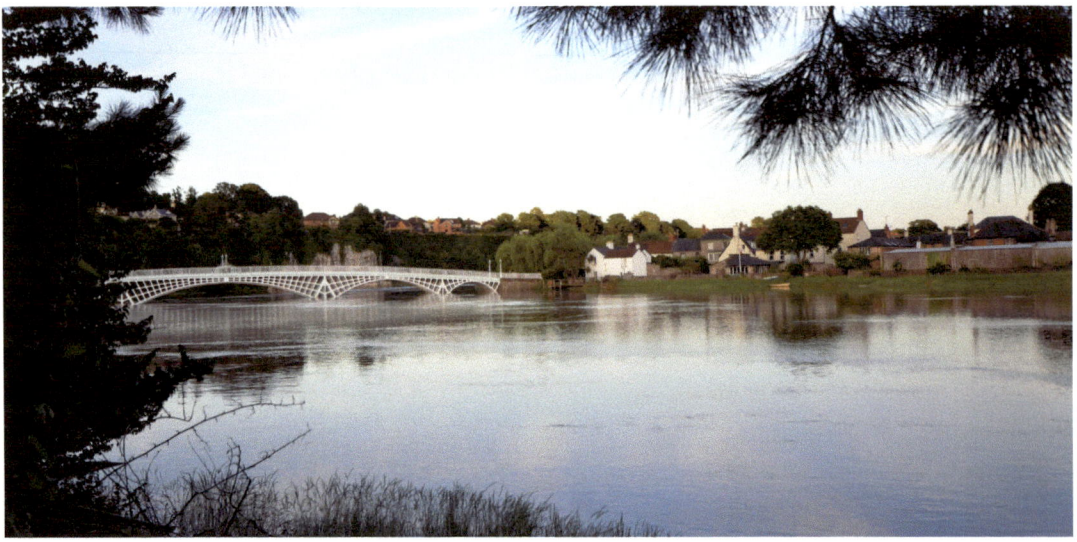

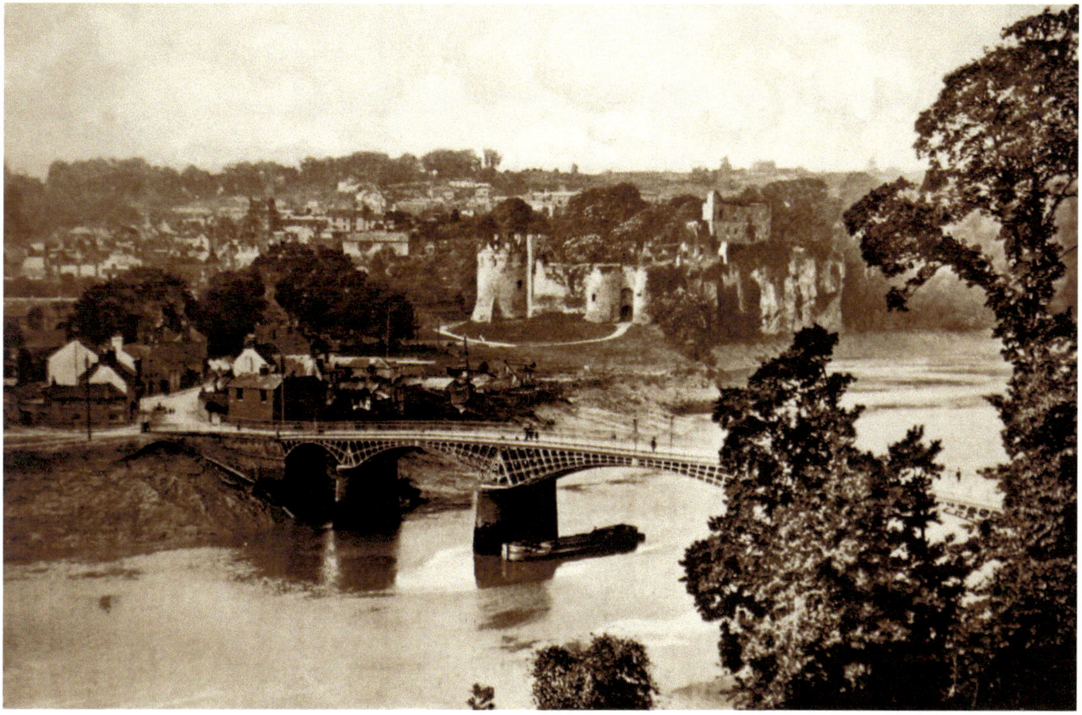

Chepstow Bridge
The bridge was designed by John Urpeth Rastrick and built at the Bridgnorth Foundry, of which he was the managing partner. Constructed of cast iron, it is 372 feet (113 metres) long with a central arch span of 112 feet (34 metres) and is Grade I listed. With its five arches rising to the centre of the river, it is the most graceful of all the Georgian-Regency iron arch road bridges and the largest remaining from that time anywhere in the world.

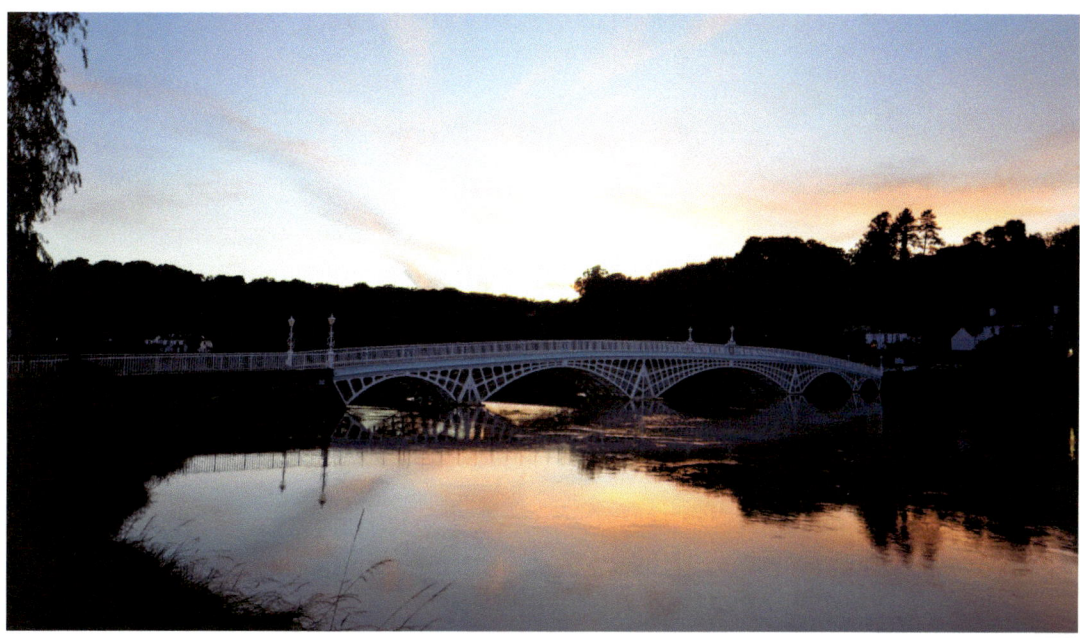

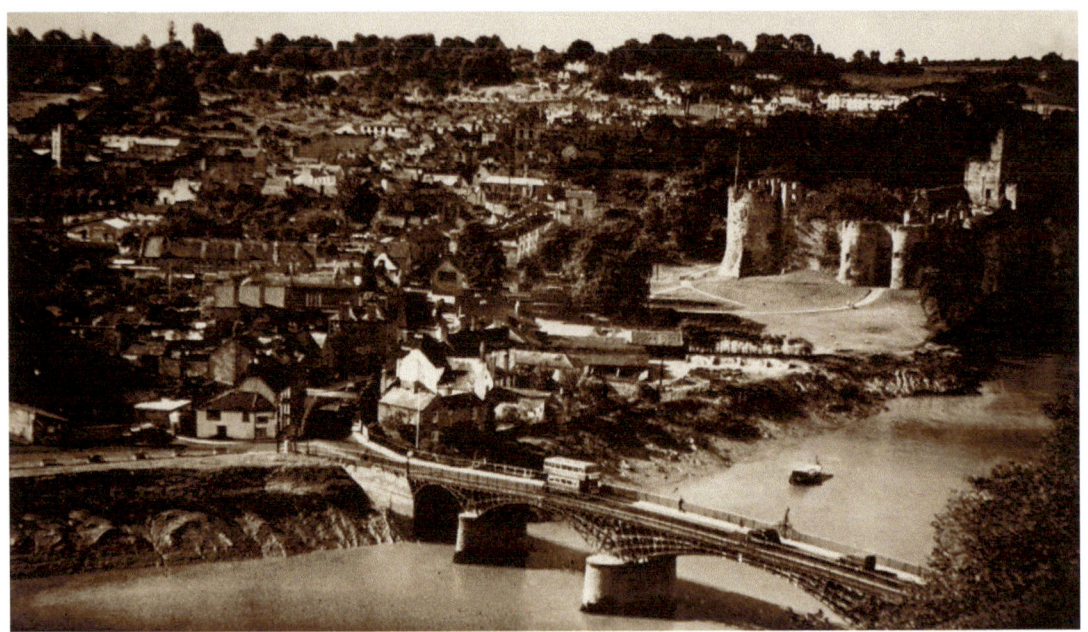

Chepstow Bridge

Until 1988, when a new road bridge was built downstream to take the Chepstow A48 Inner Relief Road, the Chepstow Bridge was the main highway across the Wye River. For 175 years, the cast-iron bridge carried the A48 main road traffic between Wales and England as well as all the traffic using the Beachley–Aust Ferry. The top postcard, which is franked 2 December 1951, shows a double-decker bus crossing the bridge. The Red & White headquarters were once in Chepstow so it was appropriate that two Vintage R&W buses took part in the opening re-enactment on 24 July 2016.

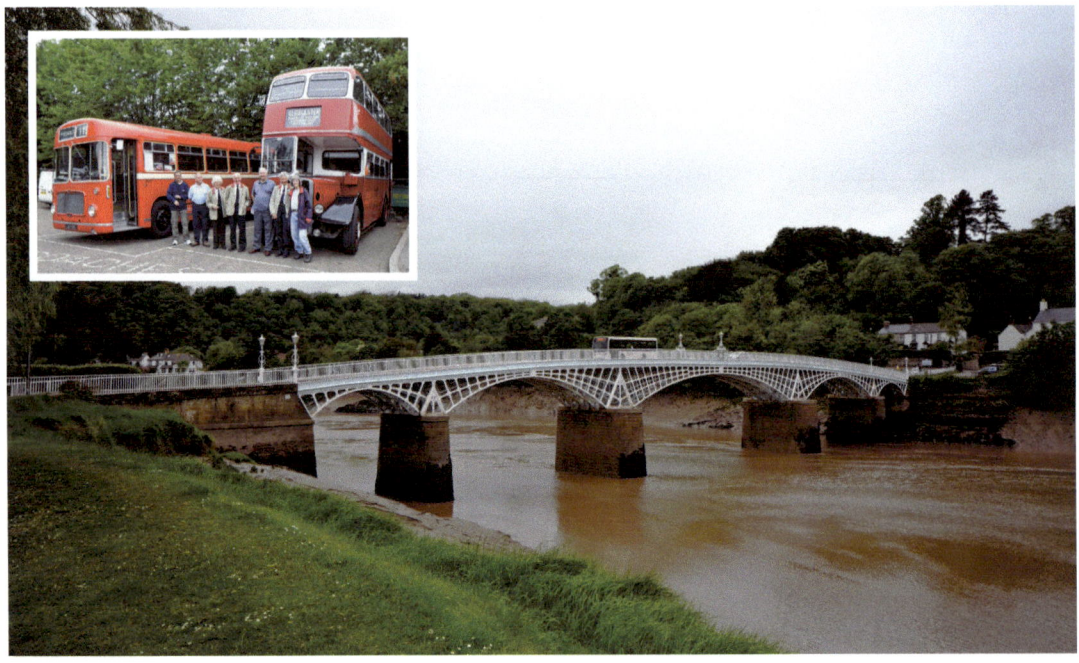

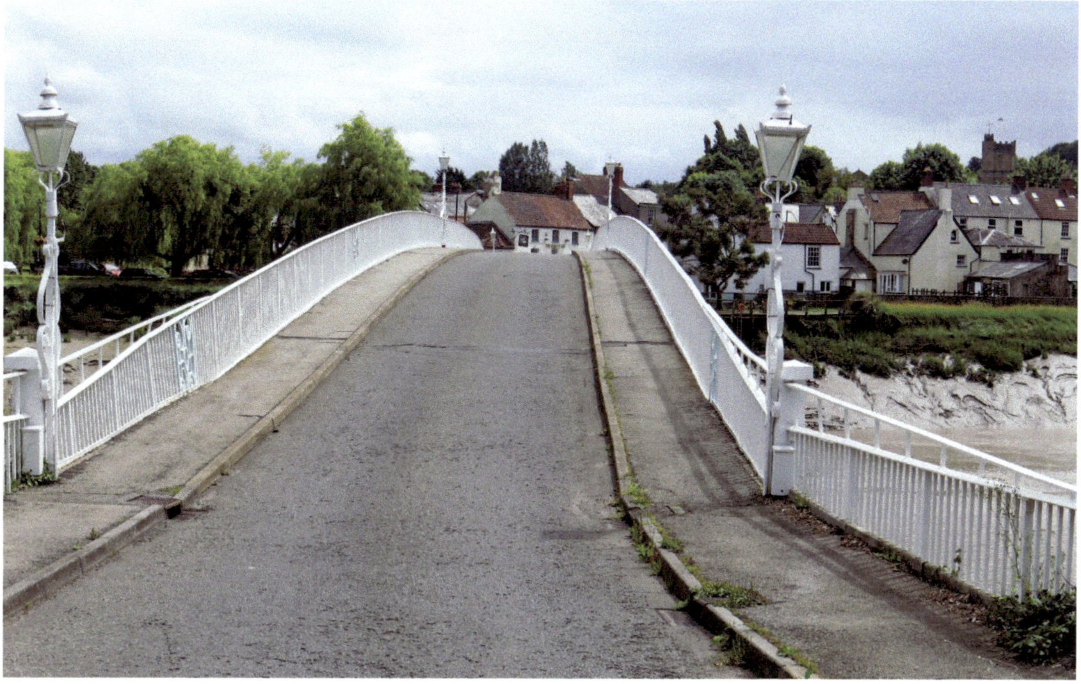

Chepstow Bridge
Chepstow is on the west bank of the Wye in Monmouthshire, Wales, while the adjoining villages on the eastern bank of the river, Tutshill and Sedbury, are located in Gloucestershire, England.

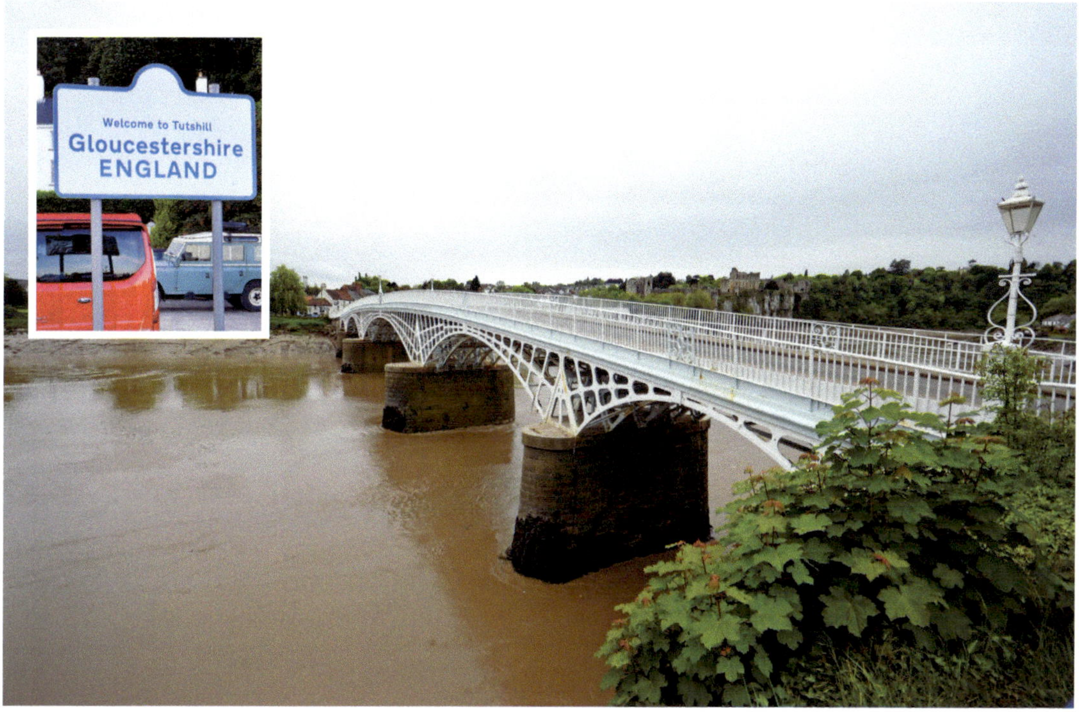

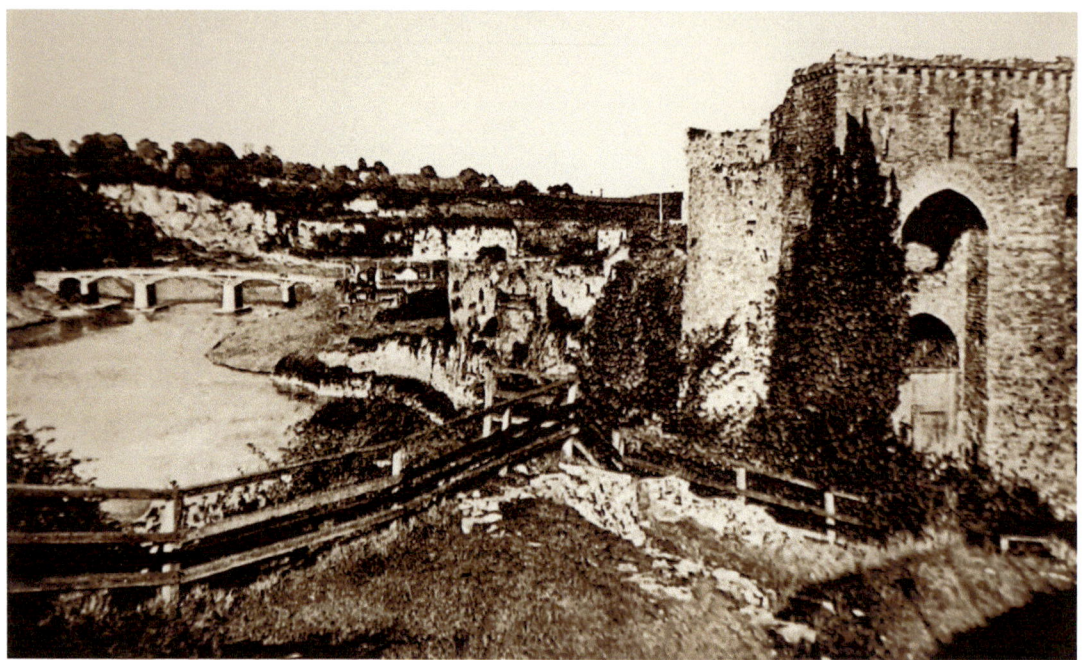

Chepstow Castle
The top image is taken from a postcard published sometime in the mid-1900s. Showing a different perspective of Chepstow Castle, it gives a clear view of the length of the fortification past the Upper Barbican to the bridge below. The inset photograph is of the latrines located in the domestic block while the lower picture is what you see when you look down the latrines to the river below; sewerage was obviously no problem to the Normans or their successors.

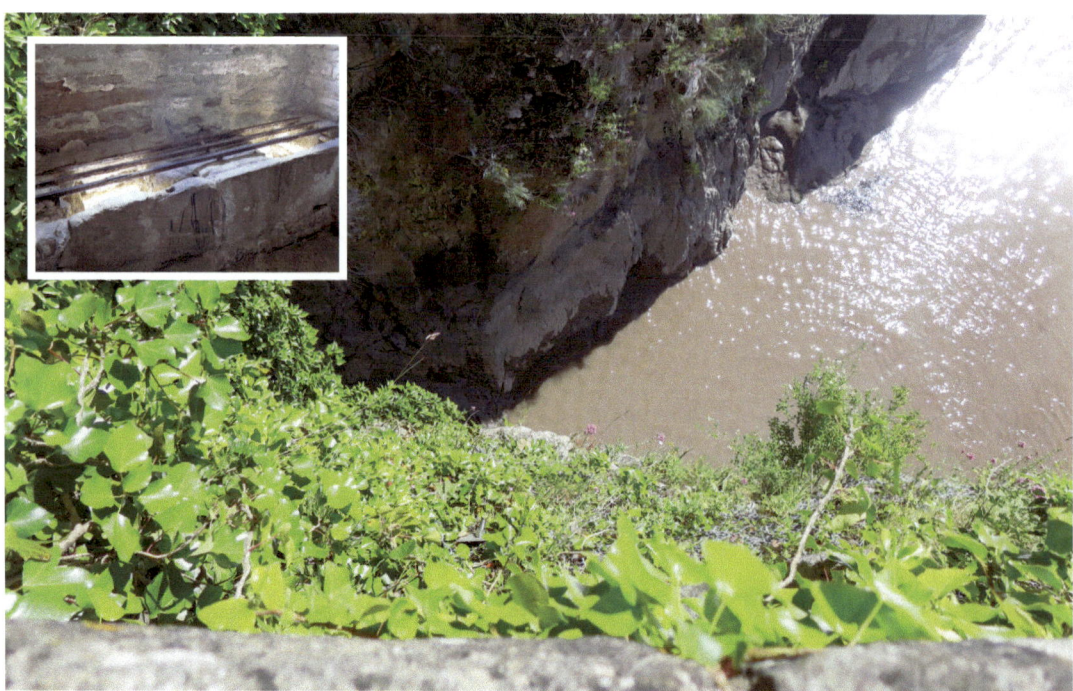

16

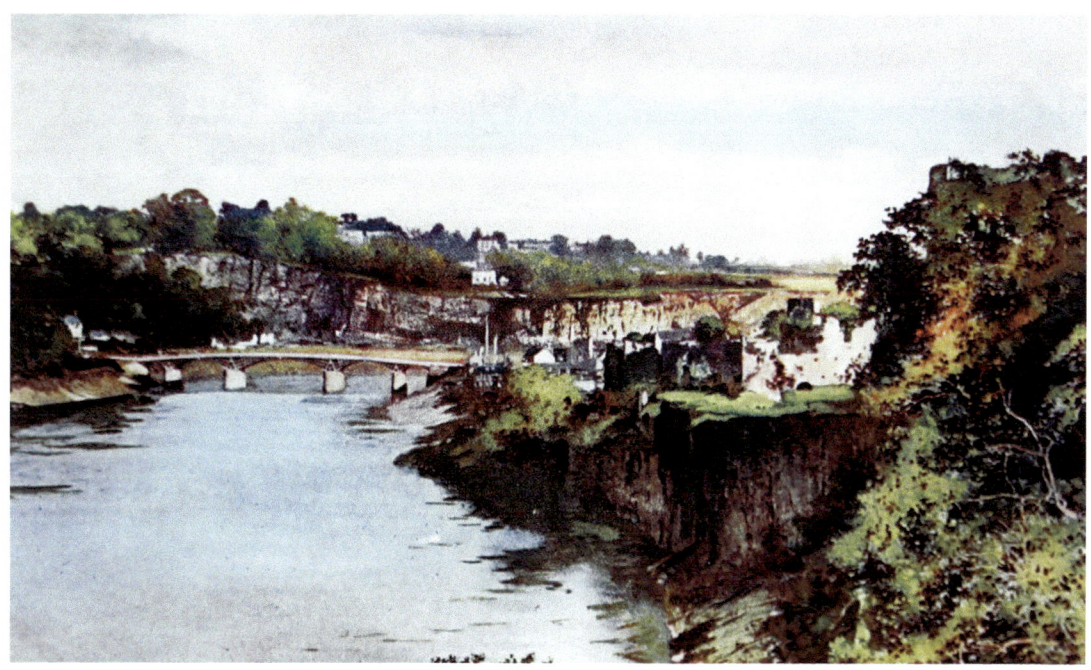

Chepstow Castle
Produced by the Great Western Railway as a sales promotion, the upper picture is again one taken from the clifftop heights above the bend in the River Wye. This panoramic view captures the whole length of Chepstow Castle down to the Chepstow Bridge at its end. Like the top picture on the previous page, neither of these two photographs can be reproduced today because of the dense undergrowth and extensive tree canopy in this area from where the originals were taken. The best that can achieved is from the castle itself just below the Upper Barbican.

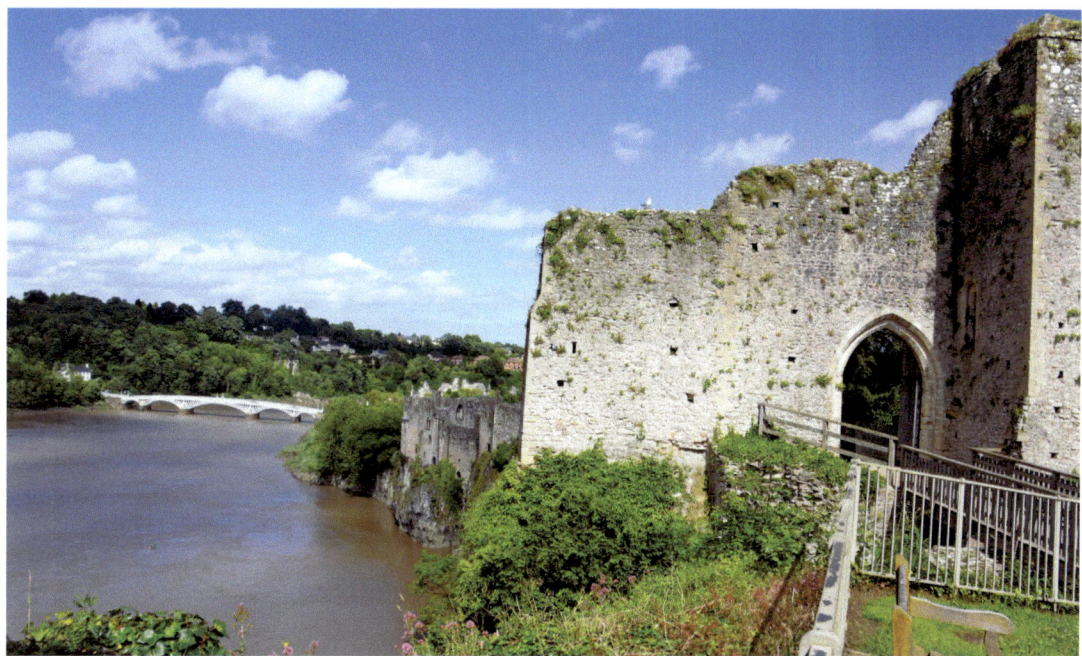

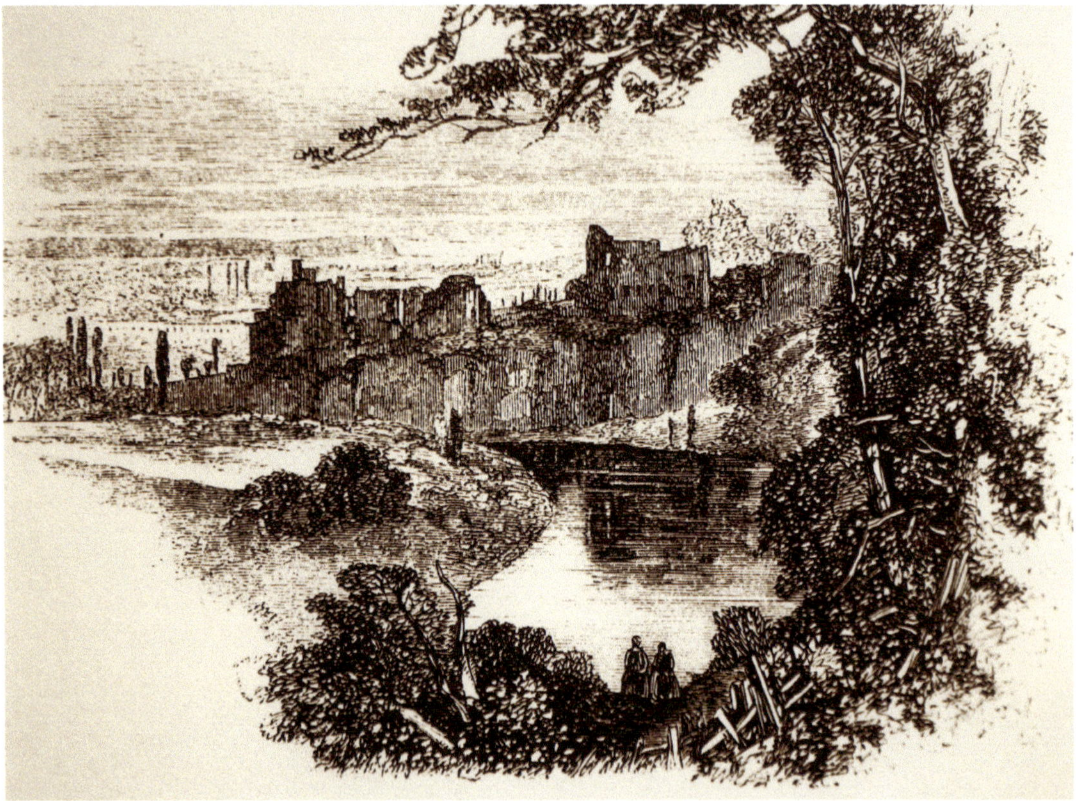

Chepstow Castle

The top sketch, which was drawn in about 1861 and has been taken from *The Book of the Wye*, shows Chepstow Castle from the north. In contrast, the lower photograph, taken by Patrick Hogan from roughly the same viewpoint on the banks of the Wye, has captured the whole vista of the castle in sharp relief with the M48 Severn Suspension Bridge standing out clear against the sky.

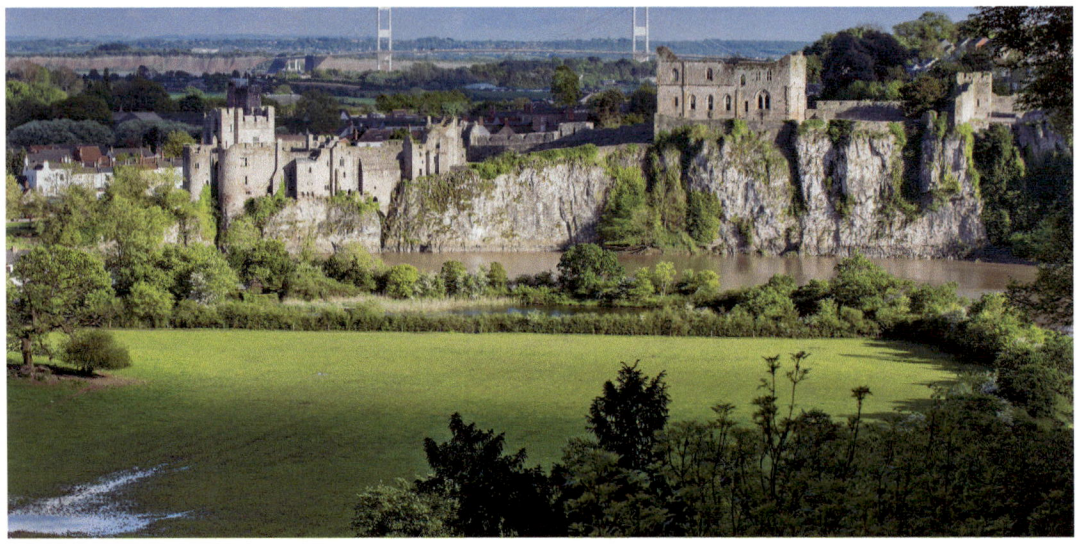

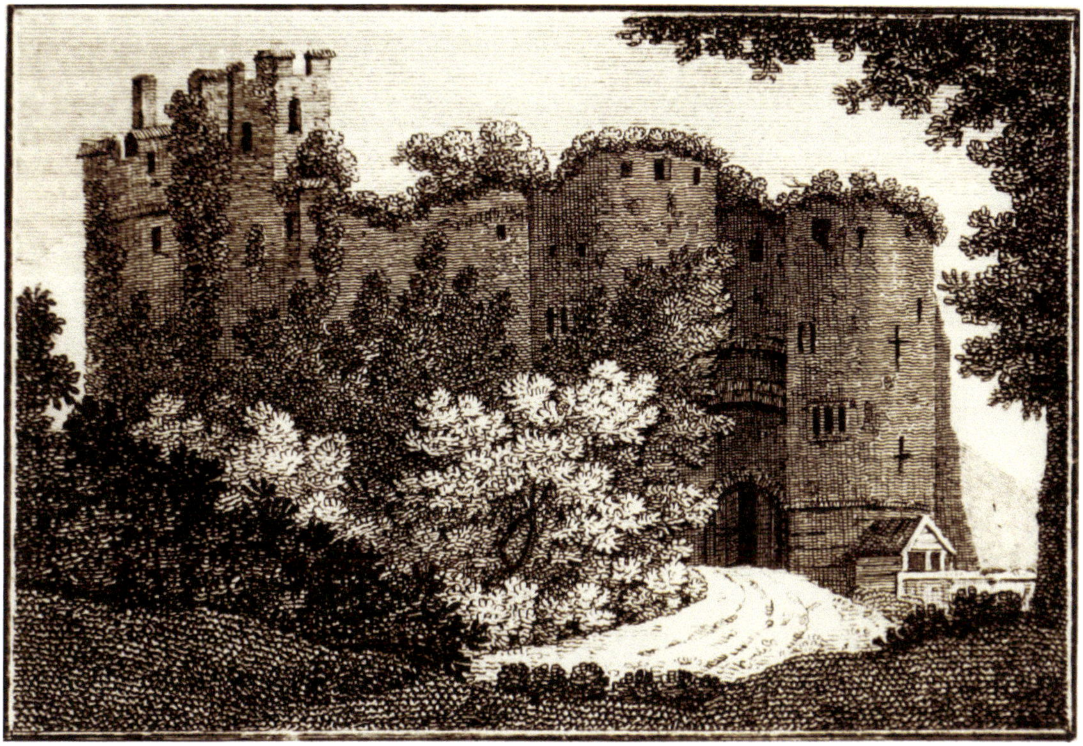

Chepstow Castle

Chepstow Castle was begun in 1067, just one year after the Battle of Hastings. That it came so soon is testament to the castle's strategic importance for the Normans to spread their power into Wales. The precipitous limestone cliffs afforded an excellent defensive location for the building of a fortress overlooking an important crossing point on the River Wye. A major artery of communications inland to Wales, it was also a route that could be taken by a Welsh attack into England. The print and photograph illustrate the main gatehouse and Marten's Tower.

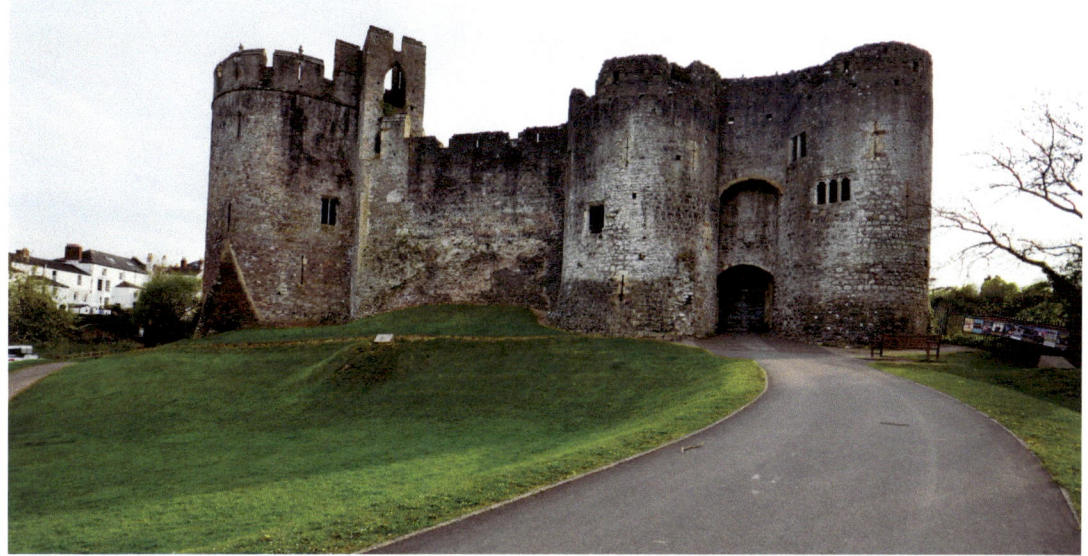

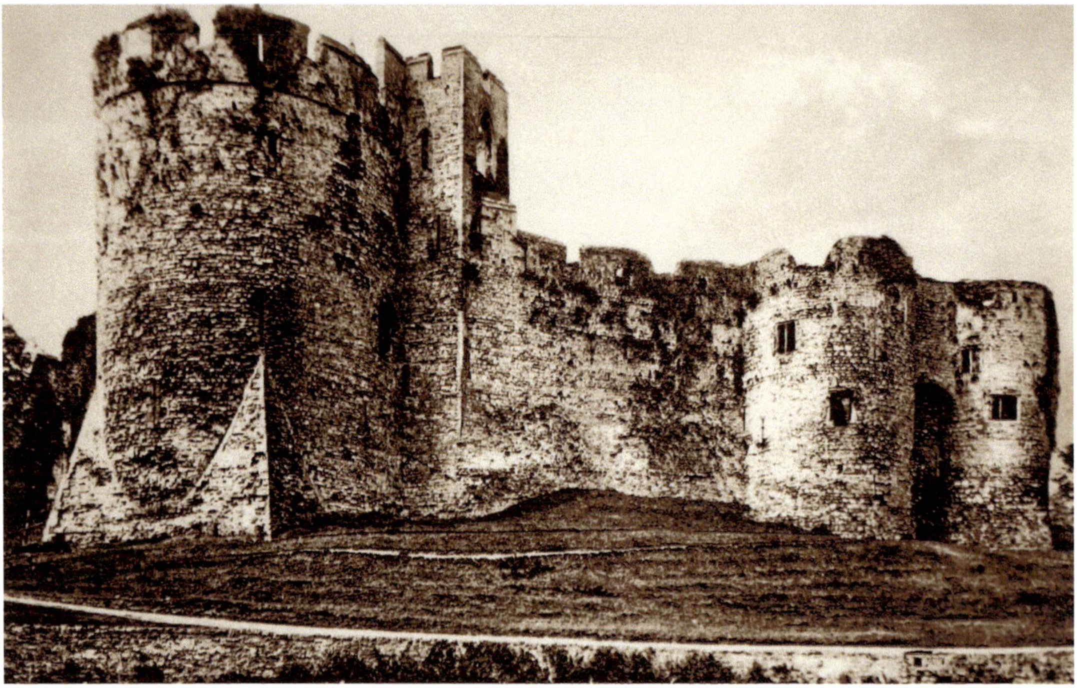

Chepstow Castle

Here are two further views of the castle's main gatehouse and Marten's Tower (on the left). Unlike most other Norman motte and bailey castles, which were first built of wood, Chepstow Castle was constructed from local quarried stone right from the start. Under the instruction of William fitz Osbern, building began on the Great Tower around 1067 and was completed in about 1090; it was possibly intended as a show of strength by William the Conqueror in dealing with the local Welsh king, Rhys ap Tewdwr.

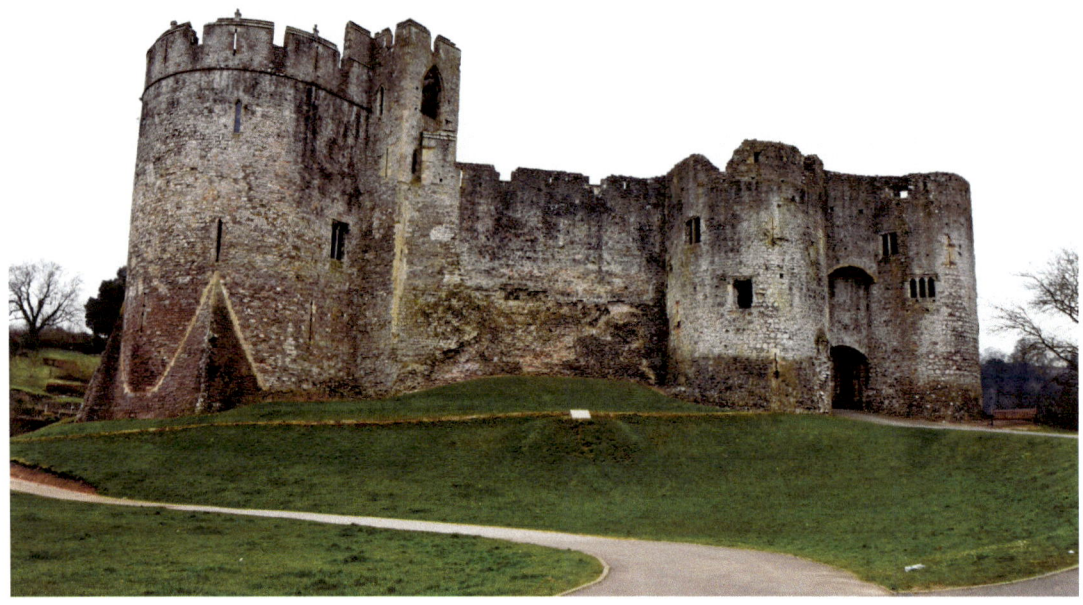

Chepstow Castle
The defence offered the landward side of the ridge on which the castle is built can be appreciated by the two views taken from the Dell, a natural valley which runs the full length of the fortification on its southern side. The inset photograph shows the first round tower to the left of Marten's Tower being refurbished by CADW in March 2013.

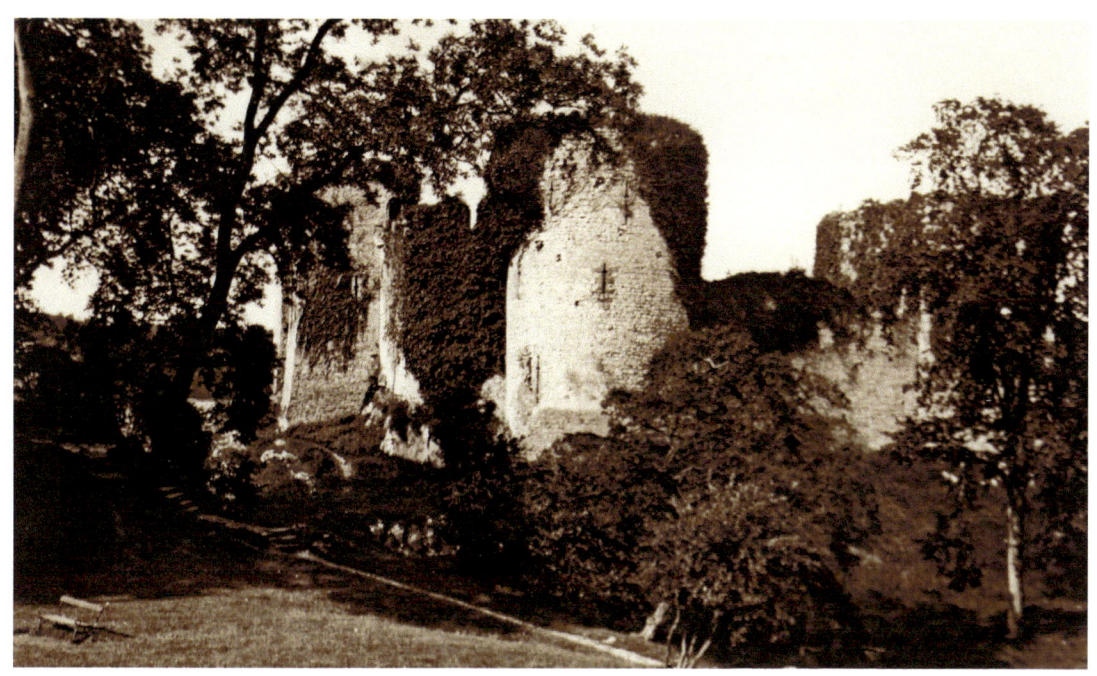

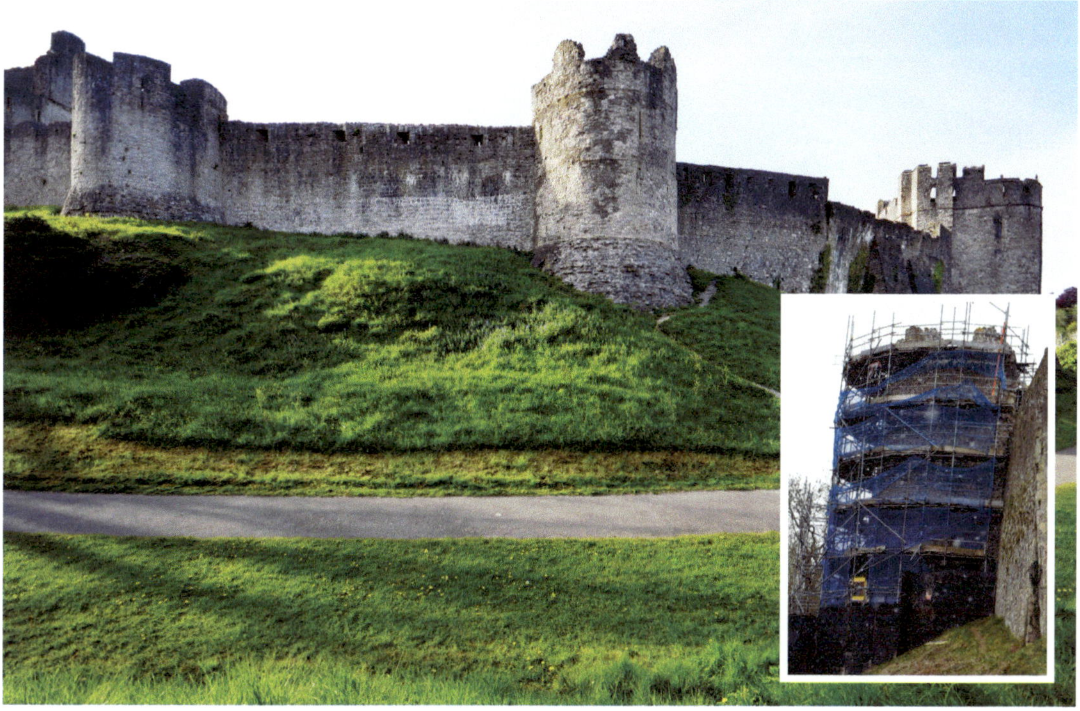

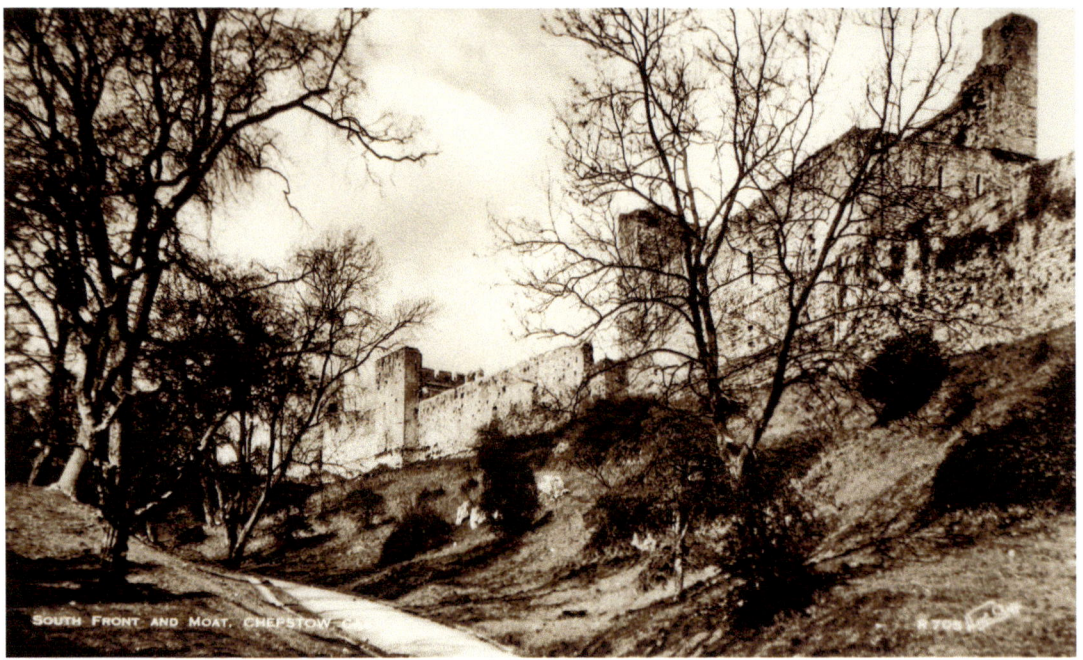

Chepstow Castle

Here are two more photographs that highlight the defence offered by the awe-inspiring stone walls of Chepstow Castle high on the bank of the ridge on which it stands. The Great Tower takes centre stage, extending even higher above the stone defences. Note the use of the red Roman tiles that girth the Great Tower along its length, as seen in the inset photograph. The tiles probably came from Caerwent, the Roman Town to the west of Chepstow as also did some of the foundation stones.

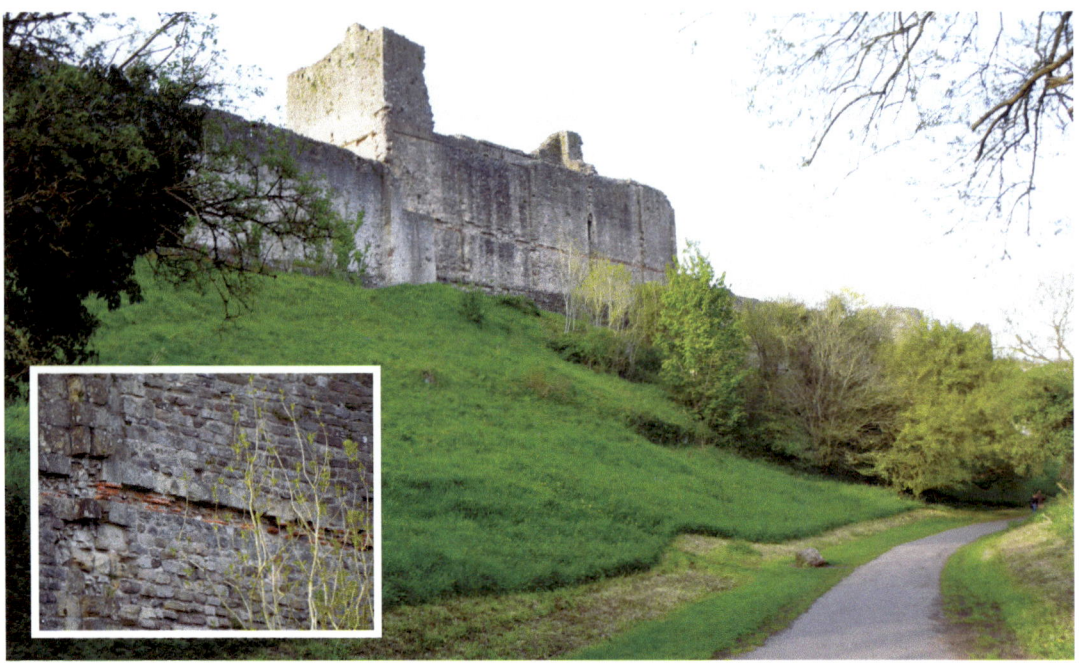

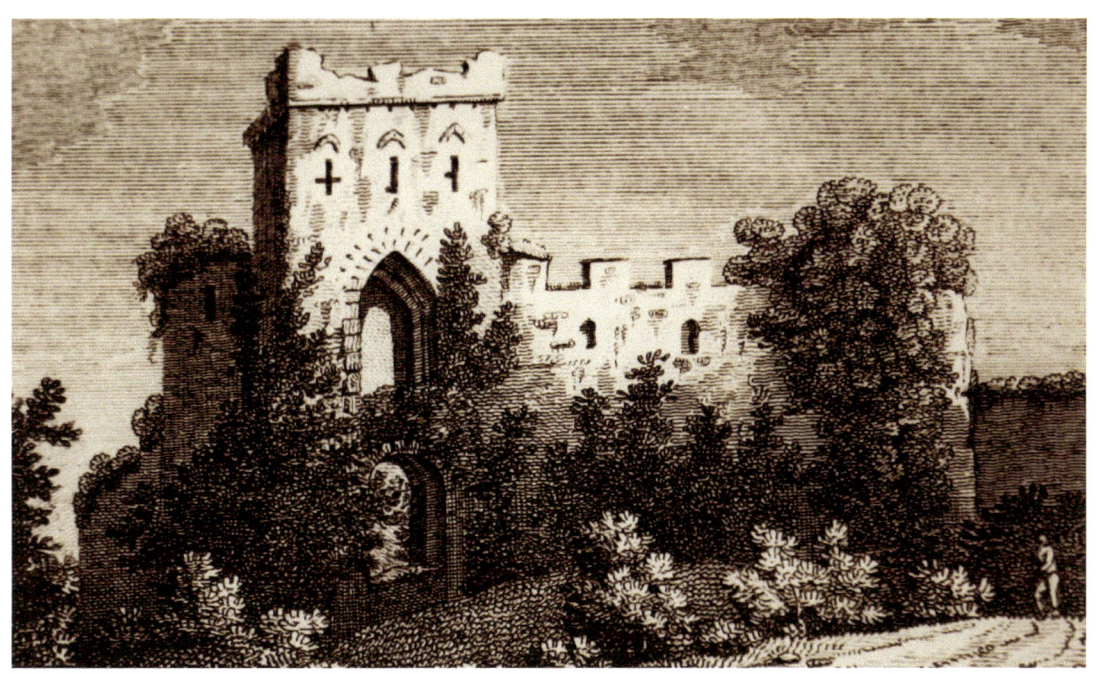

Chepstow Castle

The castle has four baileys, added in turn through history. The foundation of Chepstow Castle is considered to have taken place from 1067 to 1188. Further expansion and building work was carried out successively by William Marshall and Roger Bigod between the years 1189 and 1300. It was during this period that the Upper Bailey defences, shown in the two photographs, were rebuilt.

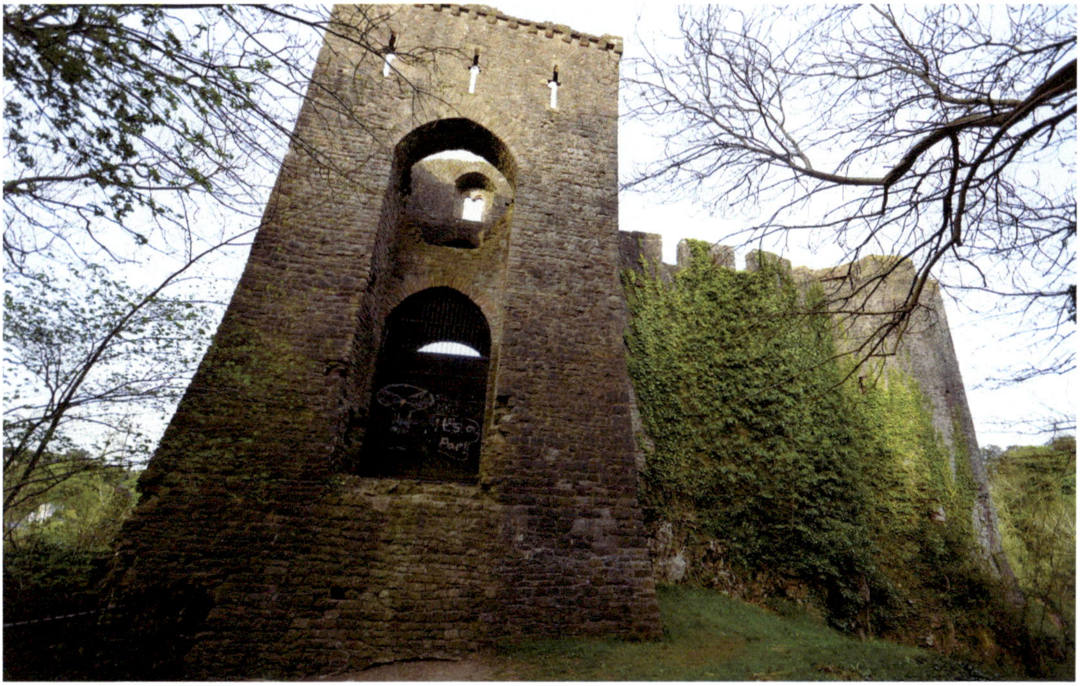

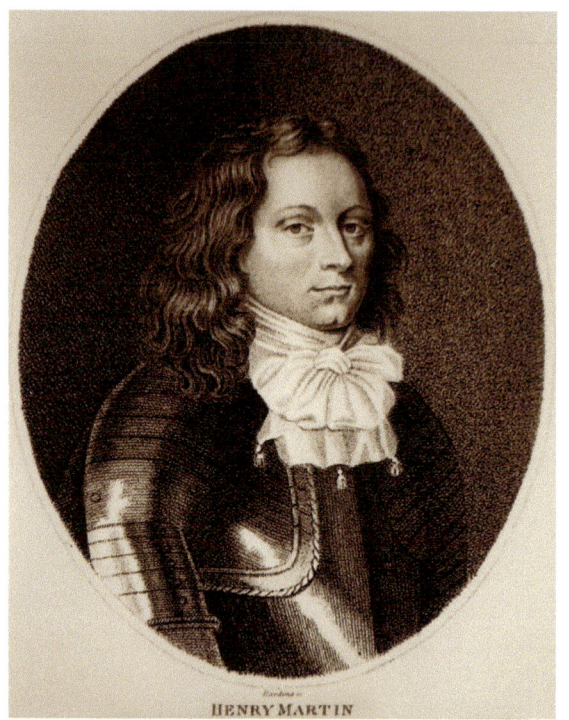
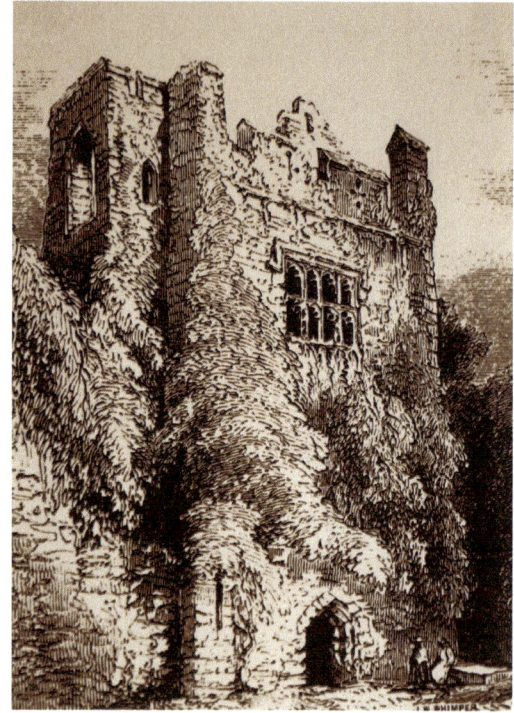

Marten's Tower

Chepstow Castle was inherited by Roger Bigod in 1270. He constructed a new range of buildings in the Lower Bailey as accommodation for himself and his family. Shortly after the visit to the castle by Edward I in 1284, Bigod built a new tower on what was certainly the site of an earlier structure. The new tower was later to become known as Marten's Tower after it had been made into fine Tudor apartments, which also served as the prison for Henry Marten, regicide of Charles I, between 1660 and his death in 1680.

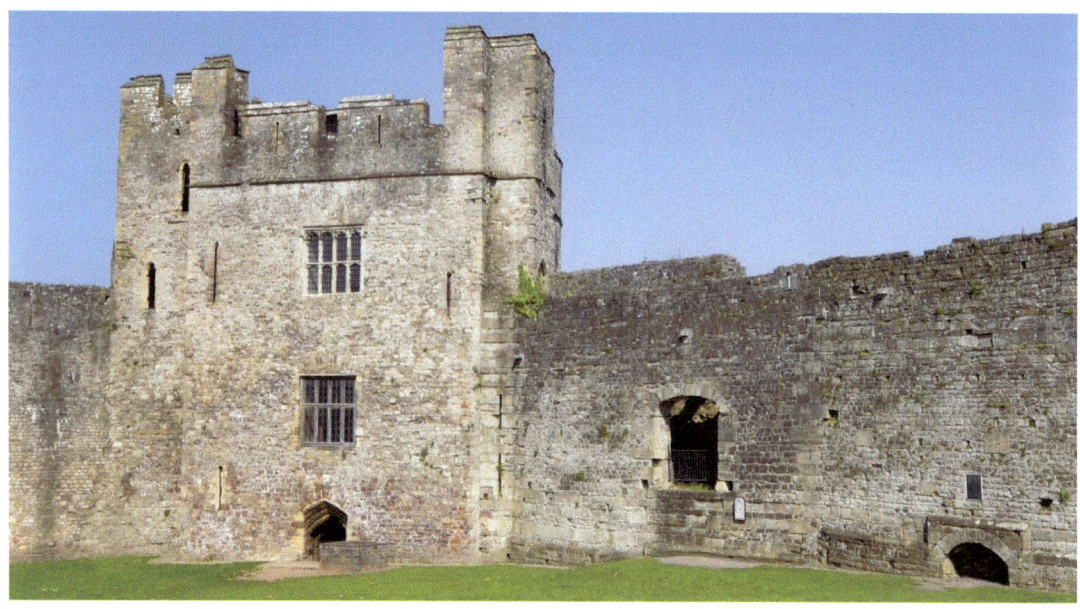

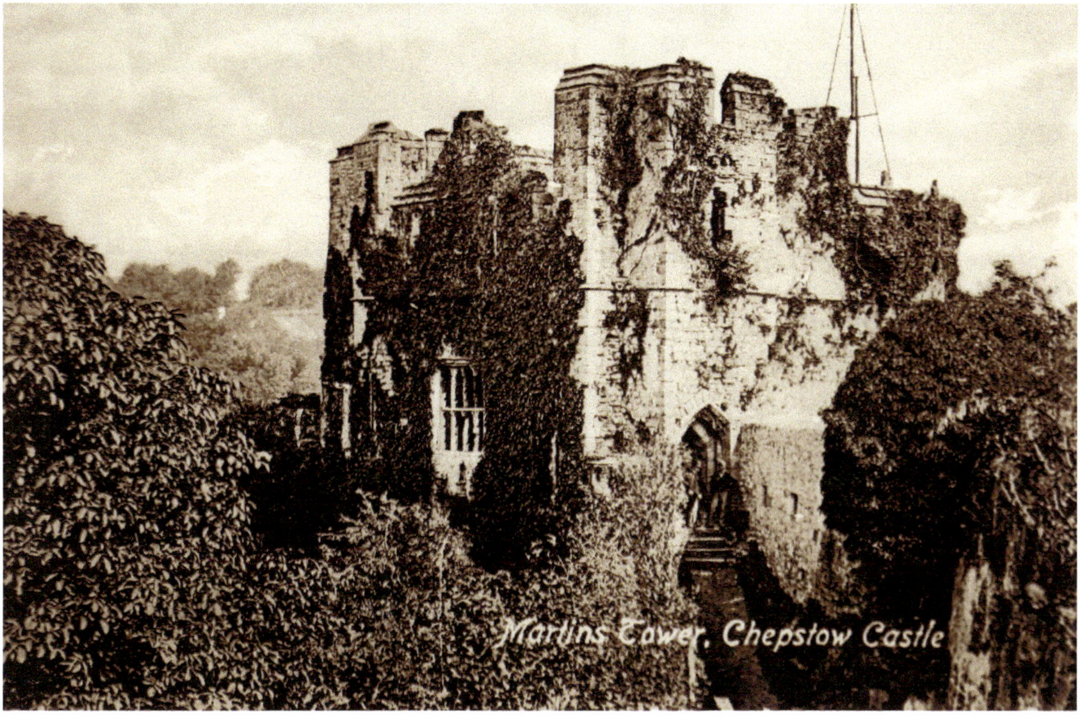

Marten's Tower

Two more views of Marten's Tower – the top from inside the castle; the lower photograph from outside. Although showing defensive strength from the outside, the inside of the tower contained well-appointed apartments for Roger Bigod and his family.

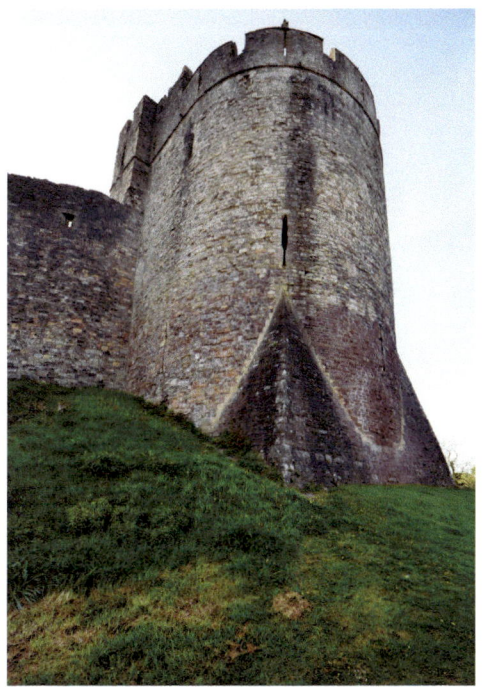
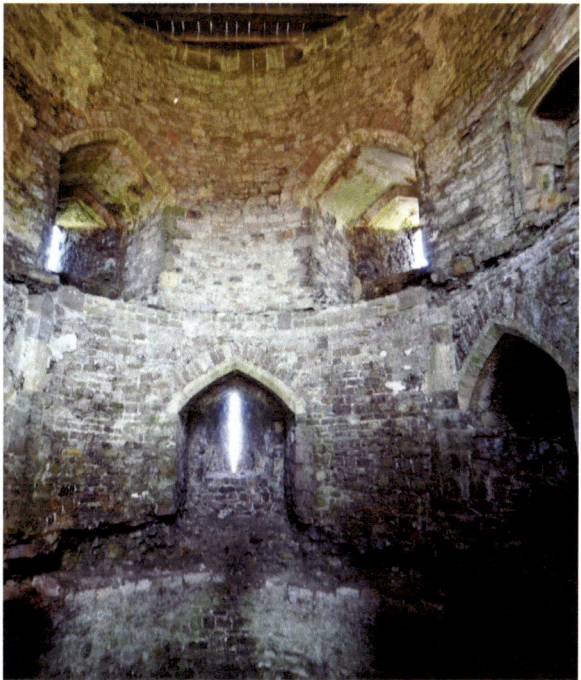

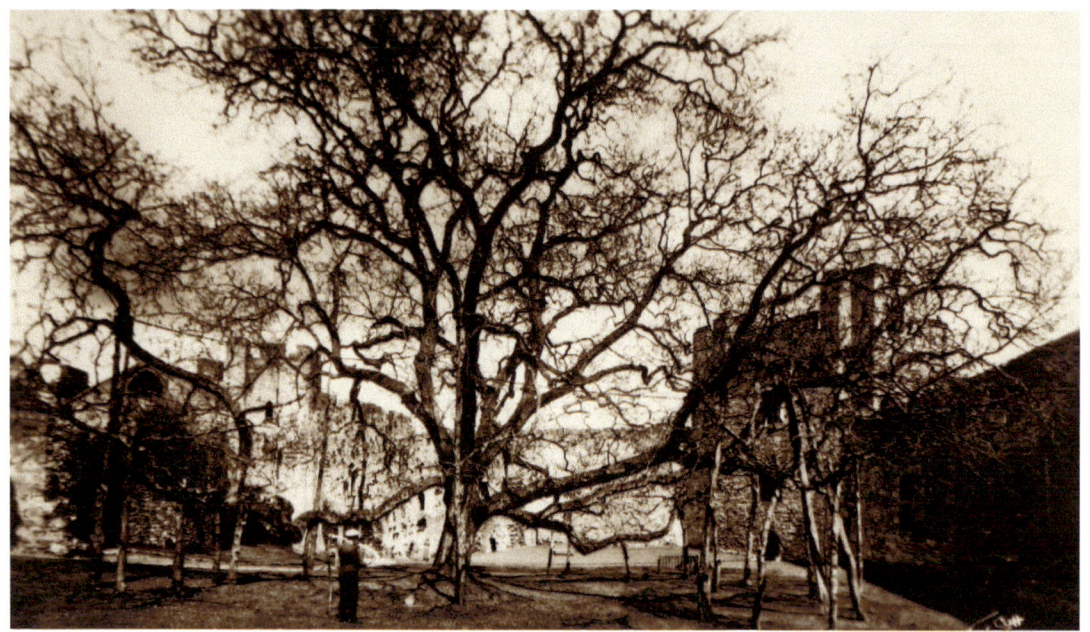

Chepstow Castle Lower Bailey

The upper postcard shows the famous walnut tree that once dominated the Lower Bailey of Chepstow Castle. It survived until the early 1960s when it finally succumbed to honey fungus. The castle saw action during the English Civil War (1642–51) and eventually fell to the Parliamentary forces on 5 May 1648. The gun port constructed during this period can be seen in the castle wall on the right in the lower photograph. Alongside there is a commemorative plaque to Sir Nicholas Kemeys who led the Royalist defence and was killed in combat after refusing to surrender.

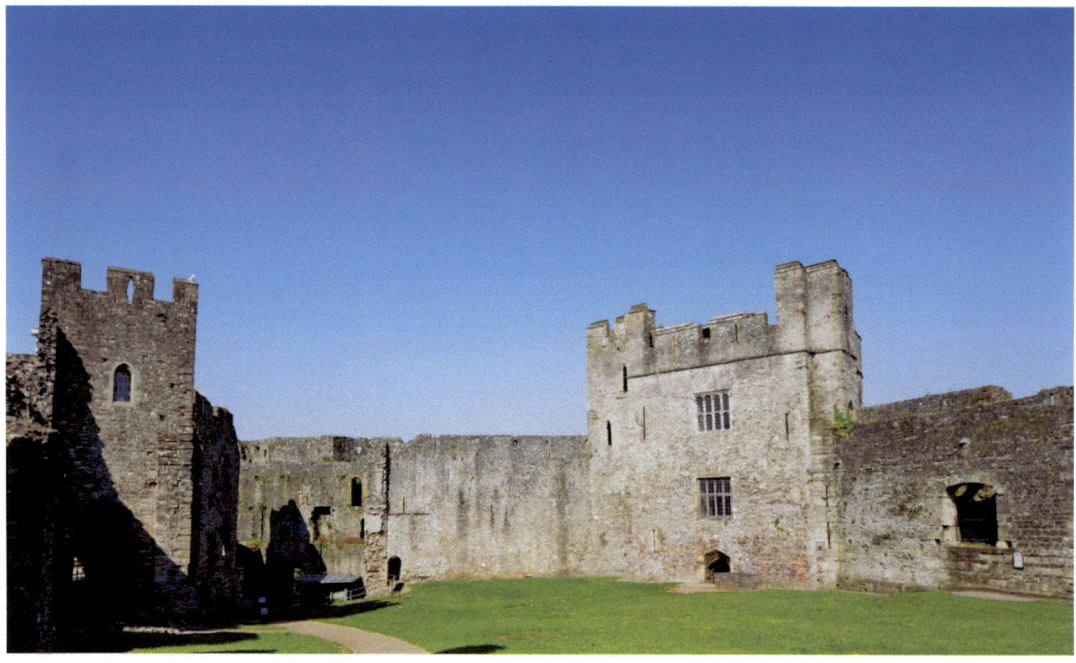

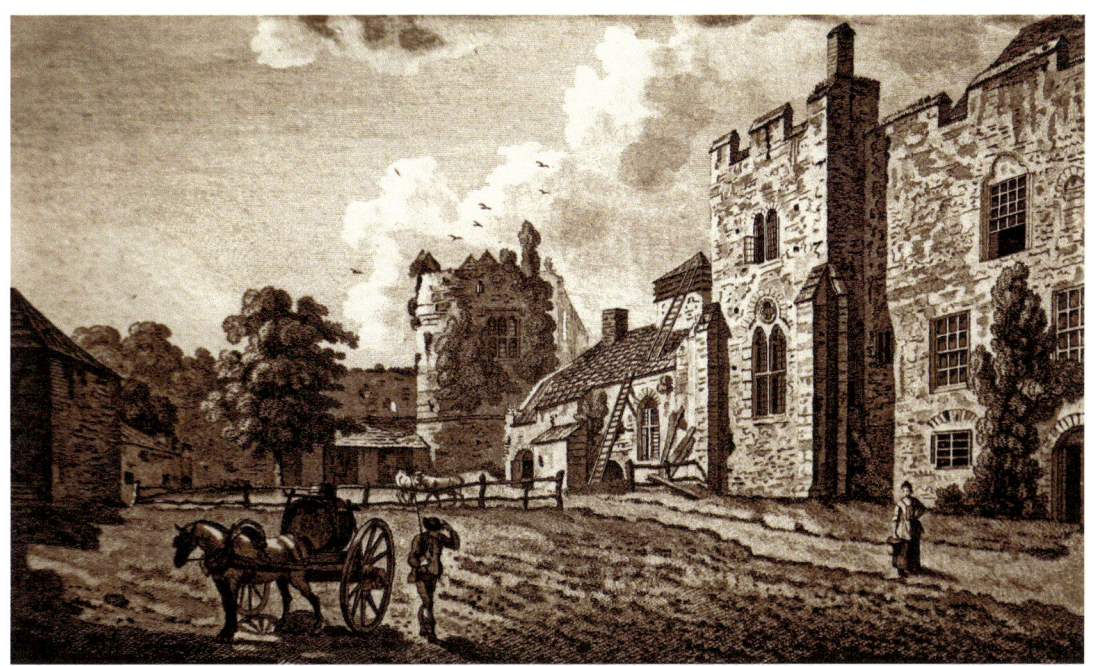

Chepstow Castle Lower Bailey

In 1682, Chepstow Castle came into the ownership of the Duke of Beaufort. Three years later in 1685, the garrison was disbanded and the buildings partly dismantled, leased to tenants and left to decay. A glass factory was installed in the confines of the castle and various parts of the grounds used as a farmyard, as illustrated in the top print. By the late eighteenth century, the castle ruins had become a 'picturesque feature' for the pleasure boats that plied the river on the 'Wye Tour'.

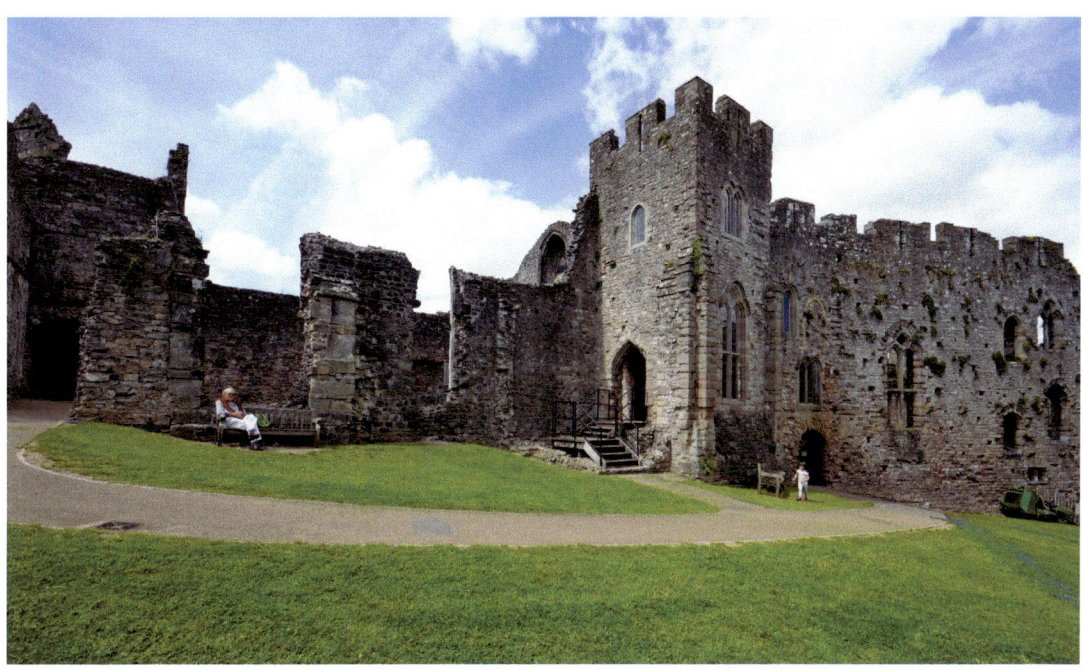

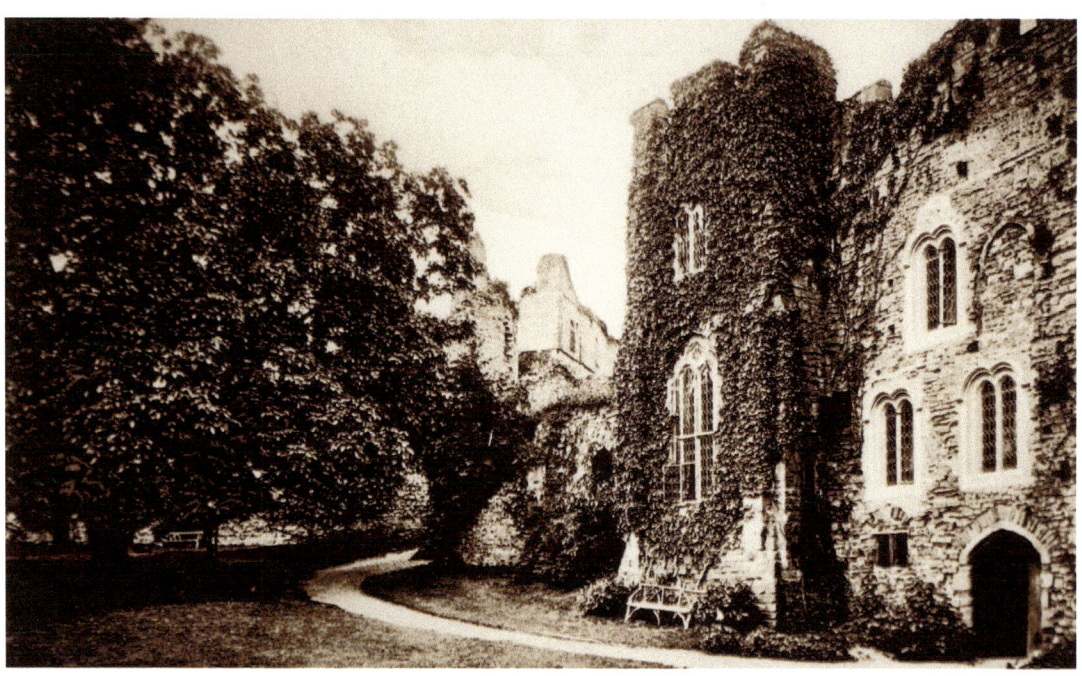

Chepstow Castle Lower Bailey
The top photograph gives a more modern perspective of the print on the previous page and shows the domestic quarters and chapel. The walnut tree is still here but most of the ivy has been removed, showing the extent of the decay on the buildings.

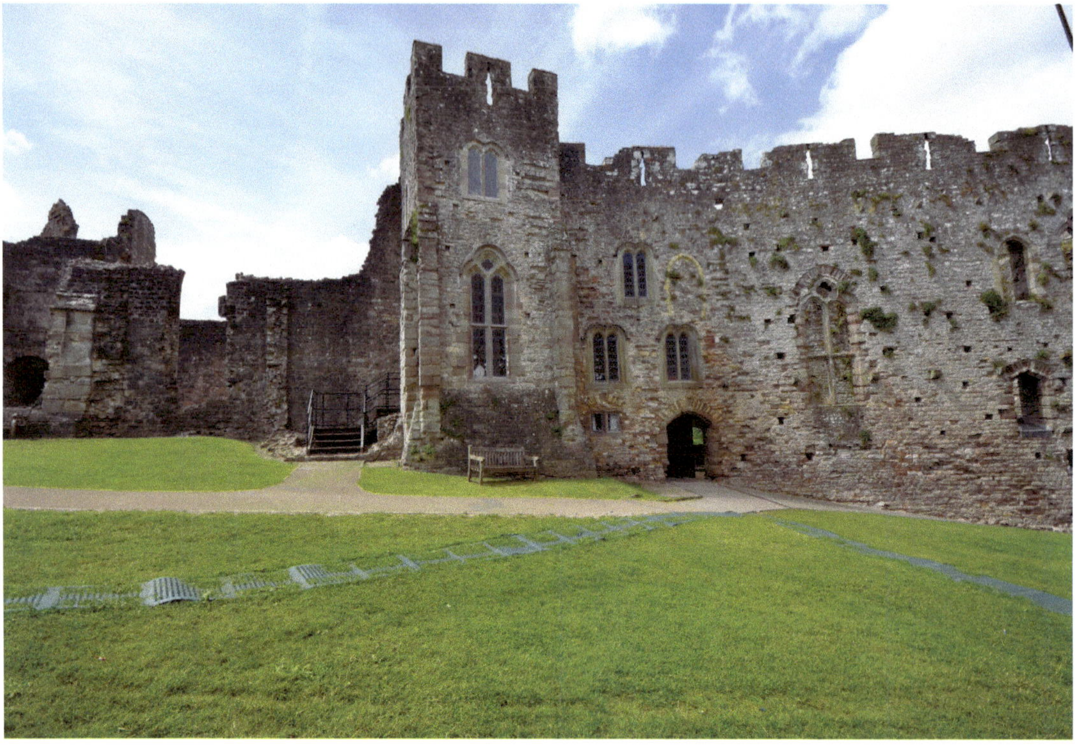

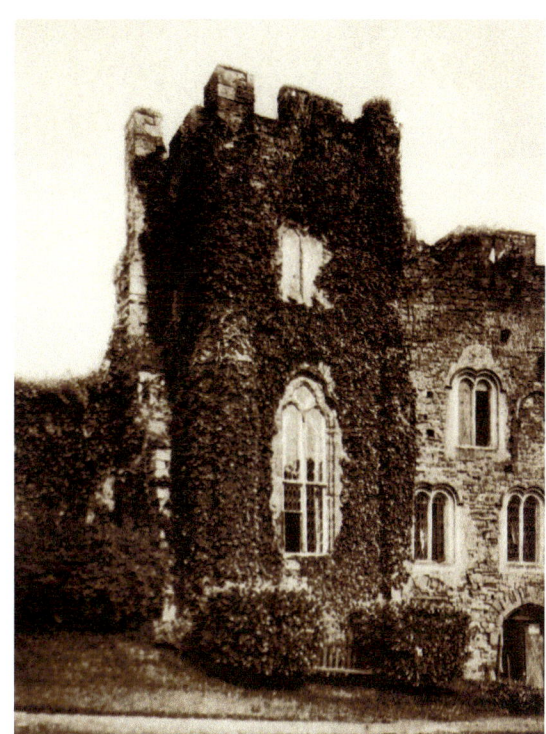

Chepstow Castle Lower Bailey

The two photographs on this page show the chapel of the domestic wing as built by Roger Bigod. The inset photograph shows the old gatehouse doors, now on display in the entrance to the chapel. The wood in the doors has been dated by dendrochronology to the period 1159–89, which is during William Marshal's time at Chepstow Castle.

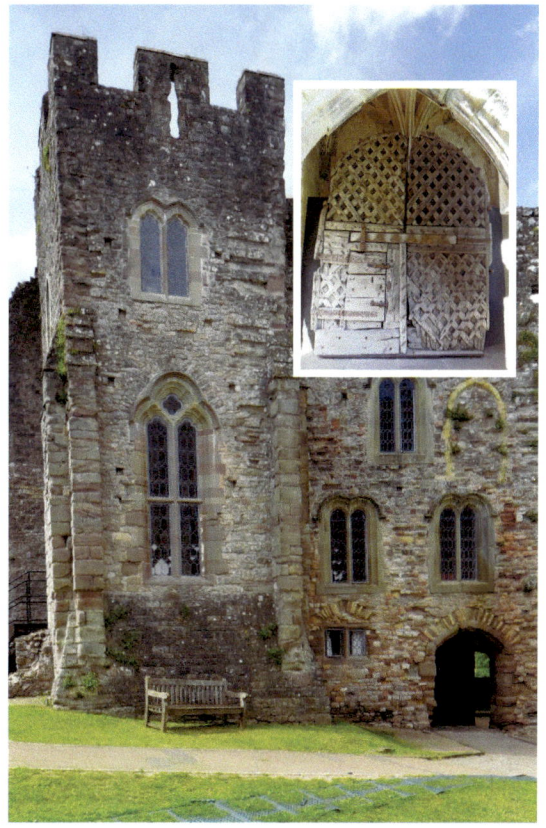

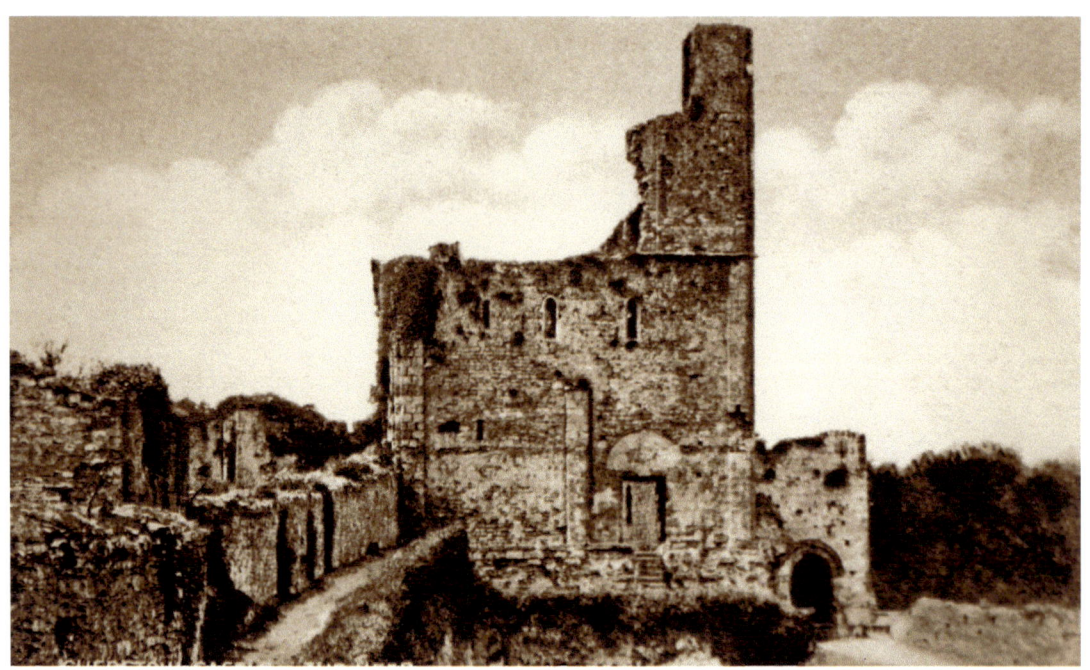

The Great Tower – Roman Evidence

When William fitz Osbern constructed the Great Tower between 1067 and 1090, he made extensive use of Roman tiles and possibly also worked stone. This quarrying could have come from the lost Roman fort, which is known to have existed in the Chepstow area, or from the Roman civitas at Caerwent some 5 miles to the west of Chepstow. Following Roman practice, the red clay tiles completely circumscribe the whole of the outside of the Great Tower at a level just above the top of the main doorway as shown in the insert. (*See also* page 22.)

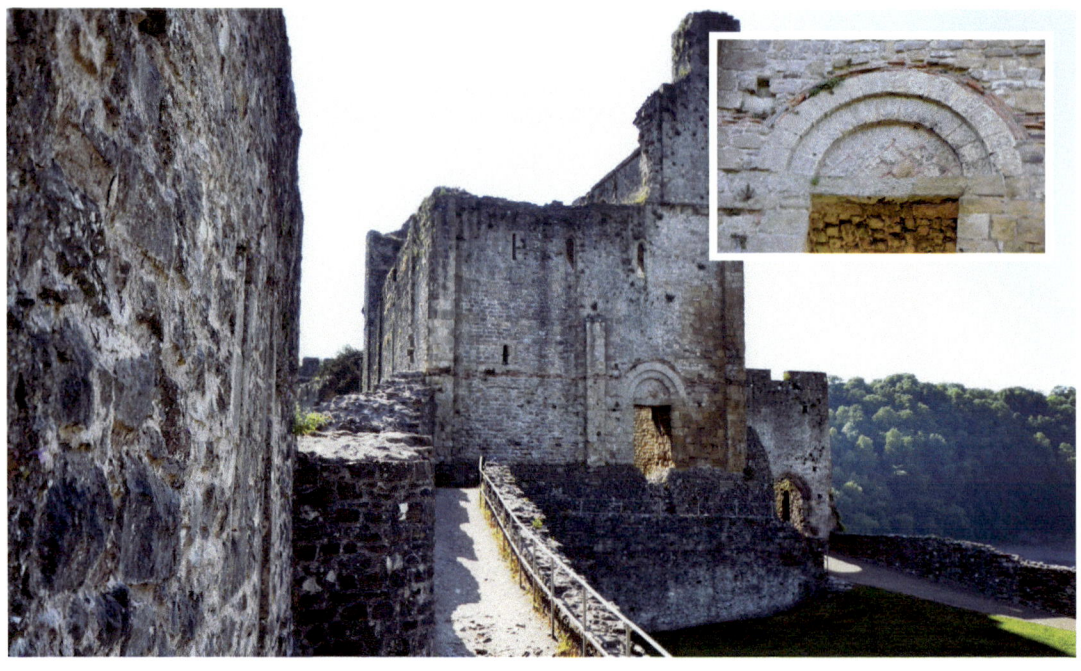

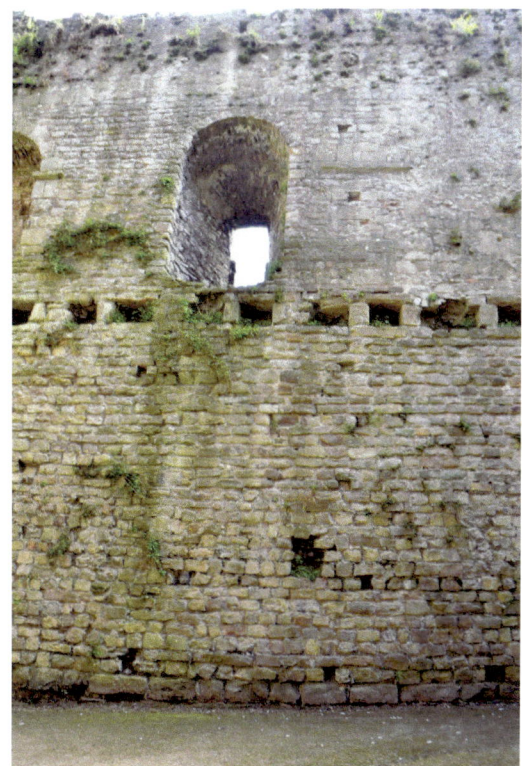

The Great Tower – Roman Evidence

Further Roman evidence is to be found in the two photographs on this page. The bottom photograph highlights a Romano-British sculpture thought to represent Venus and her nymphs, whereas the top picture locates the sculpture as being on the first floor of the Great Tower and just to the right of the window.

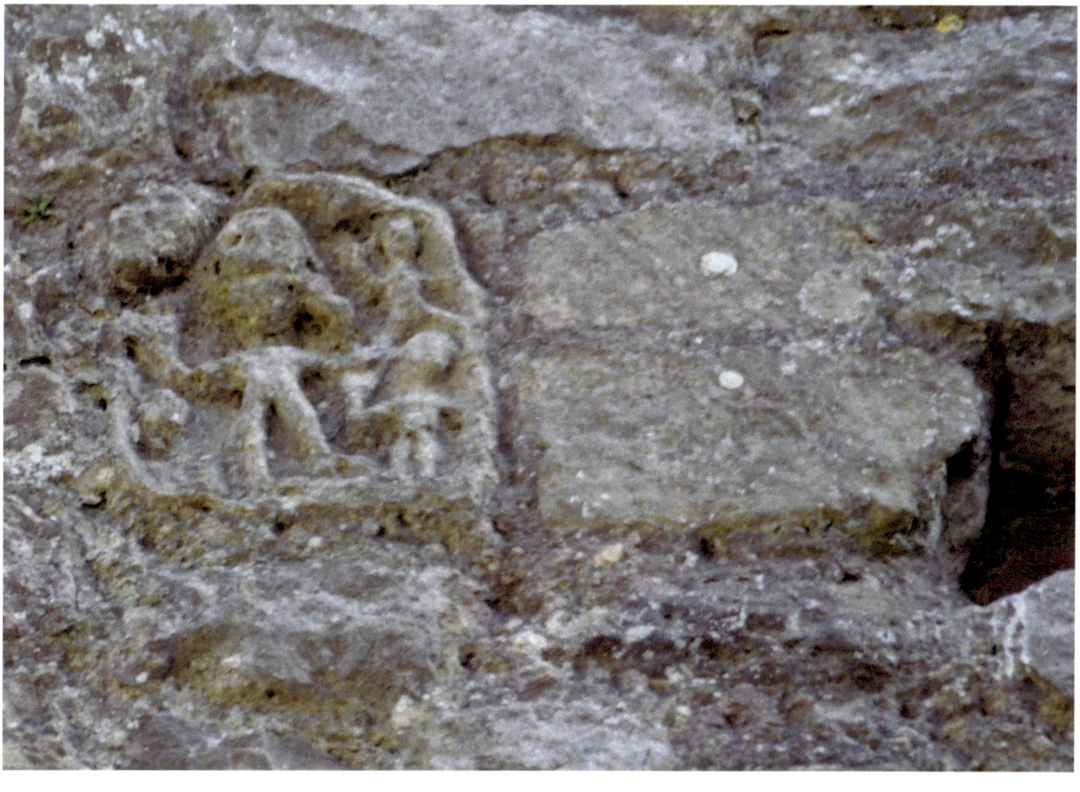

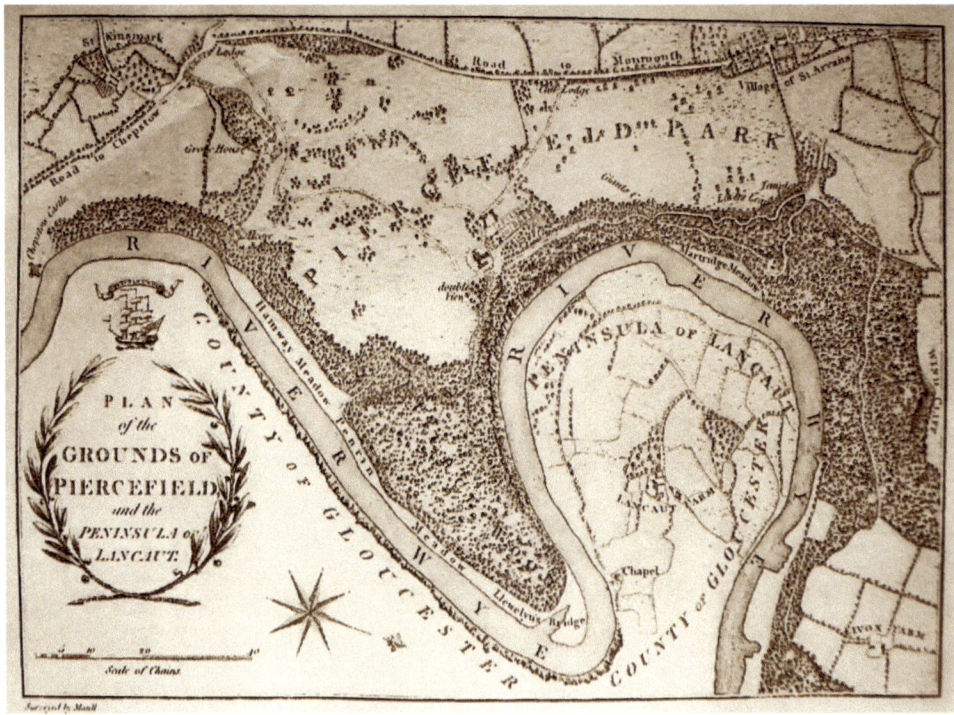

Piercefield House, Estate and Racecourse

The Piercefield estate has appeared in records under similar names since medieval times and has had many owners since. The present Piercefield House is a largely ruined neo-classical house designed by Sir John Soane on which building work began in 1792. The house is now a shell, along with its extensive stable block, and is a Grade II-listed building. Much of the estate is owned by the Chepstow Racecourse Company, who opened the new racecourse there in 1926. The inset image shows the possible site of the Roman bridge crossing of the Wye, located by the 'I' of 'RIVER' on the map above.

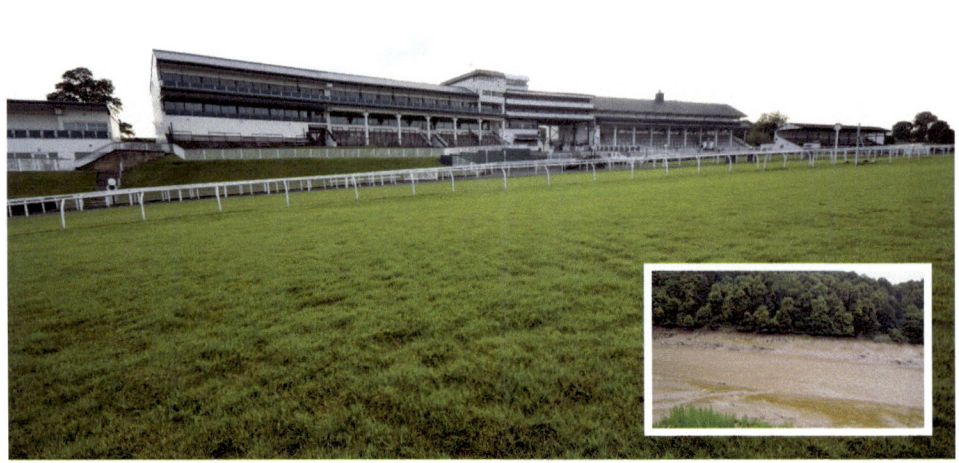

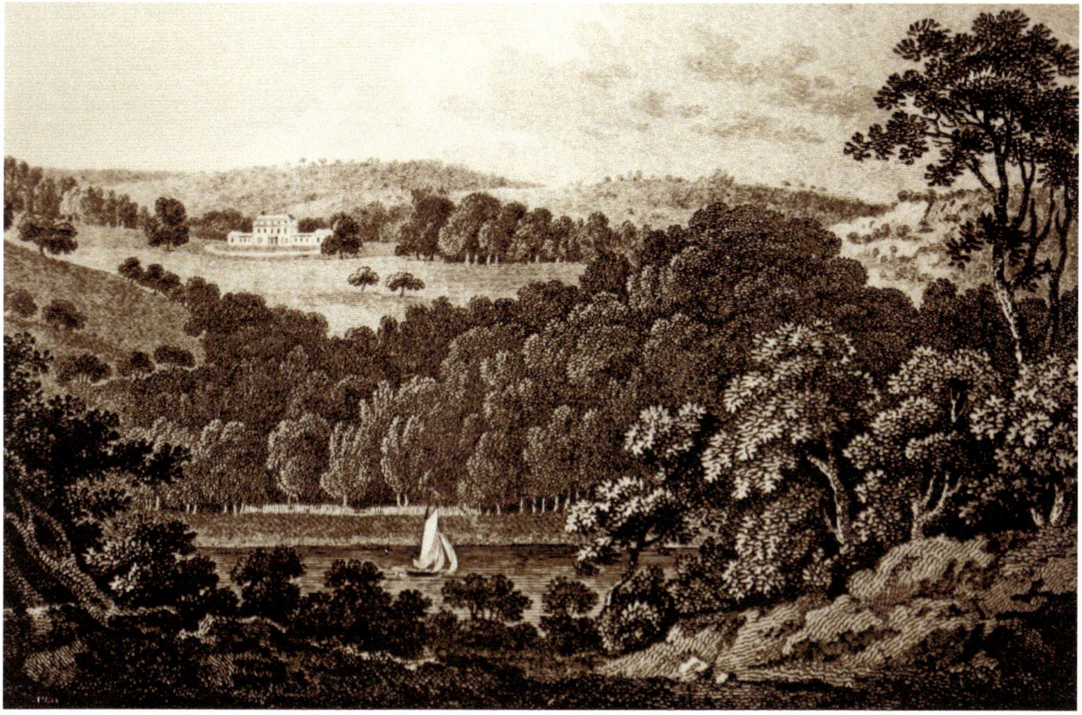

Piercefield House and Estate

The estate acquired magnificent splendour when the grounds were extensively landscaped in 1753 by owner Valentine Morris in Capability Brown fashion. Opened to visitors, it became a park of national reputation and one of the earliest examples of picturesque landscaping. Walks were laid out through the woodlands, which also included a grotto, druid's temple, bathing house and giant's cave. The top print of Piercefield Park dates to about 1753, while the lower photograph and inset show Chepstow sisters Deborah Page (left) and Helen Frost respectively in front of the ruinous remains of the house and in the Grotto.

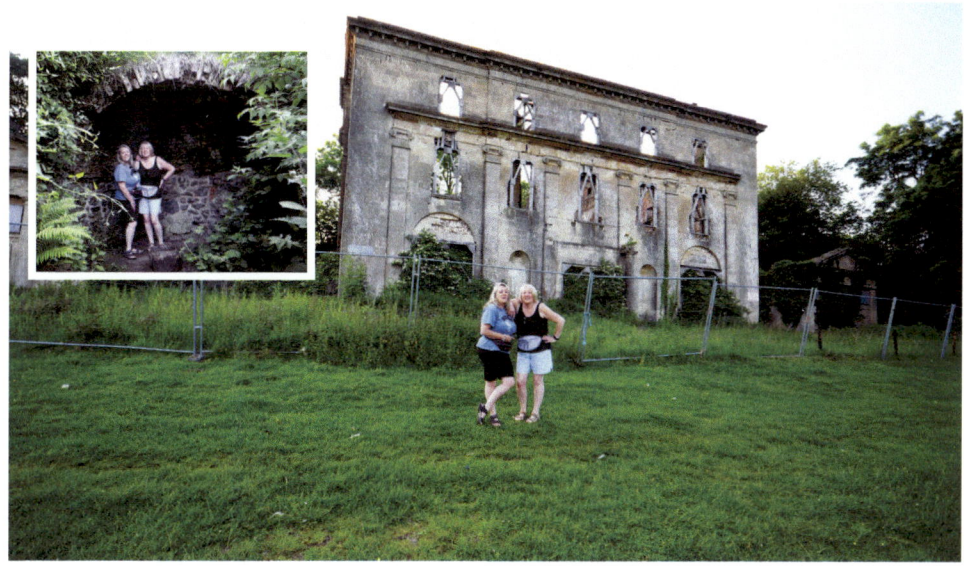

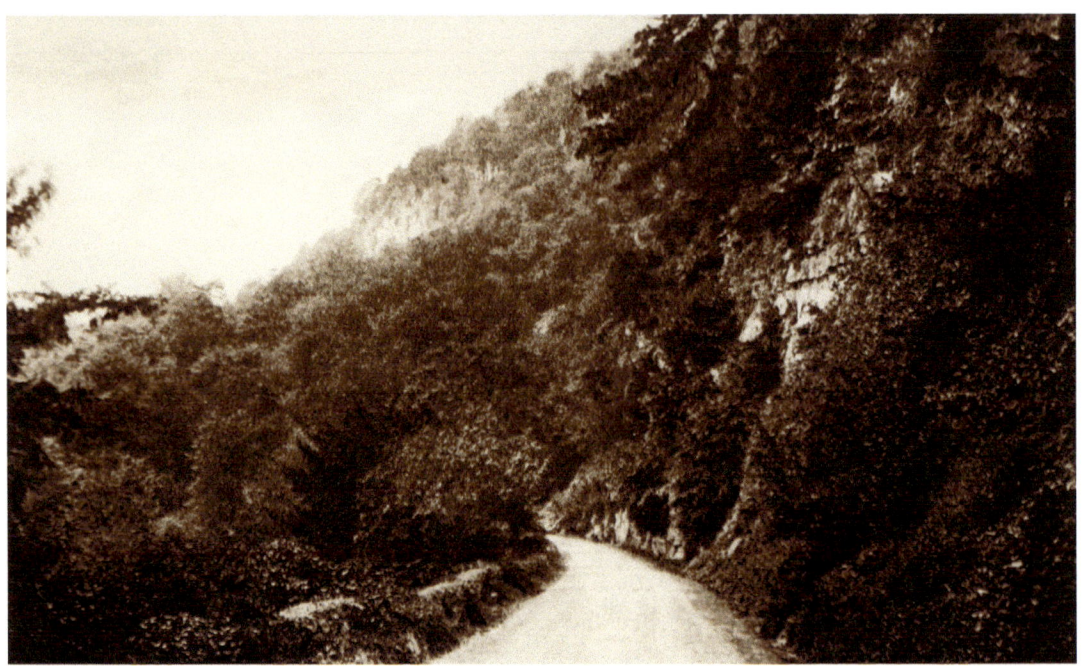

Wyndcliff

The top postcard (franked 18 June 1948), shows the limestone cliffs at Wyndcliff that overshadow the main A466 road between Chepstow and Tintern. The original photograph was taken from the direction of Tintern, but due to the tree canopy that now exists along this stretch of road, the modern photograph was taken from the opposite direction and only then could a small area of cliff be seen through the trees.

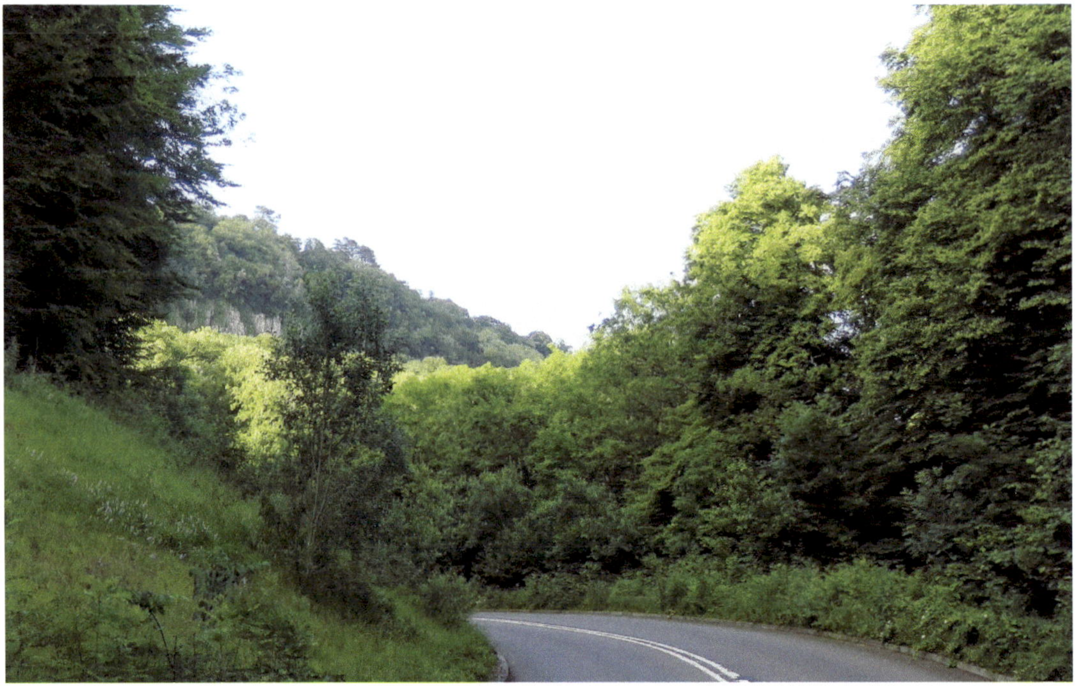

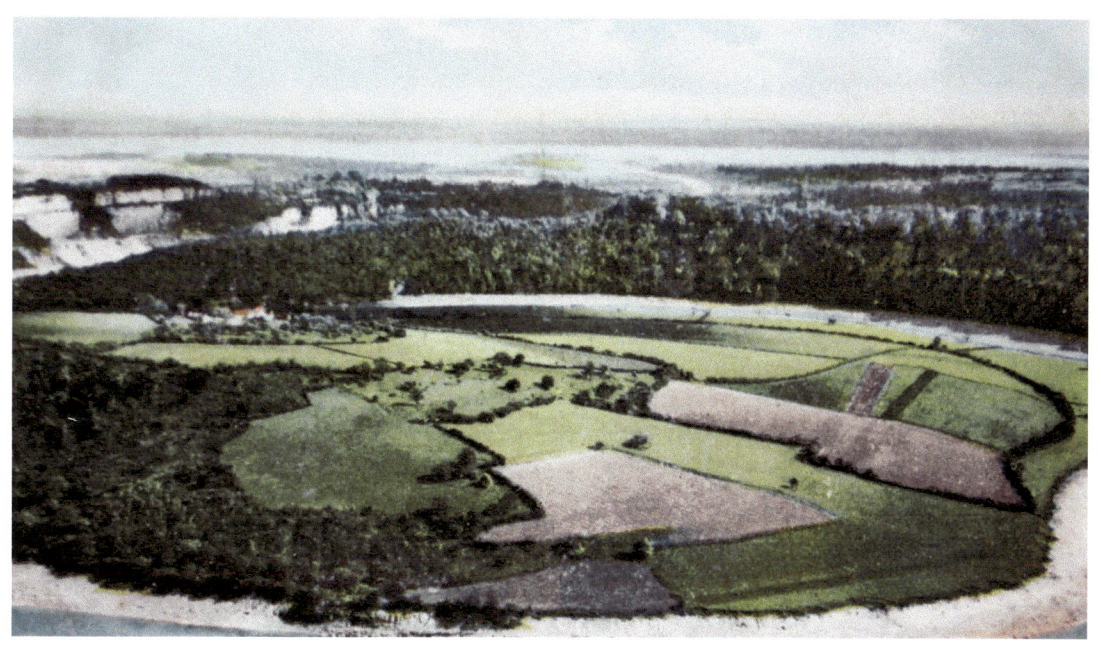

The Wye from the Wyndcliff 'Eagle's Nest'
When he landscaped Piercefield in 1753, Valentine Morris created a number of viewpoints on the cliffs above the Wye. 'Eagle's Nest' has become one of these famous viewpoints from where splendid panoramic views of the meandering River Wye can be observed, enjoyed and photographed. This is illustrated by the two pictures on this page with the top postcard dating to the early 1900s.

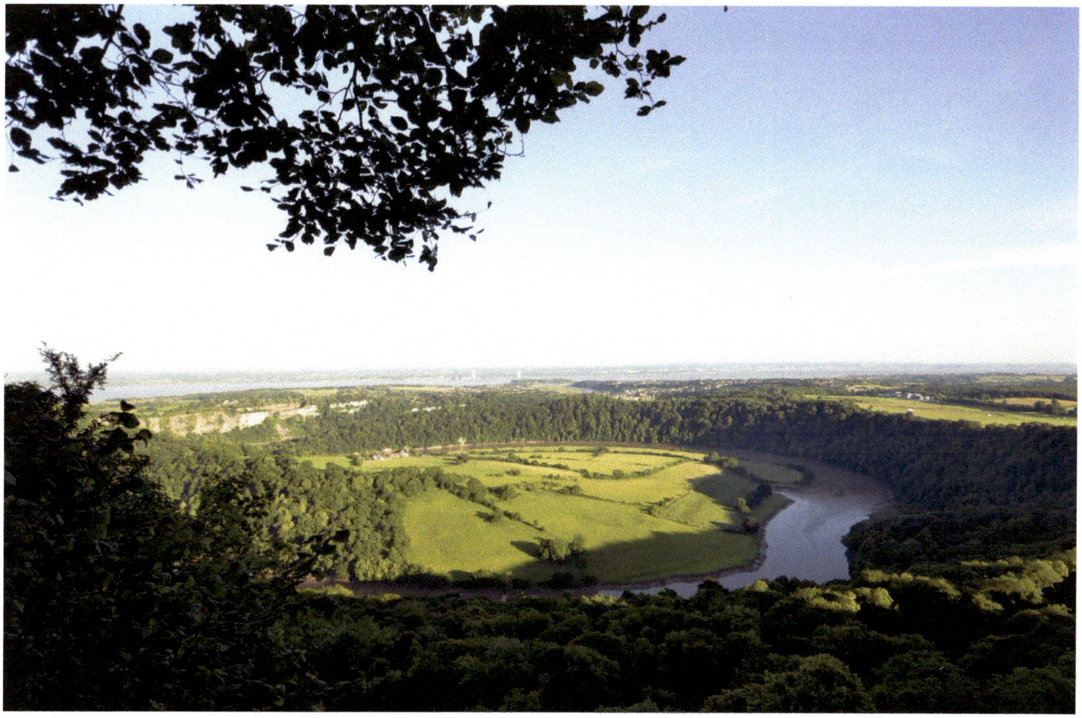

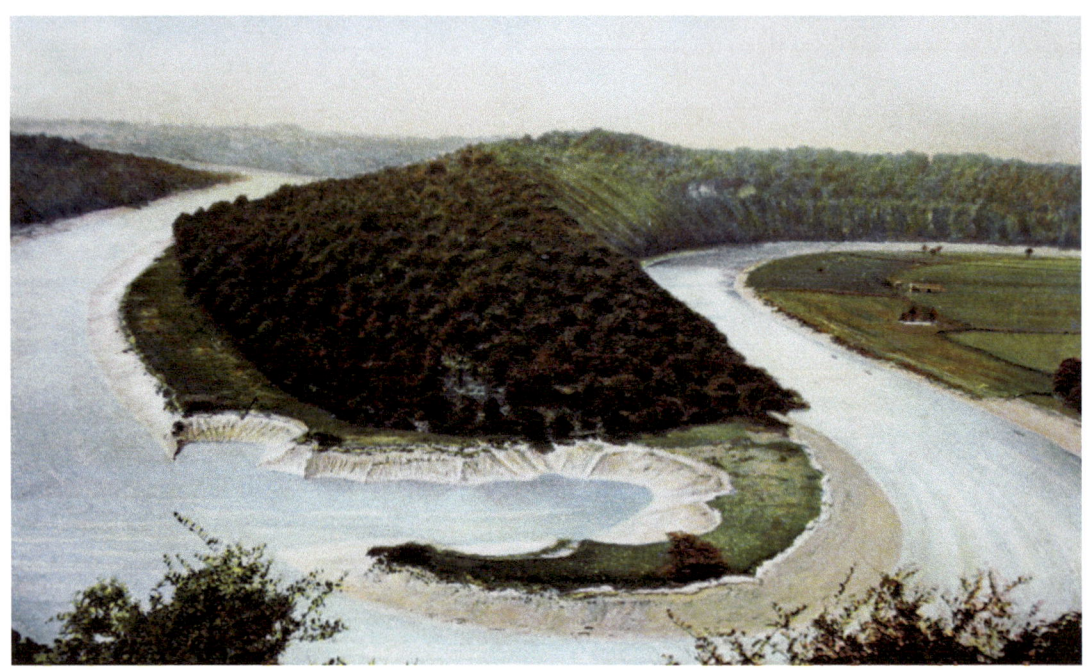

The Wye from Wintour's Leap, Broadrock

Here are two more panoramic views of the Wye at Tidenham or Horseshoe Bend, this time taken from the Offa's Dyke Path near Wintour's Leap above the limestone cliffs on the English side of the river. Beneath the massive canopy of trees, central to the view and bordered either side by the Wye, lies the remains of the very large Piercefield Iron Age fort, one of the earliest sites of occupation in the Chepstow area.

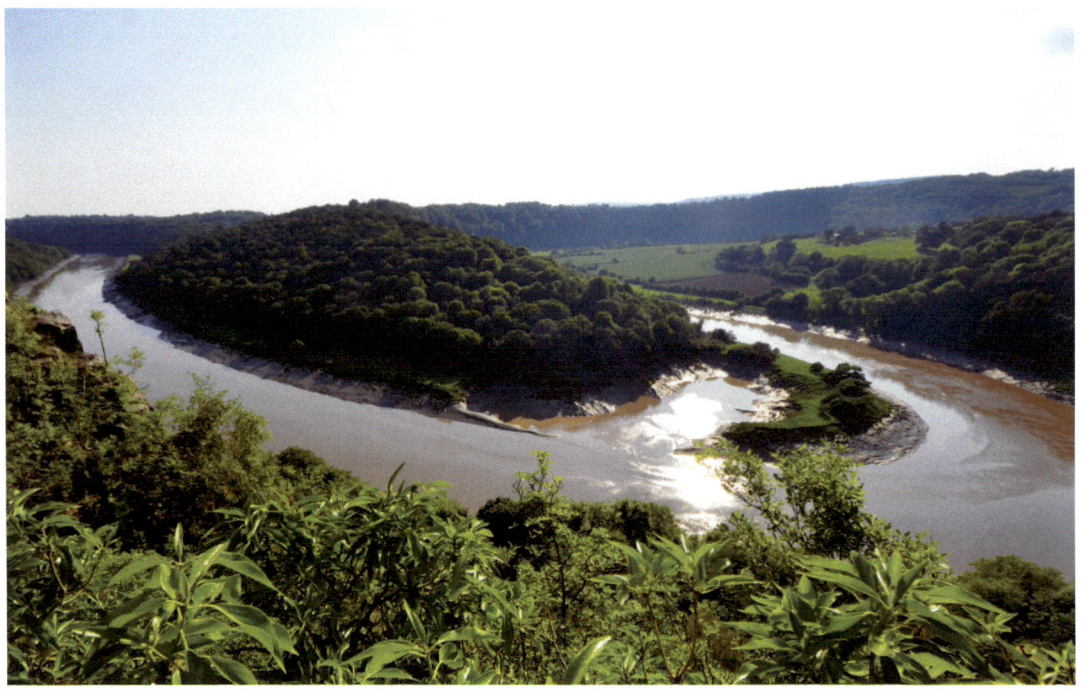

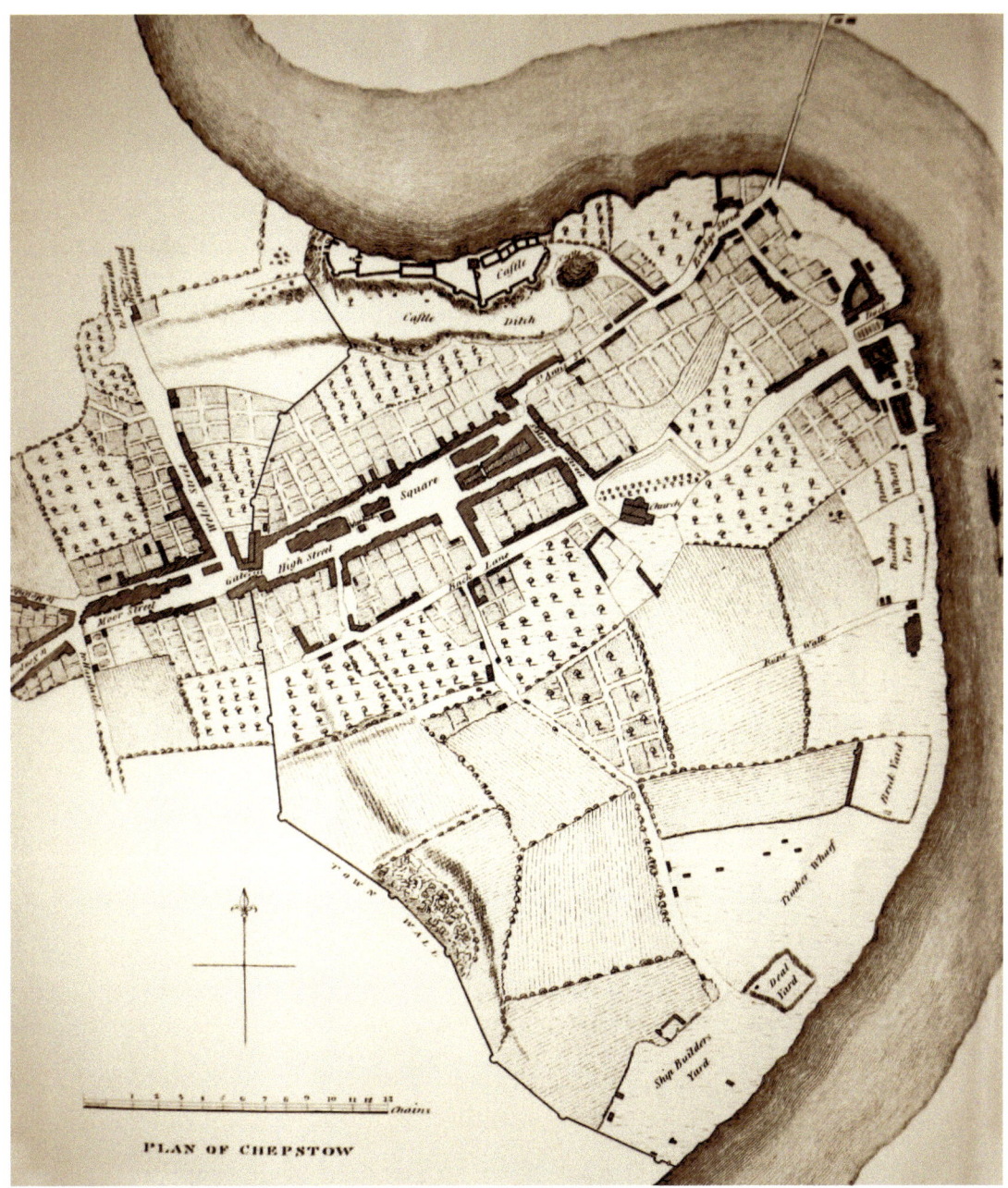

Chepstow Town

The above map is taken from William Coxe's *An Historical Tour in Monmouthshire* and shows the extent of the town of Chepstow in 1801. Until the advent of the cannon (first used by the English at the Battle of Crécy in 1346), the town must have presented itself as a formidable fortress to any would-be attacker. Defended on three sides by the River Wye and a strong Port Wall that extends from the castle in the north to the river in the south, it became a very large promontory fort.

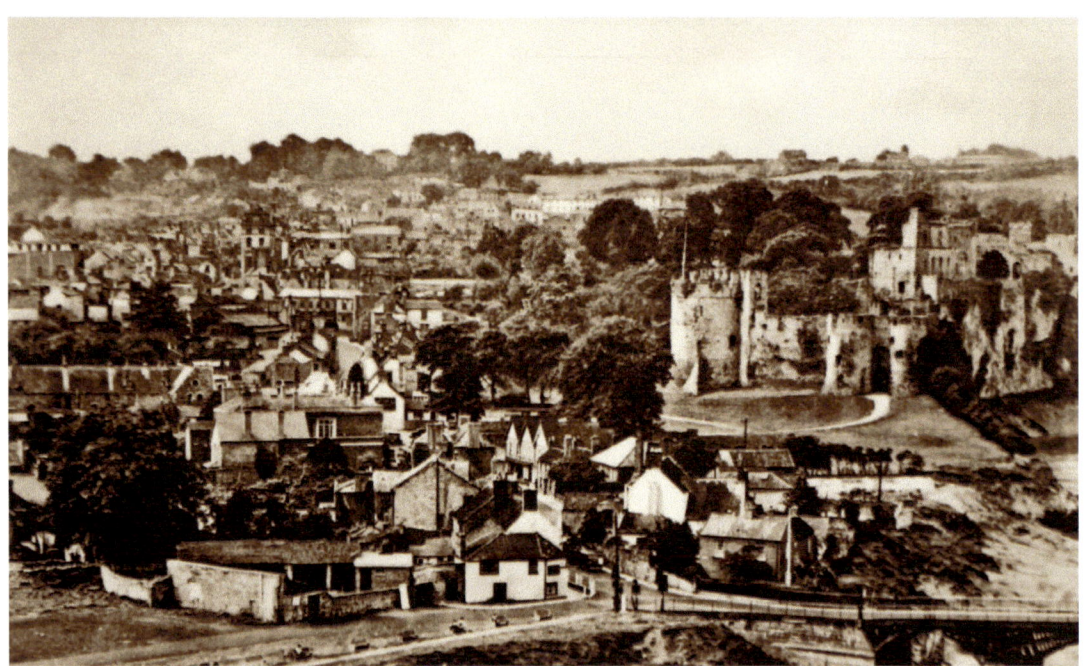

Chepstow Town
The photographs on these two pages and the map on the previous page serve to illustrate the growth of the town of Chepstow since 1801 to the present time. The name 'Chepstow' is of great antiquity and derives from the old English '*ceap/chepe stowe*' meaning market place or trading centre. The word 'stow' usually denotes a place of special significance, whilst the root 'chep' is the same as in other place names such as Chipping Sodbury and Cheapside. First recorded in 1307, Chepstow may have been used by the English in earlier centuries.

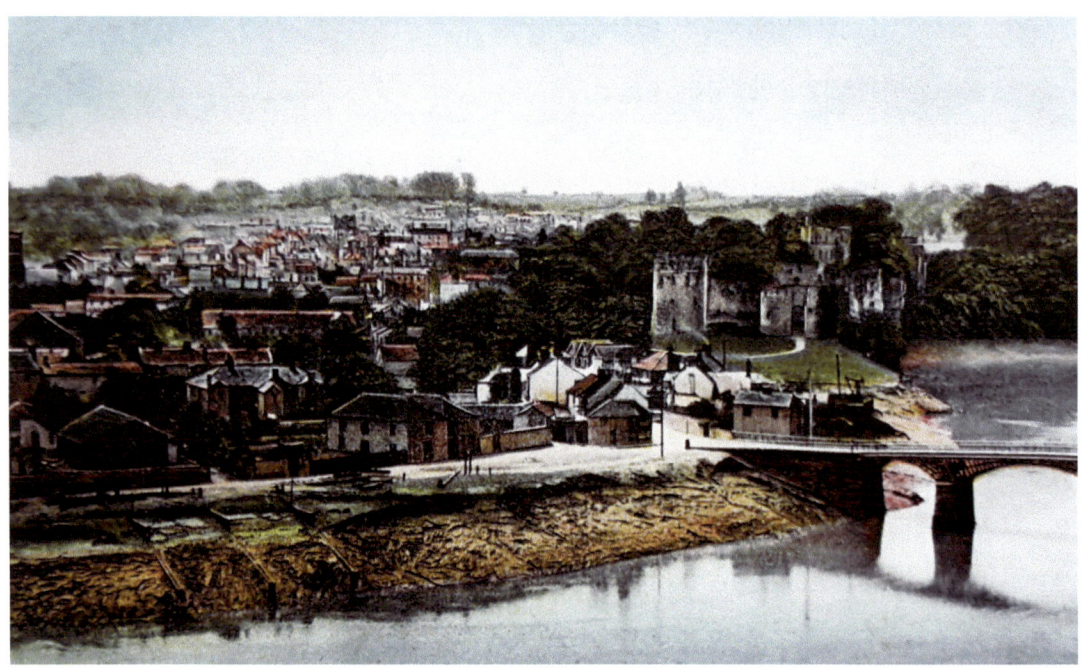

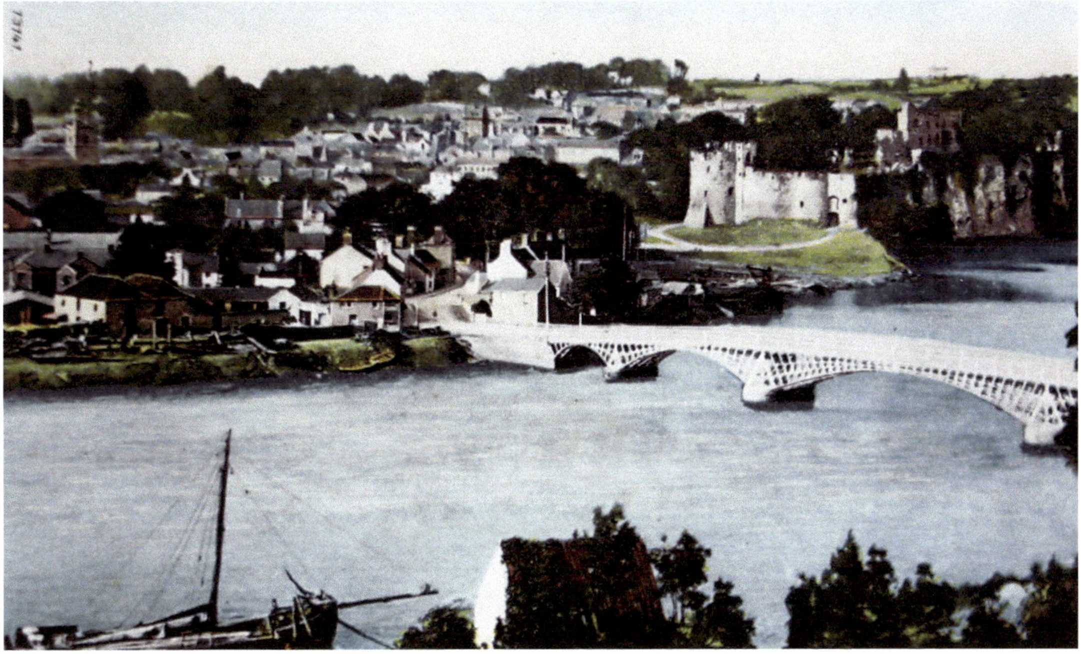

Chepstow Town

The Normans called the castle and lordship '*Striguil*' or '*Estrighoiel*' which probably derived from the Welsh '*ystraigyl*', meaning a bend in the river. The Welsh name '*Cas-gwent*' refers to the 'castle of Gwent'.

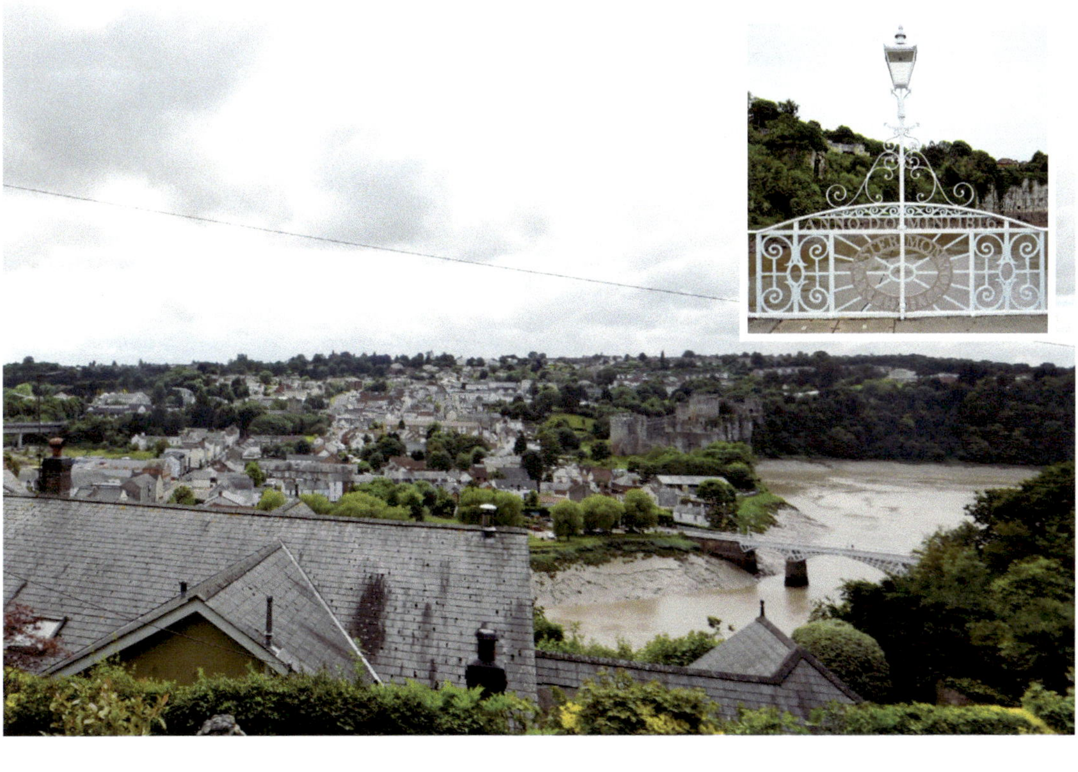

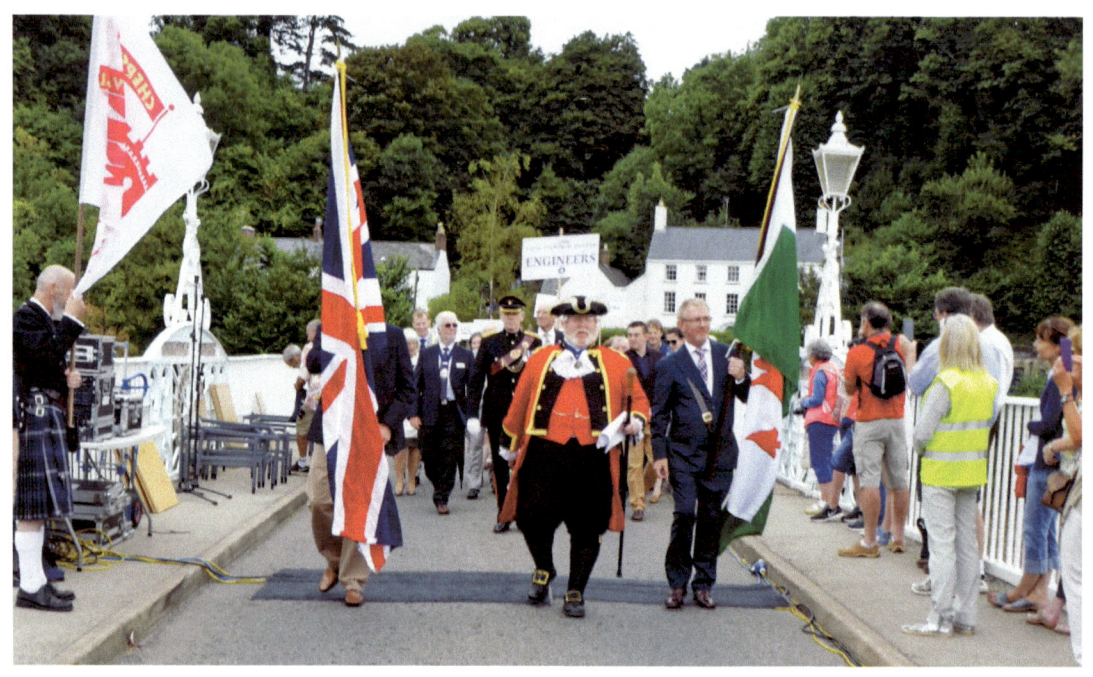

Re-Enactment of the 1816 Procession and Opening Ceremony of the Chepstow Bridge
Two hundred years to the day, a re-enactment of the opening ceremony of the Chepstow Iron Bridge was carried out on Sunday 24 July 2016. The bridge is still in constant use today, a credit to British engineering design, skills and manufacturing.

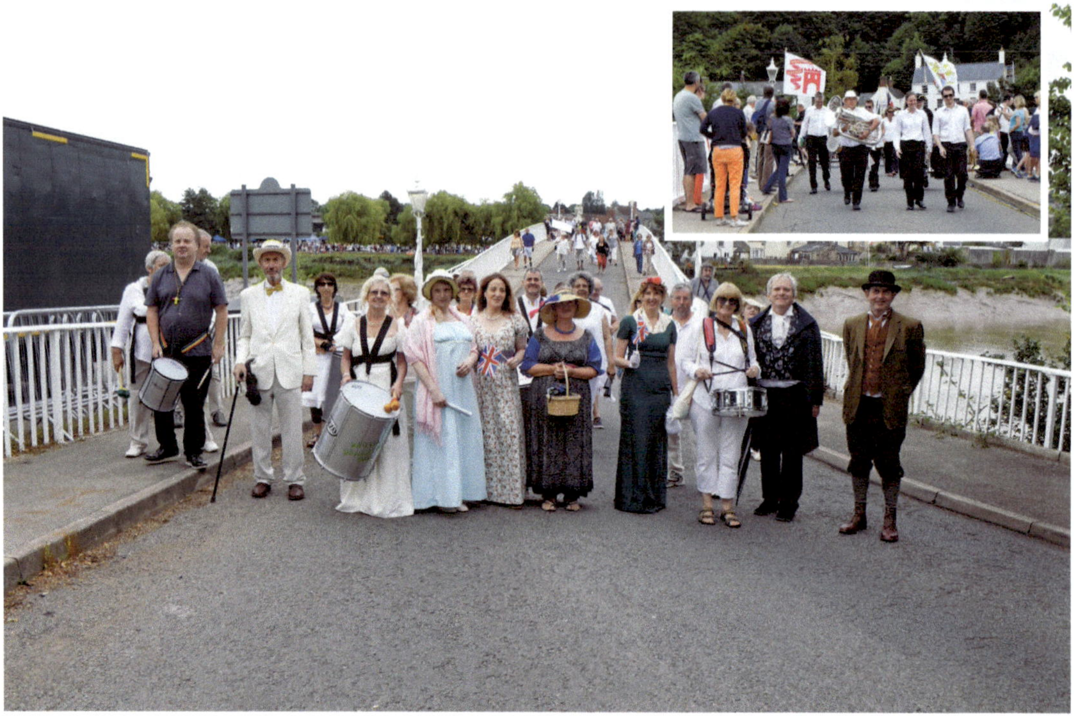

Re-Enactment of the 1816 Procession and Opening Ceremony of the Chepstow Bridge

More photographs of the re-enactment of the 1816 procession and opening ceremony. These include those showing the cavalcade of vintage vehicles crossing the bridge from the English side and their assembly after a tour of the town in front of Chepstow Castle.

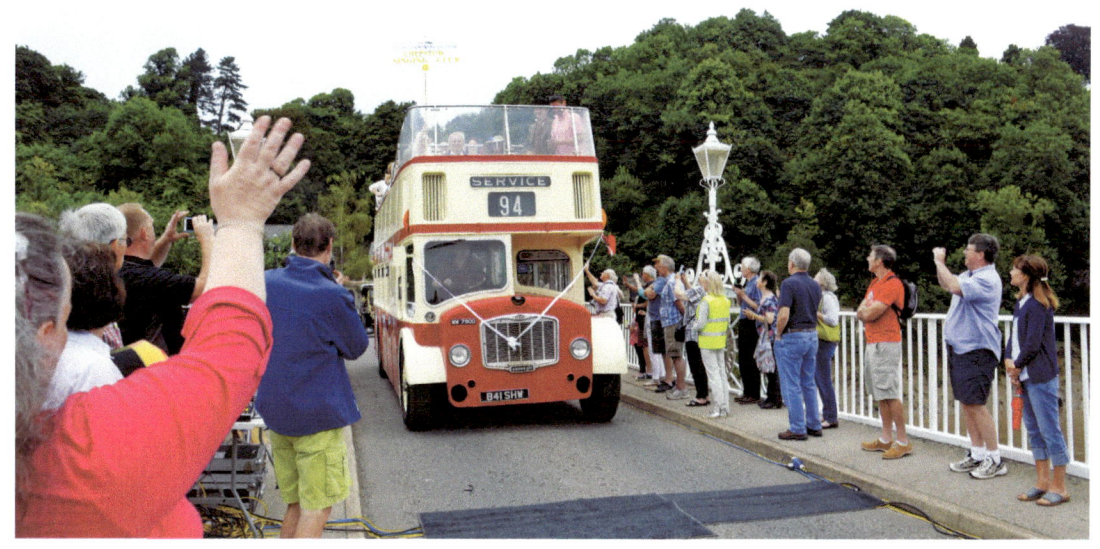

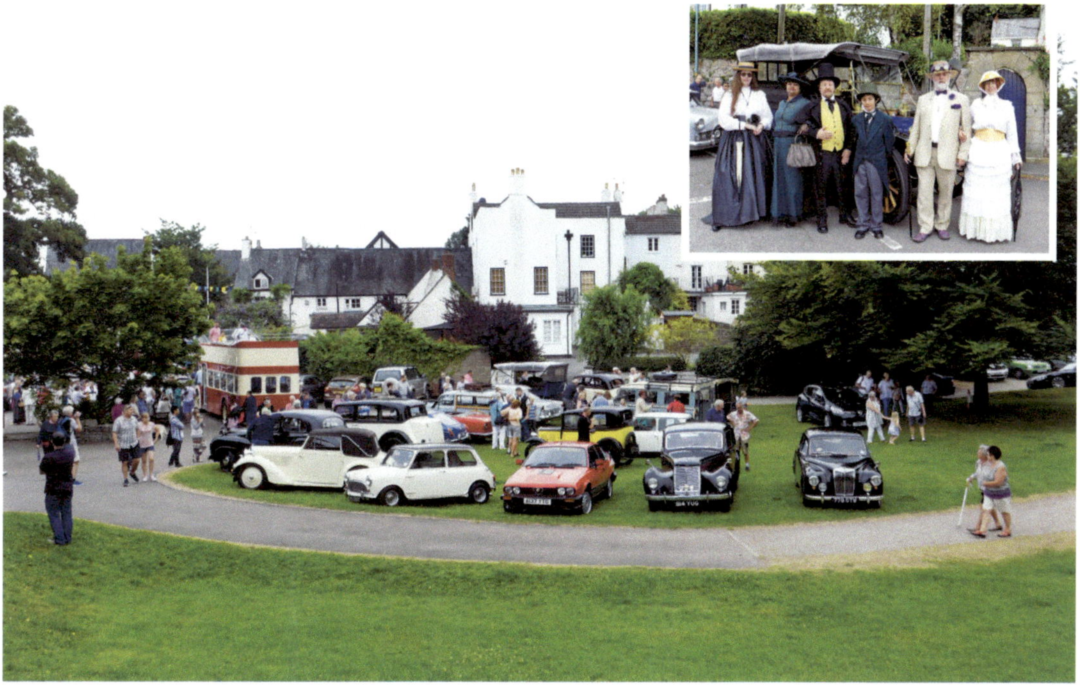

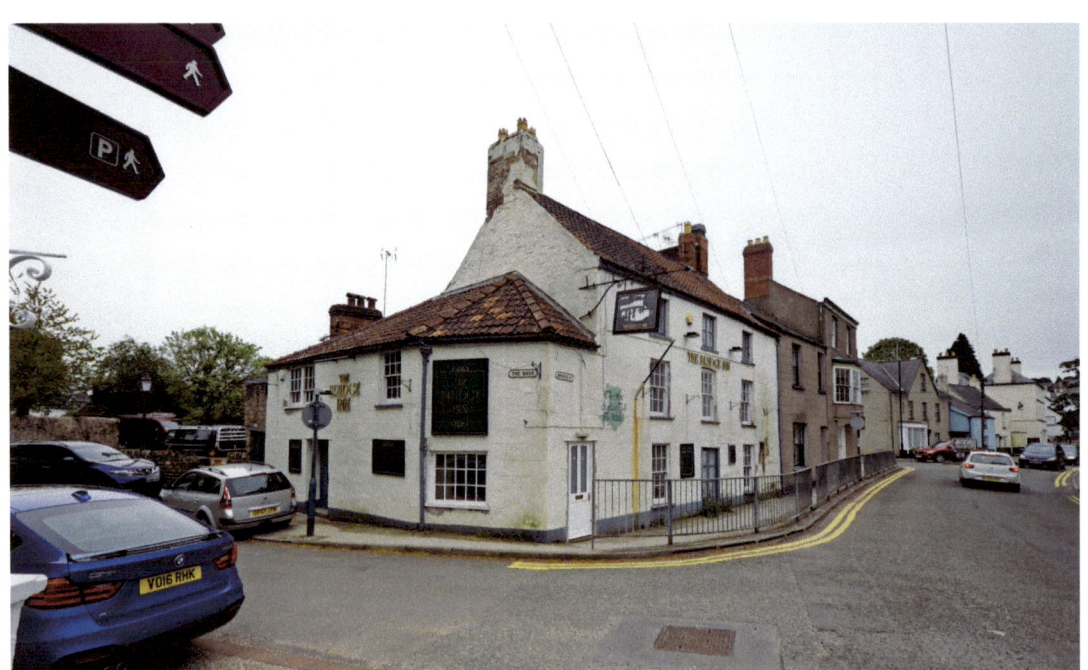

The Bridge Inn
On the Welsh side of the bridge at Chepstow, known as The Back, there is a traditional hostelry called (not surprisingly) the Bridge Inn. It is one of the surviving public houses out of a total of seventy-five that were in business in the town 100 years ago. At one period in time, this well-known watering hole was called the Ship Inn. Also at the end of the bridge at this point is a notice that advises drivers and walkers that they are now in Monmouthshire.

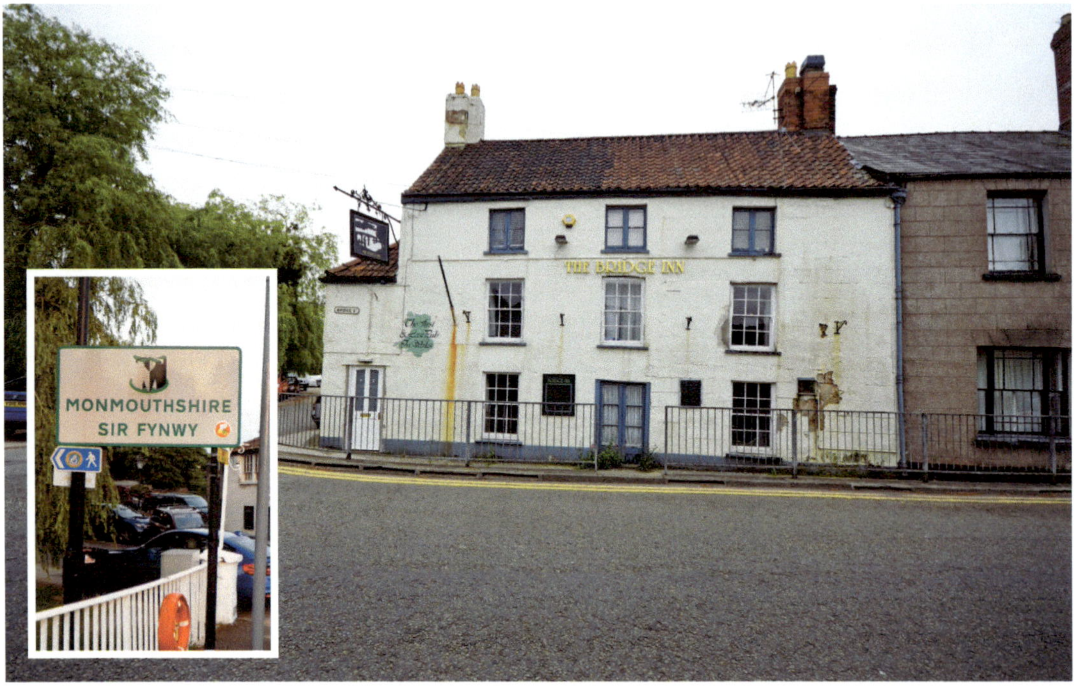

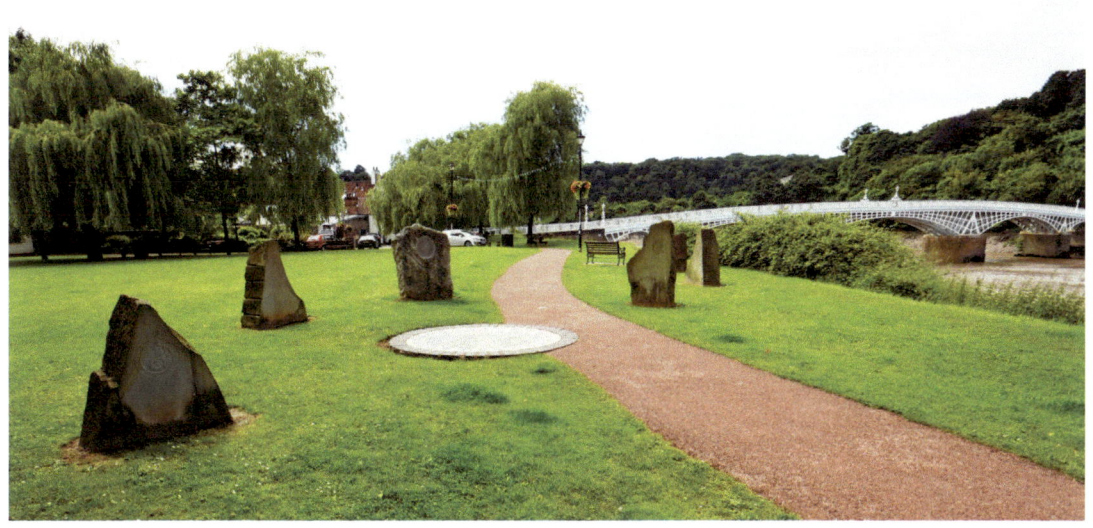

The Back
At this point on the Welsh side of the River Wye known as The Back (an old word for quay or wharf), inscribed standing stones have been erected to commemorate the start and finish of both the Wye Valley Walk and the Gloucestershire Way. There is also a loop here over the bridge from the Offa's Dyke Path that passes on the English side of the Wye. The picturesque little bandstand on the green is decorated around its base with ceramic tile murals as shown in the insert recording The Back's traditional fishing and shipbuilding heritage.

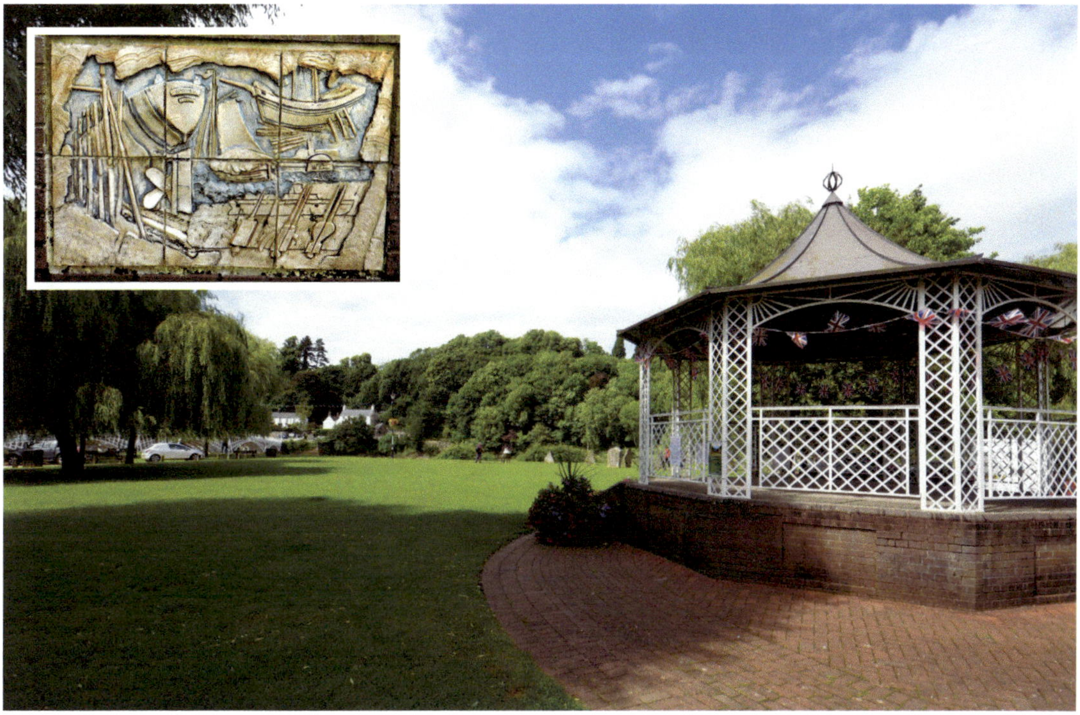

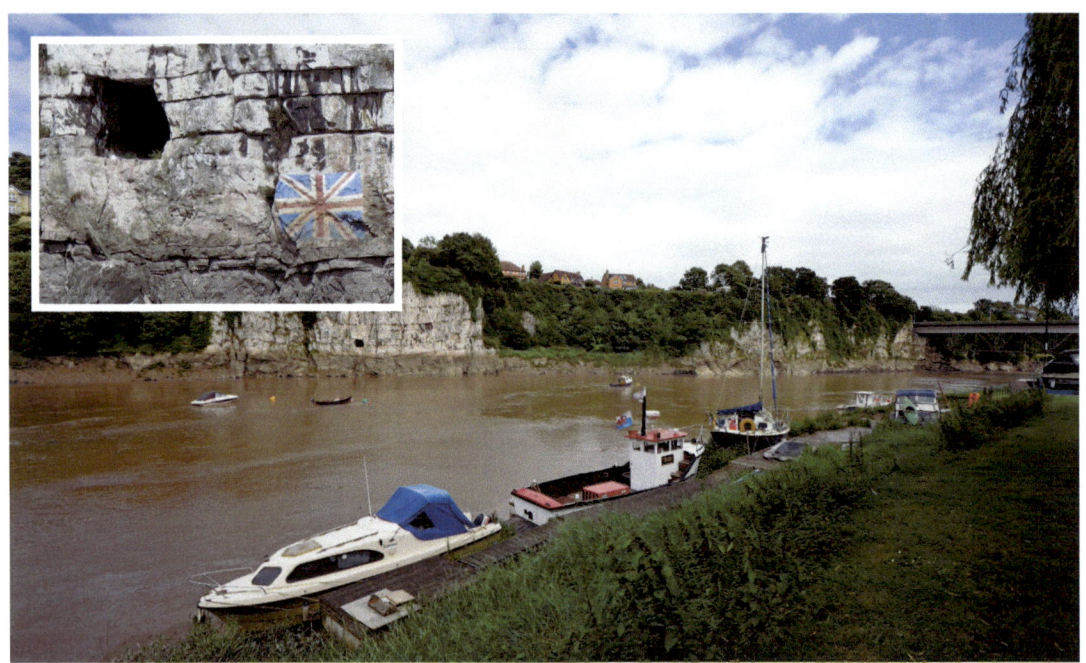

The Back

Extensive fishing and shipbuilding used to be carried out at The Back. Today, fishing still takes place, but the main business is leisure craft. All that remains of the shipbuilding is the small dry dock. The insert shows the tall limestone cliffs on the English side and Gloucester Hole, an enlarged natural cave with a Union Jack flag painted on the cliff face to its right. The high tide mark can be seen just below the cave in all photographs. The difference between high and low tide on the Wye is one of the greatest in the world.

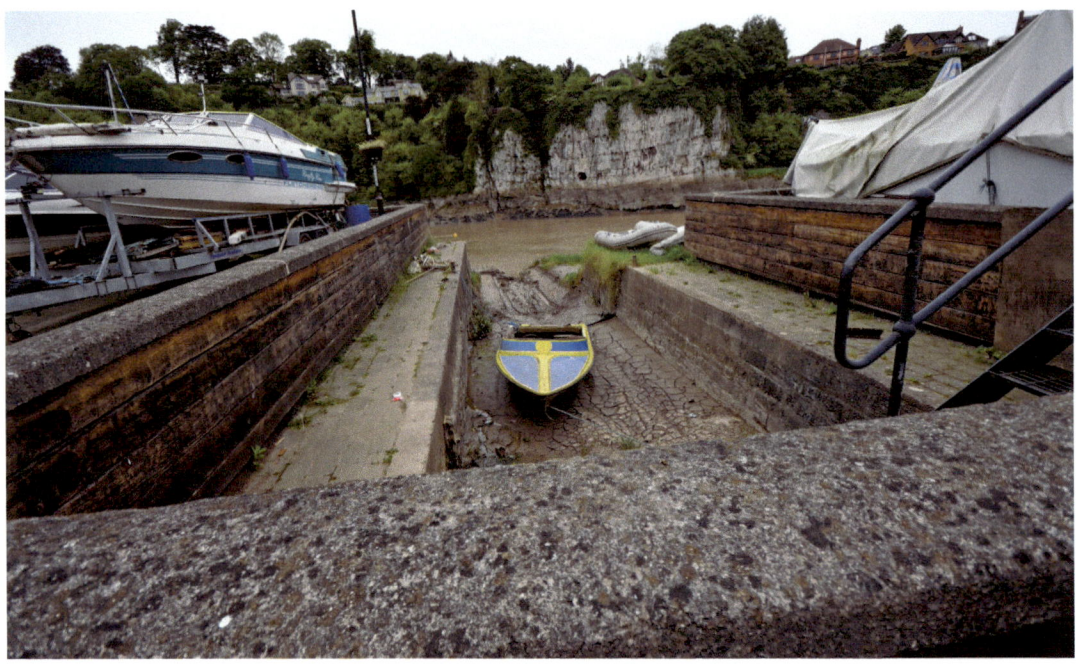

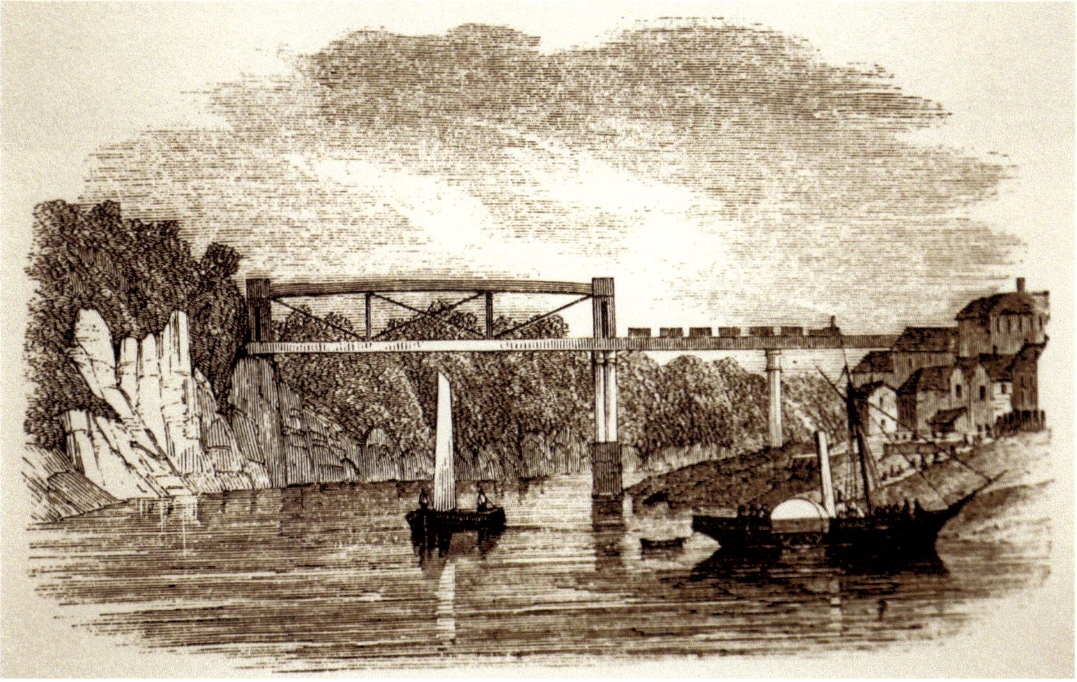

The Packet Slip

From 1822, steamers provided a regular daily service from this point direct to Bristol, greatly increasing the number of tourists to Chepstow and the Wye Valley. These pleasure cruises continued to be popular right up until the start of the First World War. The top print from about 1861 shows the Brunel Great Tubular Railway Bridge in the background with a train crossing, a sailing boat making its way upstream and paddle steamer berthed at The Packet slip on The Back quayside.

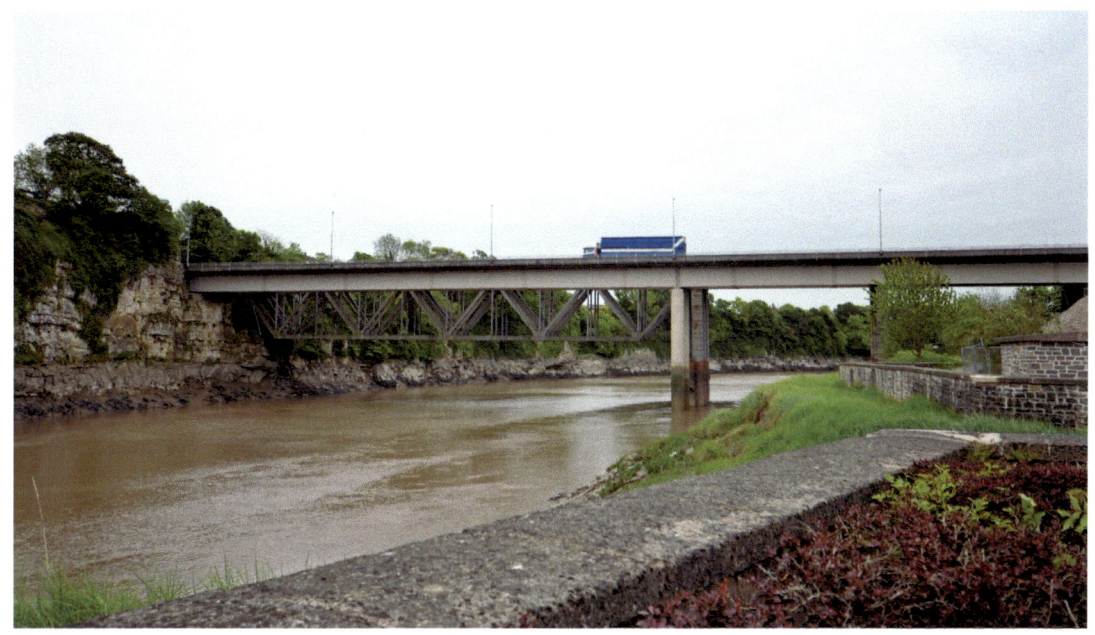

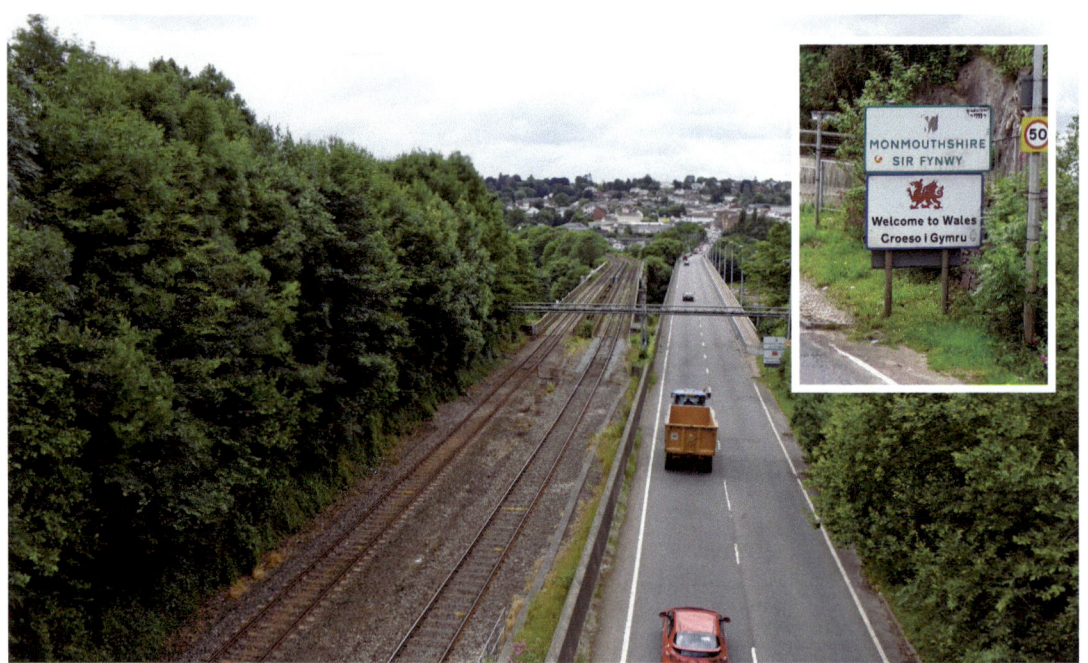

The Railway and A48 Inner Relief Road

The 7-foot broad-gauge South Wales Railway between Chepstow and Swansea opened on 19 June 1850 between Chepstow, Gloucester and Paddington in July 1852 when Brunel's Great Tubular Bridge over the River Wye was completed. Brunel's Bridge was not replaced until 1962. The A48 Inner Relief Road, which opened in 1988, runs parallel alongside the railway line (which sports a tunnel on the English side) and passes over the Wye in a steel-reinforced concrete bridge. This is another point where the traveller crosses the border separating Wales and England.

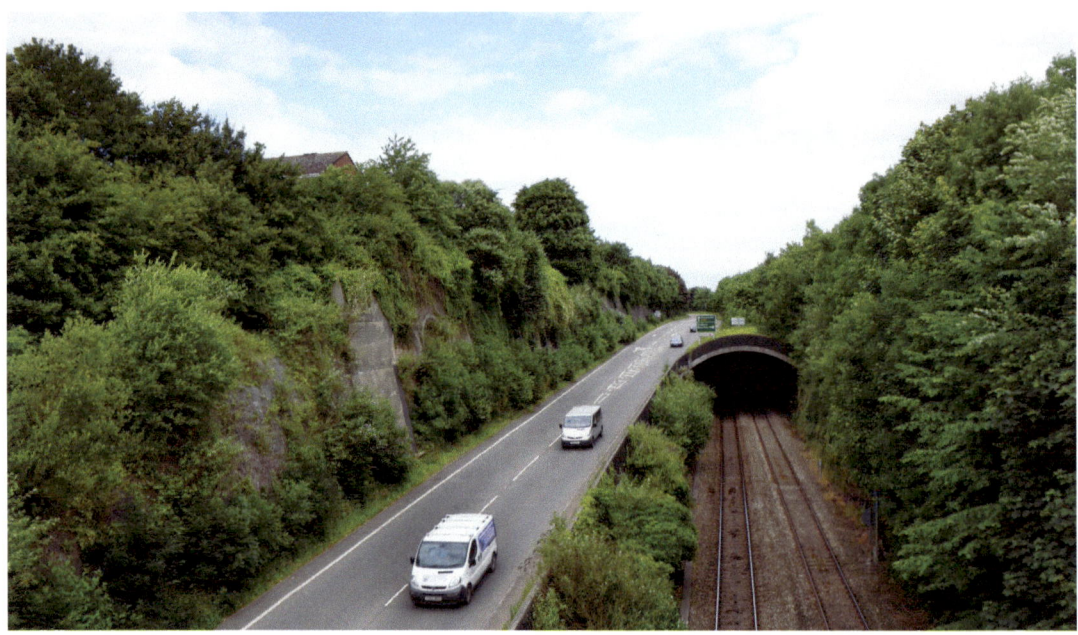

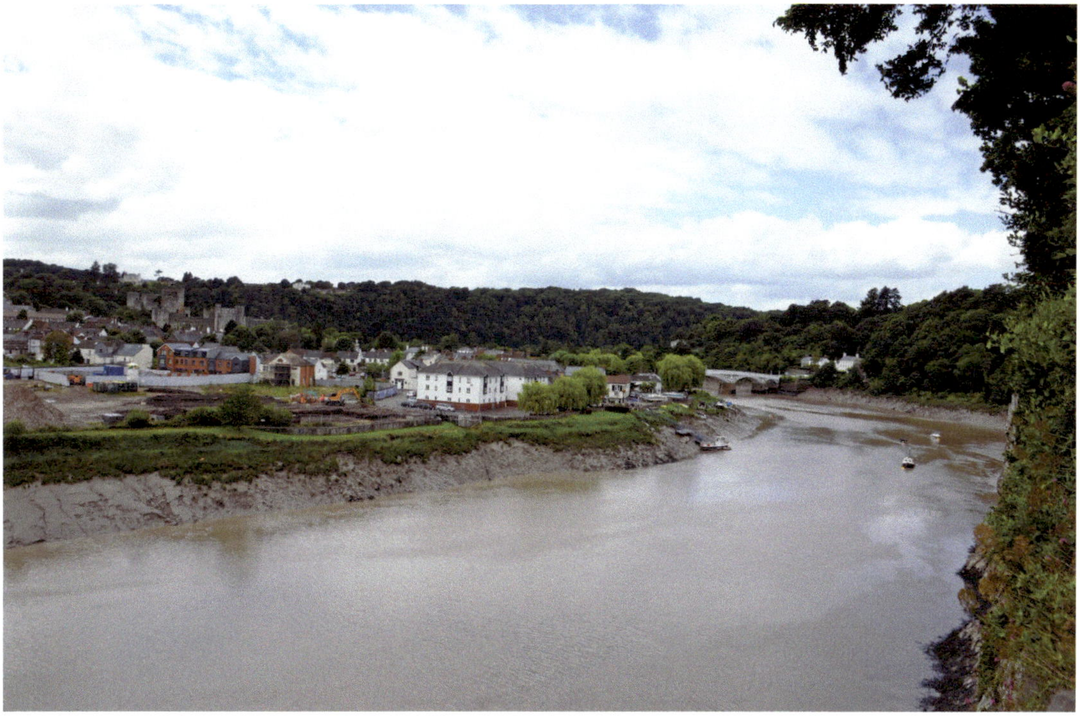

The Back
The top photograph was taken from the A48 Road Bridge looking down on The Packet Slip and The Back on what was once the very busy little port of Chepstow. Nowadays, as can be seen from the lower photograph, there are very few working boats on the river.

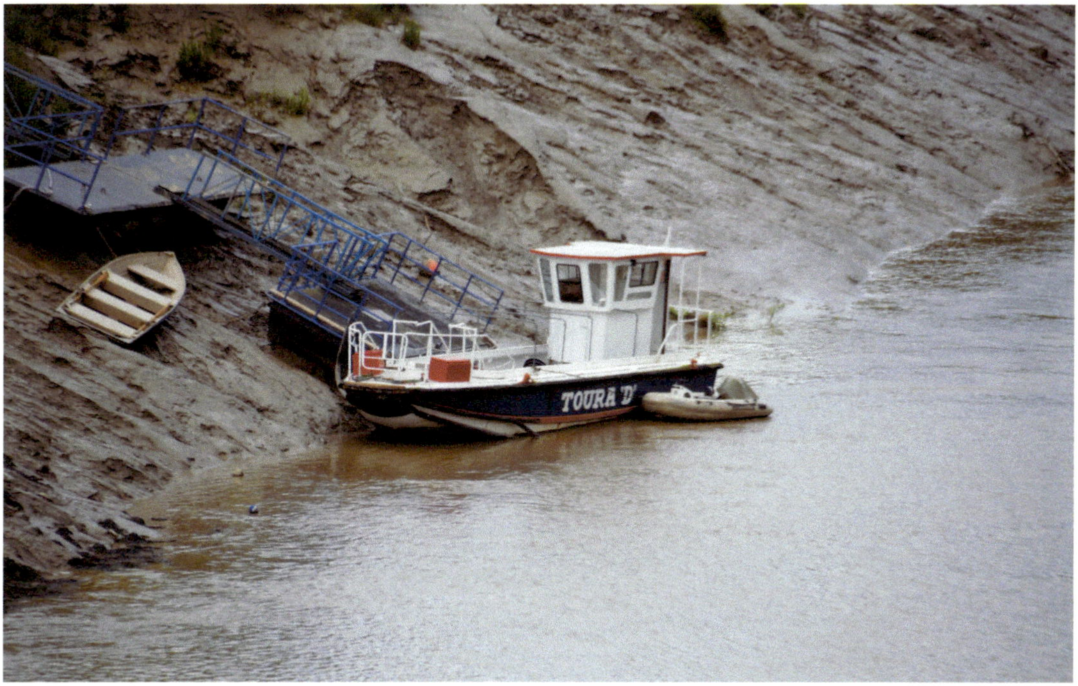

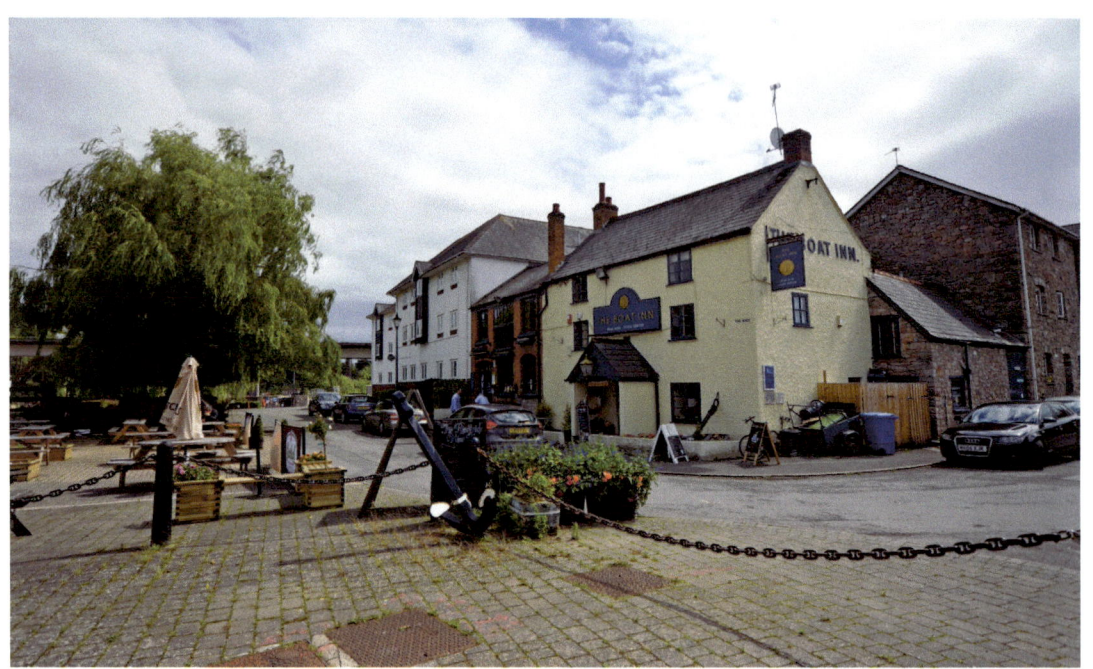

Places of Historical Interest

The top photograph shows the Boat Inn at The Back, which was constructed in 1789. It was once called the 'Chepstow Boat' and inquests were held here in the nineteenth century. In 1840 Chartists were transported from here to Australia. The lower photograph shows 'Gwy House', which was built in 1796 for a wealthy apothecary. It became a girls' high school in 1907 before serving as a Red Cross Hospital in the First World War. In 1921, it became the Chepstow & District Hospital until 1982 when it was converted to the Chepstow Museum.

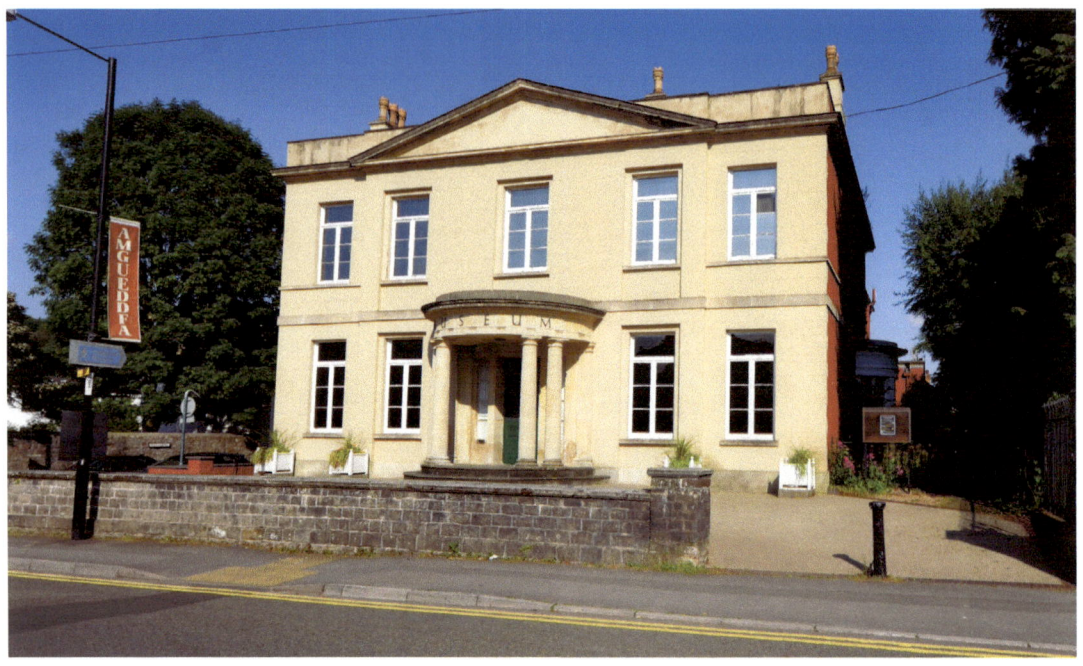

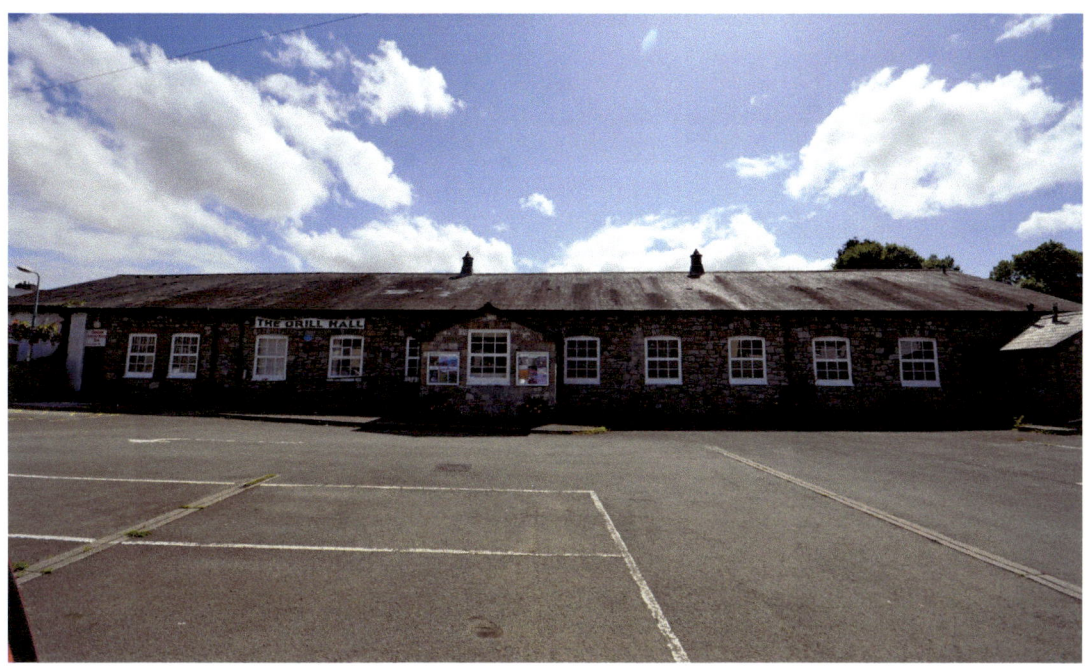

Places of Historical Interest

The former Territorial Army drill hall shown in the top photograph dates back to the early 1900s. Located in the public car park at the bottom of Church Street, it has been run by a volunteer management committee as a community and arts venue since March 2008. Just around the corner, also at the bottom end of Church Street, is Chepstow's old fire station. As seen in the lower picture, it was built in 1938 and now houses a health and fitness centre. Up to June 2007, the building still sported an air-raid warning siren on its roof.

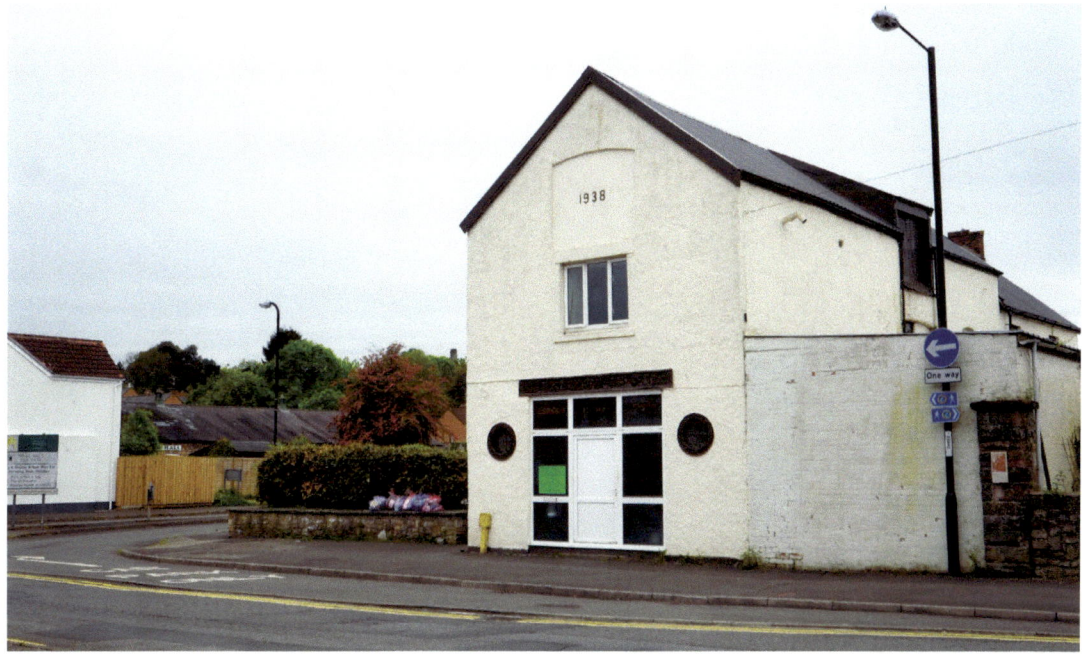

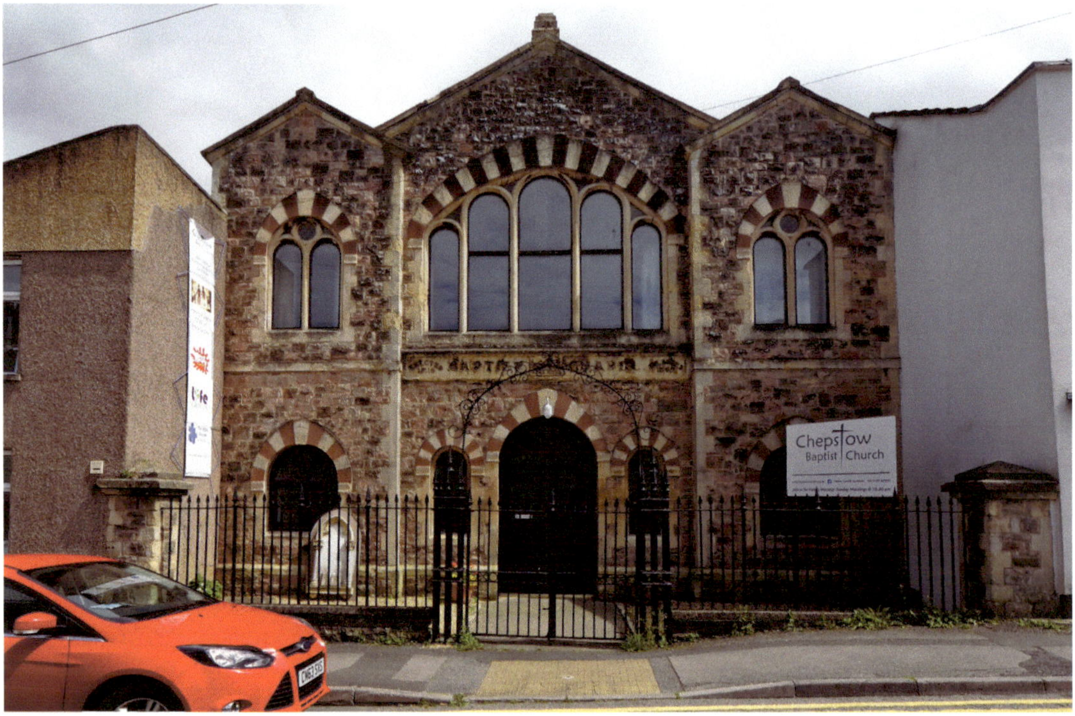

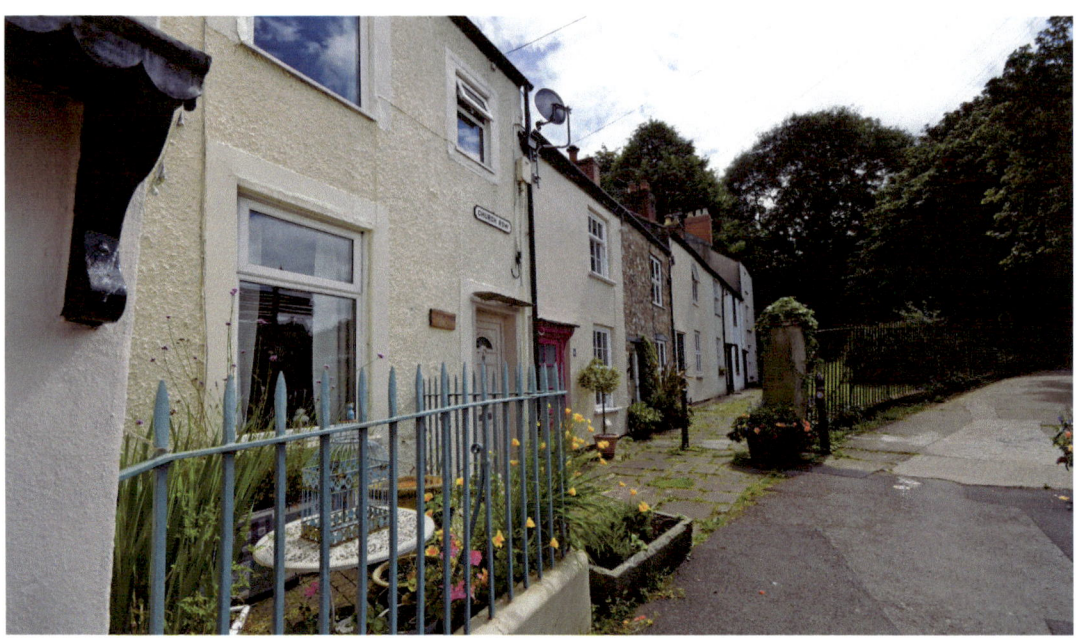

Places of Historical Interest

Somewhat more modest than St Mary's Church further up the street, the Chepstow Baptist Church of Lower Church Street (as seen in the top photograph) is nevertheless of architectural interest. It was built in 1816 and enlarged in 1867. Methodist roots in Chepstow go back to 1762 when John Wesley preached in the town. The quaint little cottages of Church Row captured in the lower picture seem to disappear under the umbrella of trees into the churchyard itself at their far end.

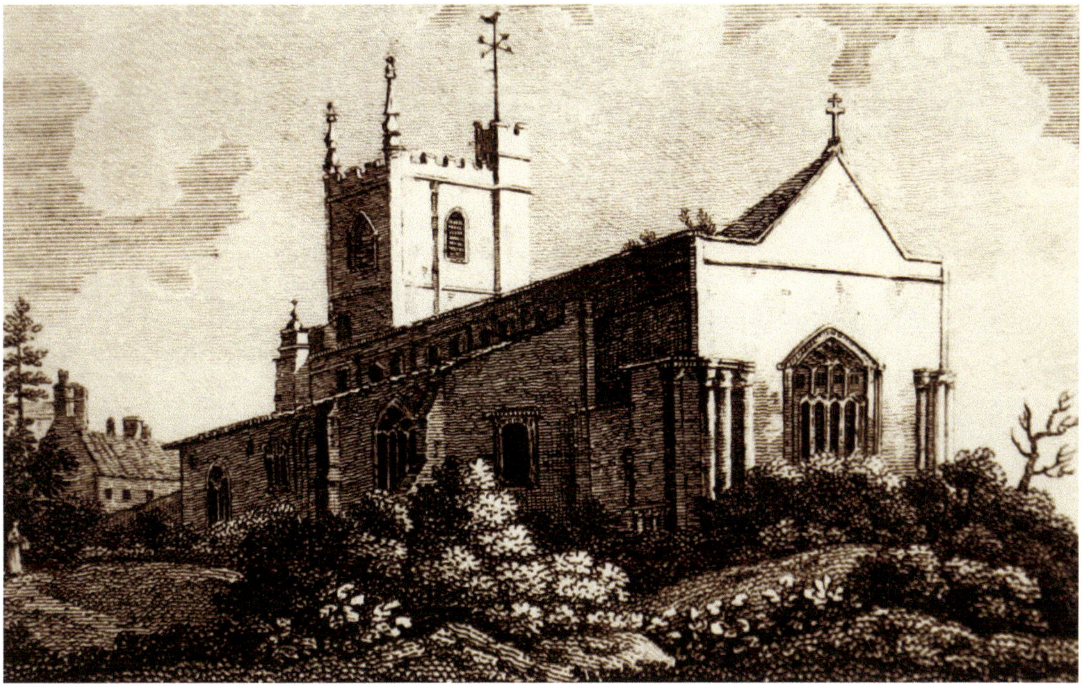

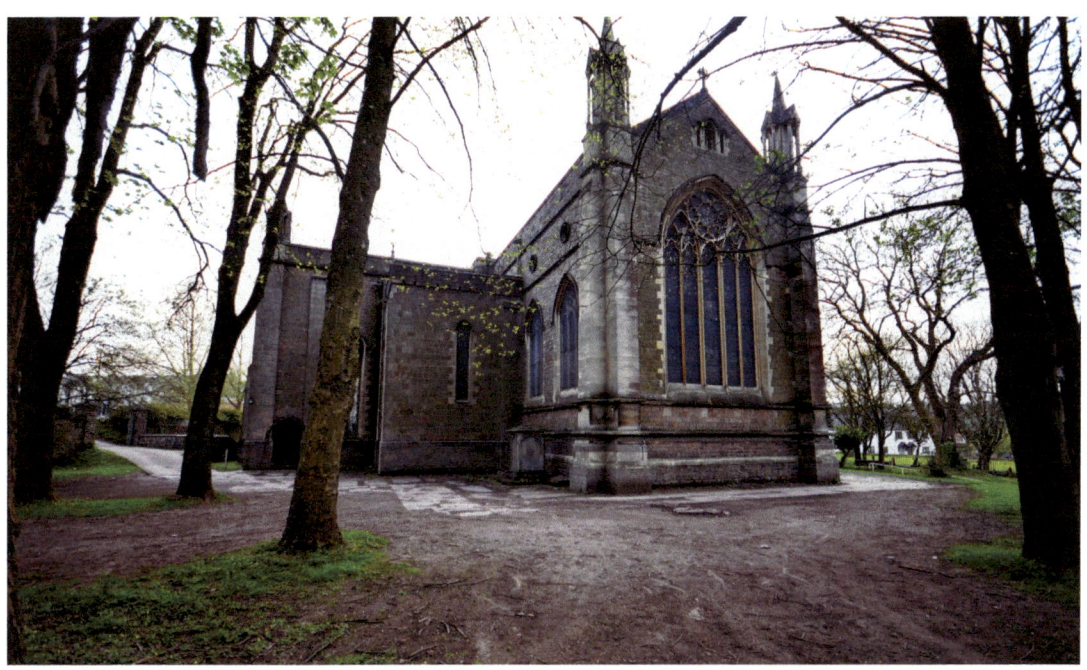

St Mary's Priory Church

The top print, produced on 2 March 1800, shows St Mary's Priory Church from the east. It was substantially rebuilt in 1841 and this is when the ornamental pinnacles shown in the lower photograph were probably added to the structure. The church was founded as a Benedictine priory by the Normans in about 1072 and it still retains its ornamental west entrance doorway. The priory was suppressed during the Dissolution of the Monasteries when it became the parish church.

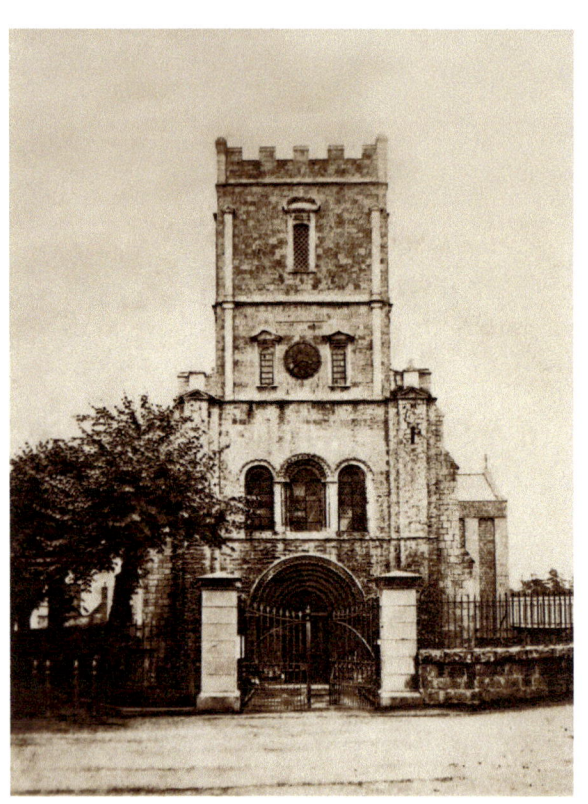

St Mary's Priory Church

The two photographs on this page show St Mary's Priory Church from the west, which retains its ornamented Norman entrance doorway and windows decorated with zigzag and lozenge patterns. Few changes have taken place over the 111 years since the top postcard was posted in Weston-super-Mare on 23 July 1905 following a visit to Chepstow and the church.

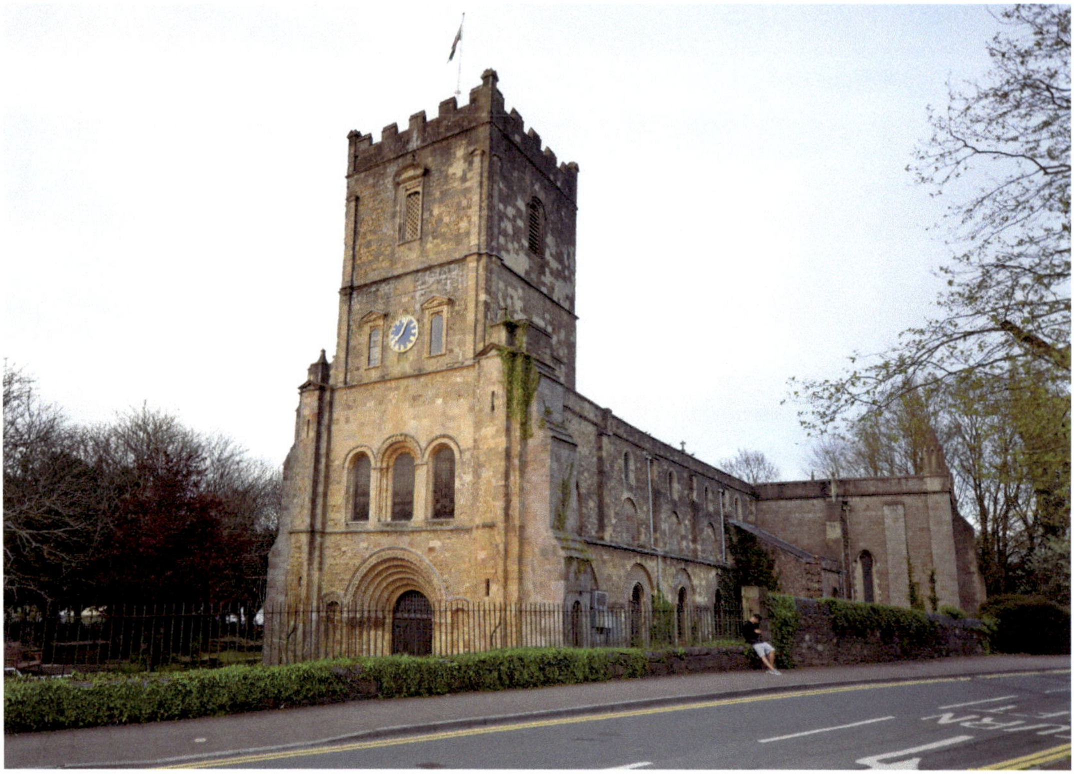

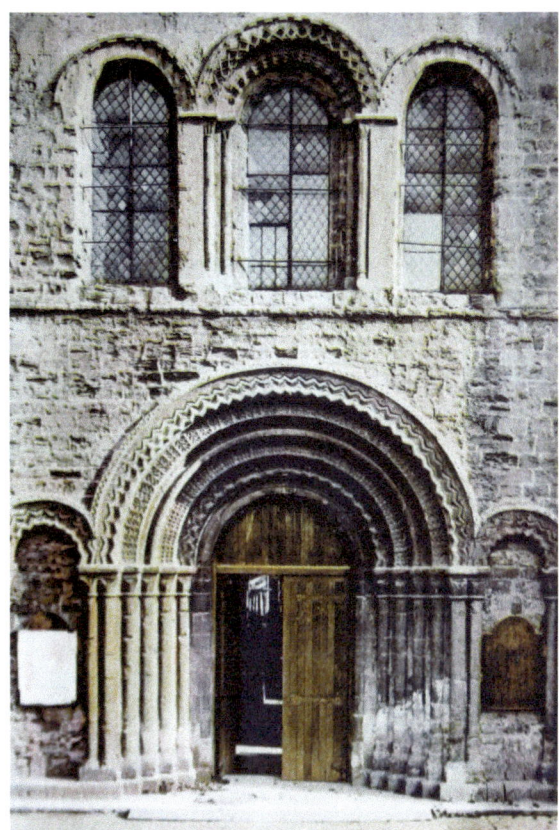

St Mary's Priory Church

Details of the very ornate Norman west doorway are shown in these two pictures, with the top tinted one probably dating from the early 1900s. The elaborate zigzag and lozenge patterns of the distinctive Norman arch standing on a series of columns clearly stand out over the church's west doorway and above where the design is echoed in the three windows.

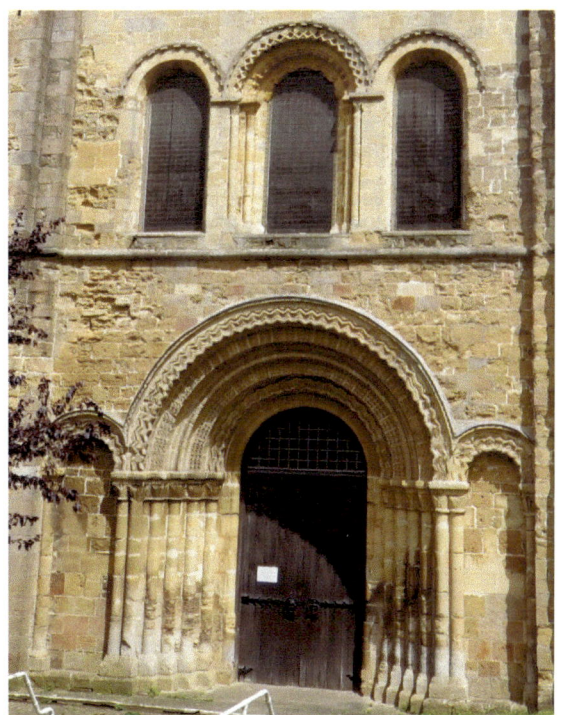

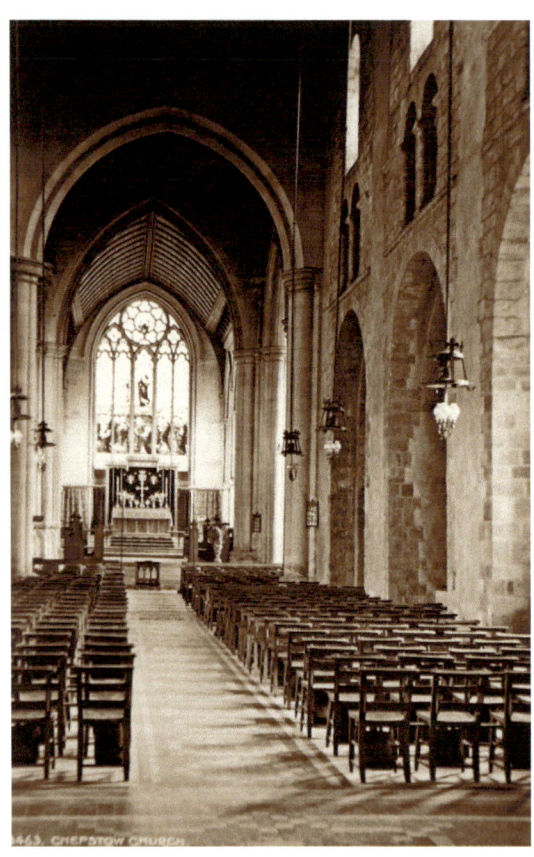

St Mary's Priory Church

The top photograph shows the chancel of the Priory Church in the early 1900s. Following its rebuilding in 1841 by the Victorians, there is little left to reflect its original Norman foundation. A little more unusual is the lower modern picture, which has been taken of the north less-photogenic side of the Priory Church, the design of which reflects that of the south vista of the building.

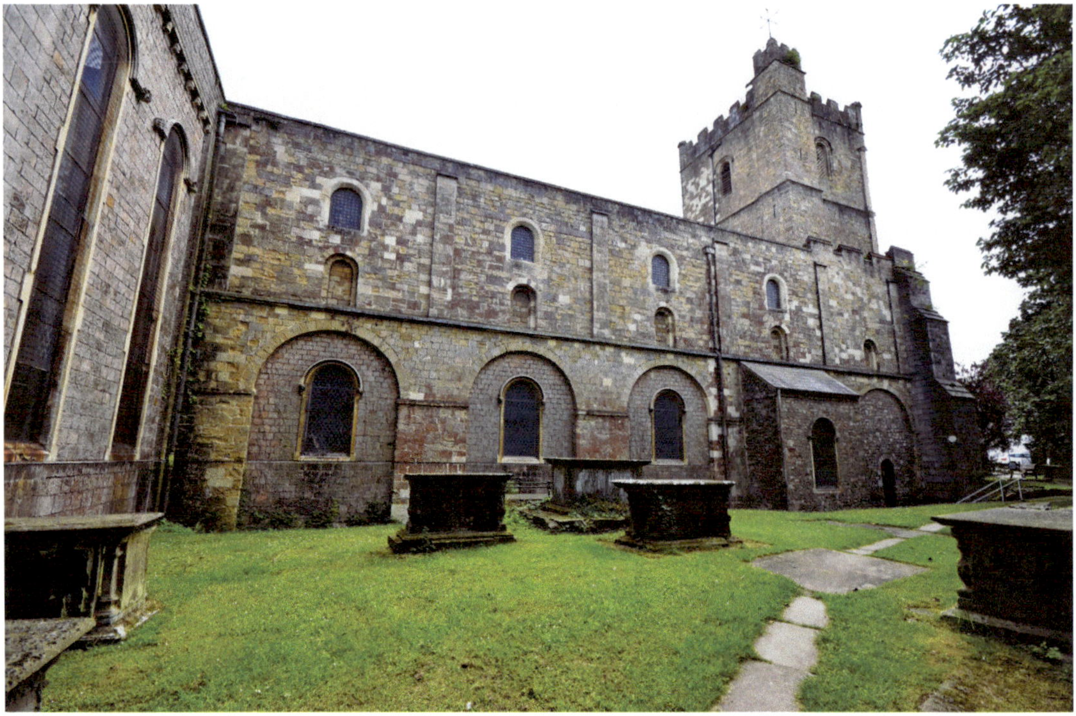

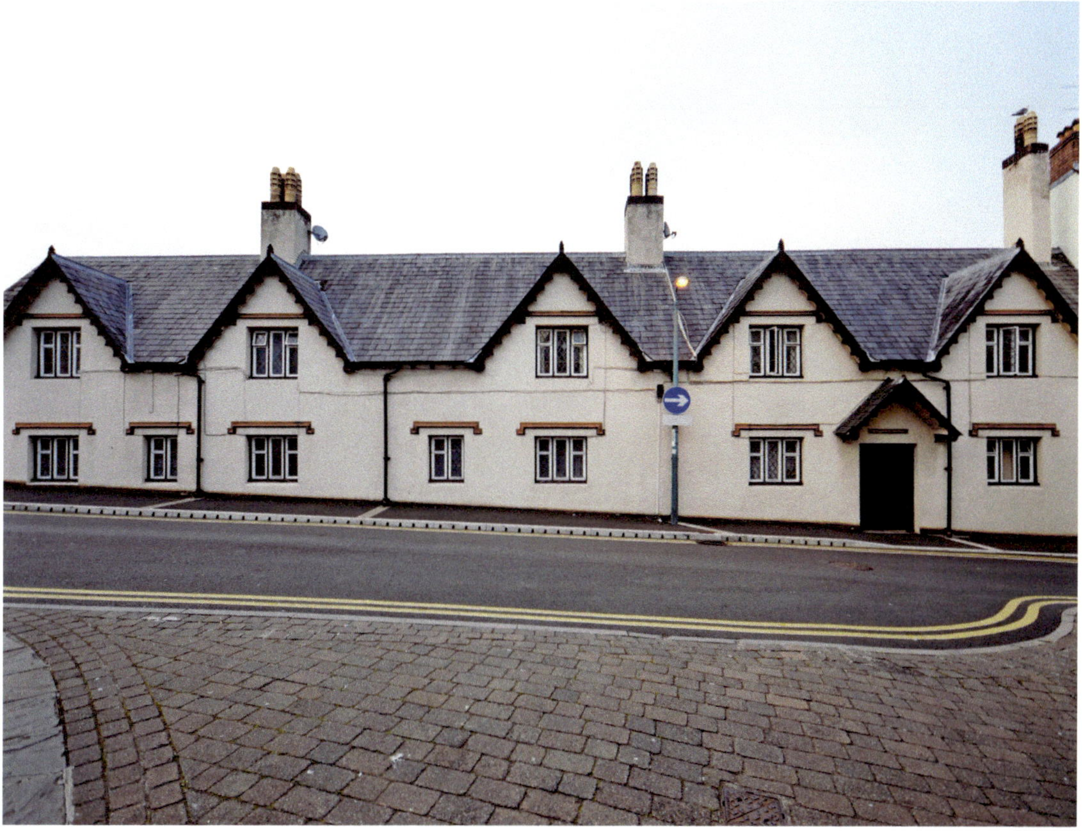

The Montague Almshouses

As indicated in the commemorative plaque reproduced in the lower photograph, the almshouses were originally built at the request of Sir Walter Montague who, in his will of 1614, left his house and gardens to be converted into almshouses for '10 or 12 poor people' after his death. Sir Walter died in 1615 and the institution was founded in 1616. After many years of decay, and following local campaigning, the almshouses were rebuilt as flats to the original design and reopened in 1958.

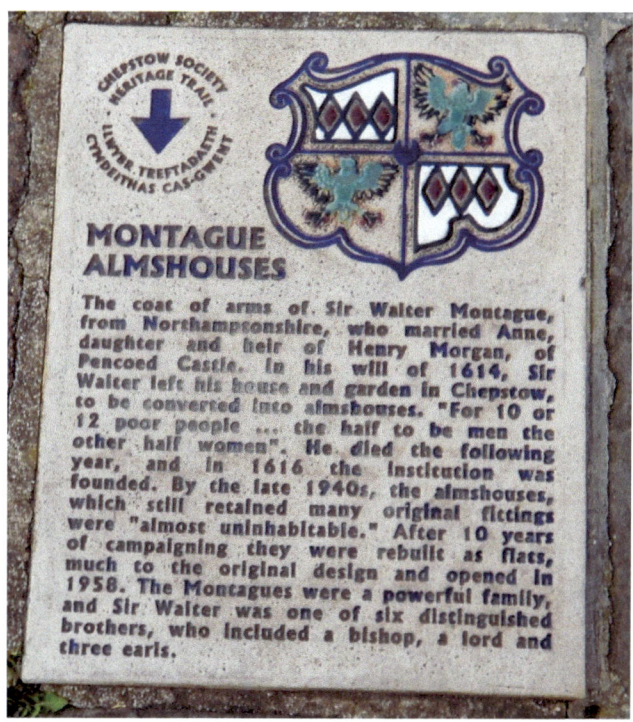

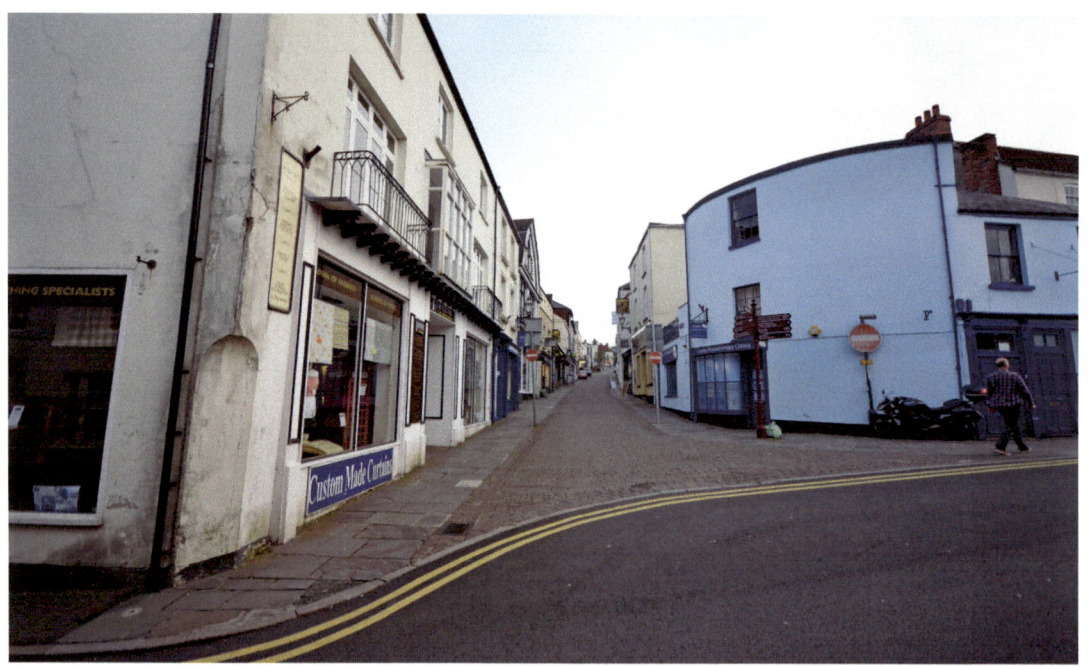

St Mary Street and Beaufort Square

Two views of St Mary Street are seen here. The top picture looks up the picturesque little shopping precinct from Upper Church Street and the Montague Almshouses to a distant Beaufort Square at the top. The second photograph gives a somewhat panoramic view of St Mary Street where it merges in with the lower end of Beaufort Square. The building on the right used to be the old Gaumont Cinema and to its left is the Beaufort Hotel. The building on the left was successively the Provincial Bank and then a NatWest; now it is a Costa Coffee outlet.

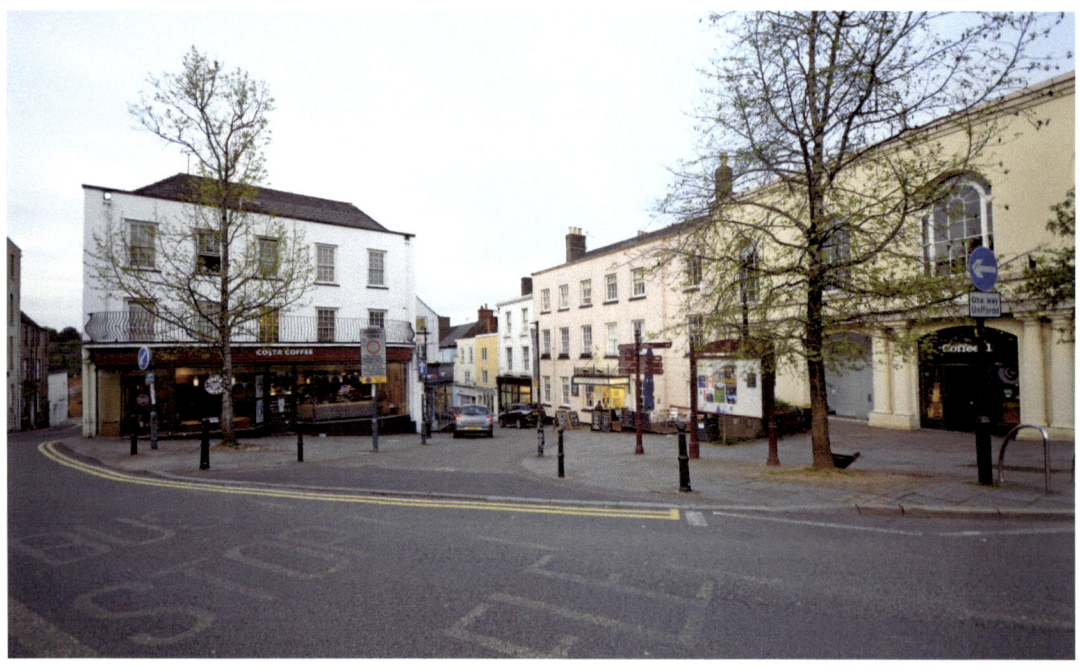

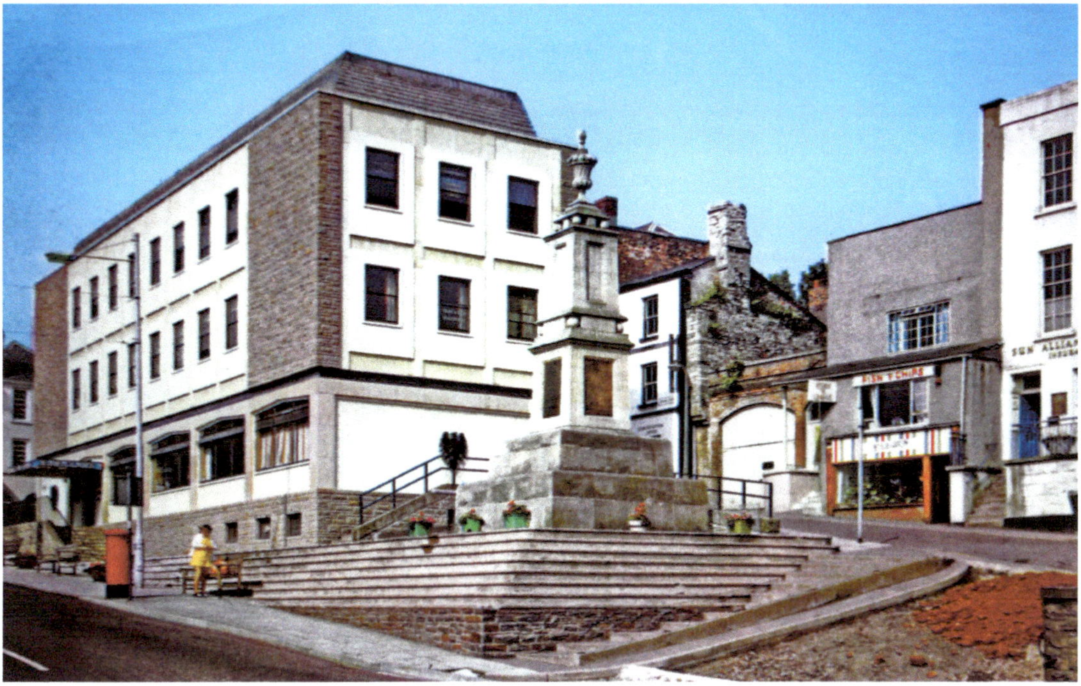

Beaufort Square and the High Street
Beaufort Square forms the centre of the town of Chepstow. The traditional markets were held here for decades until moved to a new site by St Mary's Church and many of the old buildings were demolished to make way for more modern structures or for the necessities of twentieth-century road traffic. The war memorial was erected in 1922 to commemorate the First World War.

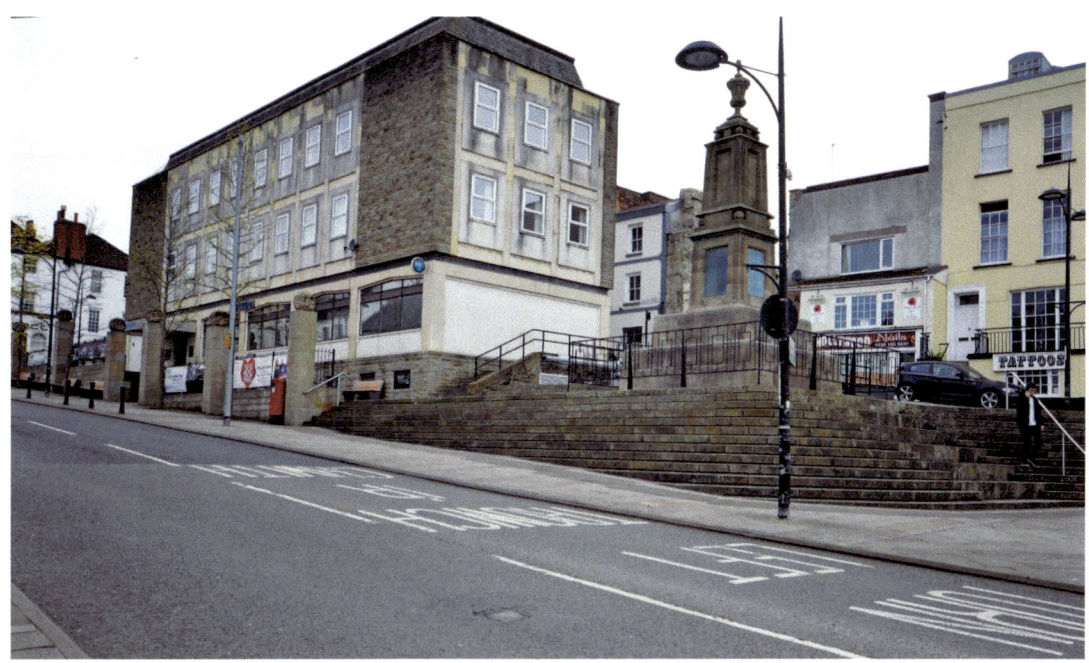

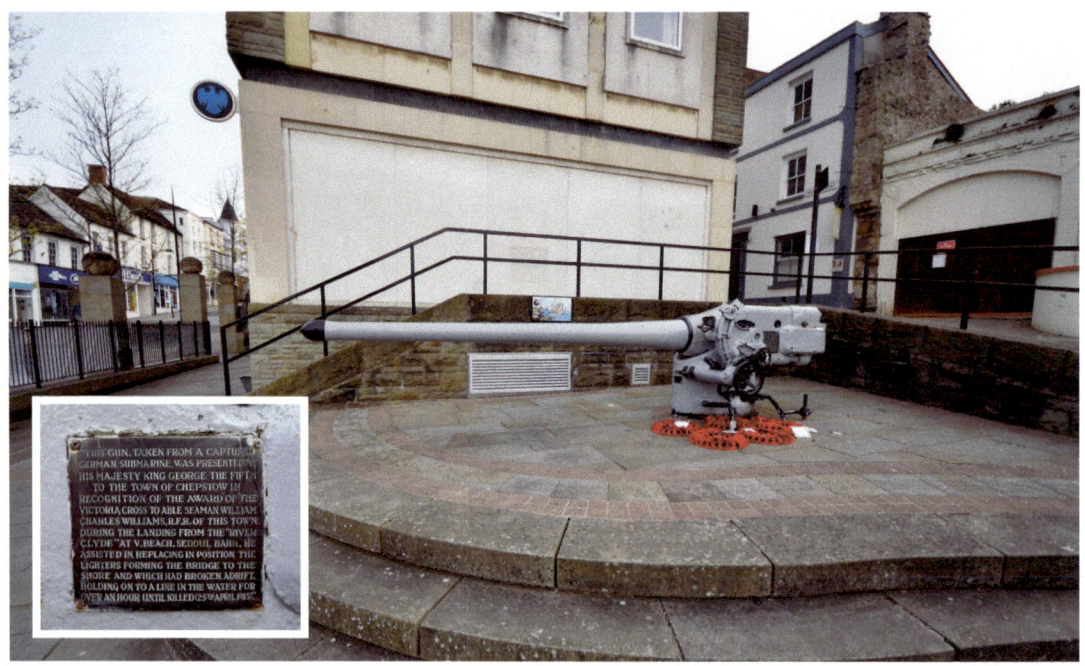

Beaufort Square

Just behind the War Memorial there is a further memorial of the First World War – a gun taken from a captured German U-boat. It was presented to the town by George V in memory of Able Seaman William Charles Williams who was posthumously awarded the Victoria Cross for action in the Dardanelles Campaign. A little further up the High Street is the solitary larger-than-life bronze sculpture of a naked man entitled *The Boatman*. The work of sculptor André Wallace, this controversial piece was put in place in 2005 as part of Chepstow's regeneration scheme.

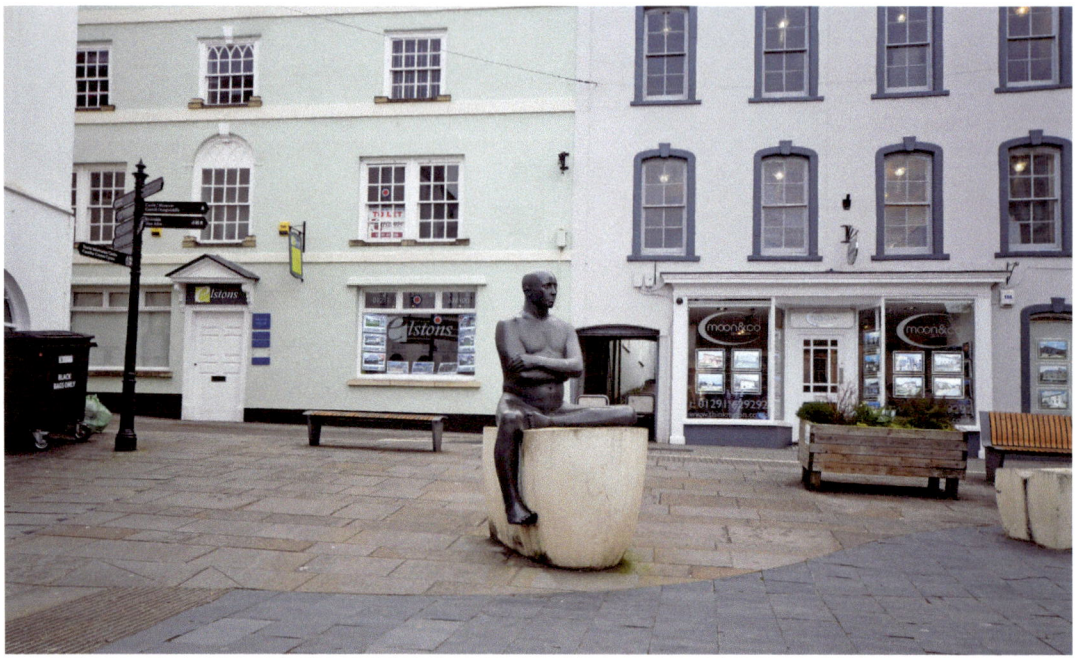

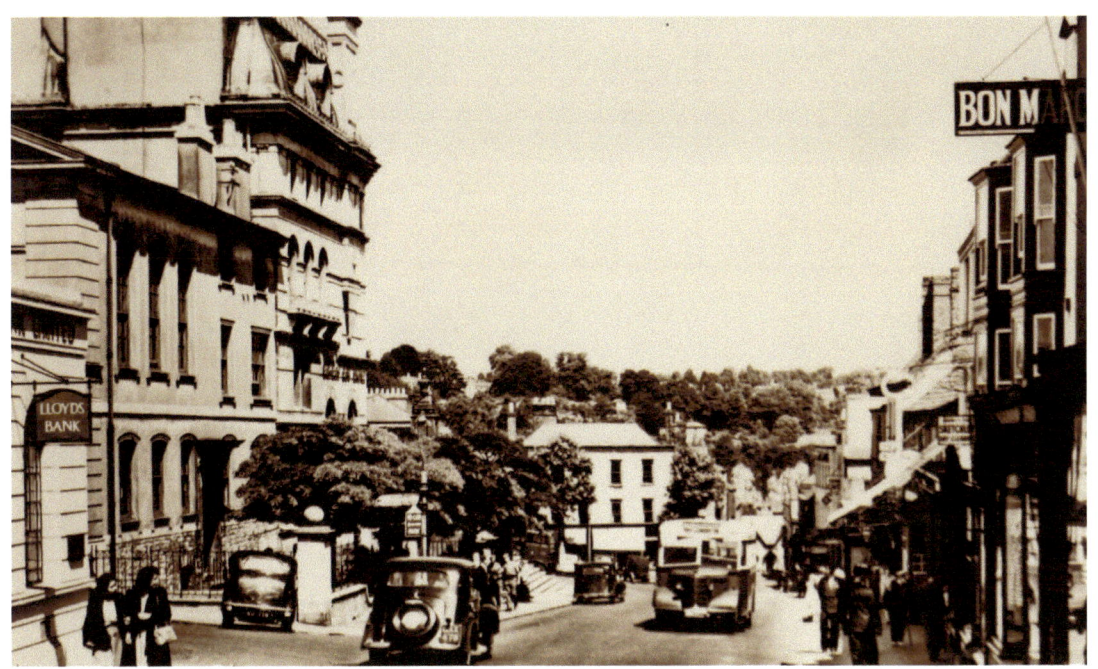

The High Street
Looking down a crowded High Street to Beaufort Square in the late 1950s, a visitor to Chepstow would have been impressed by the architectural lines of the large building occupied by Barclays Bank on the centre left. Alas, it was demolished to make way for a much less impressive modern building, which took centre stage in the photographs on page 57. Otherwise, other than the shop fronts, little has changed.

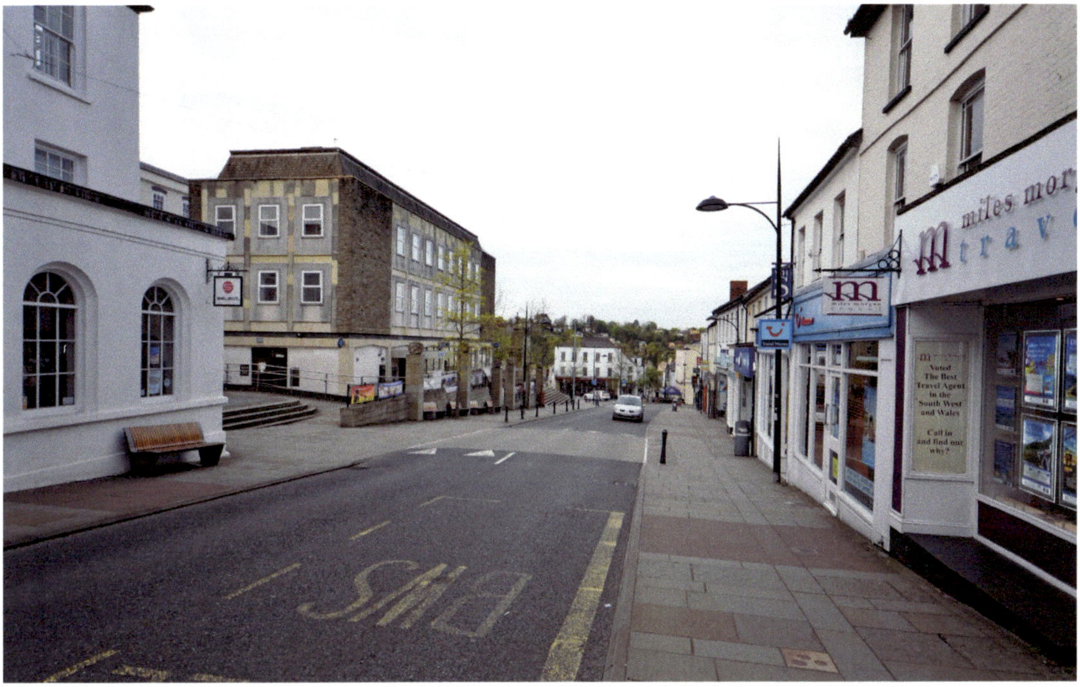

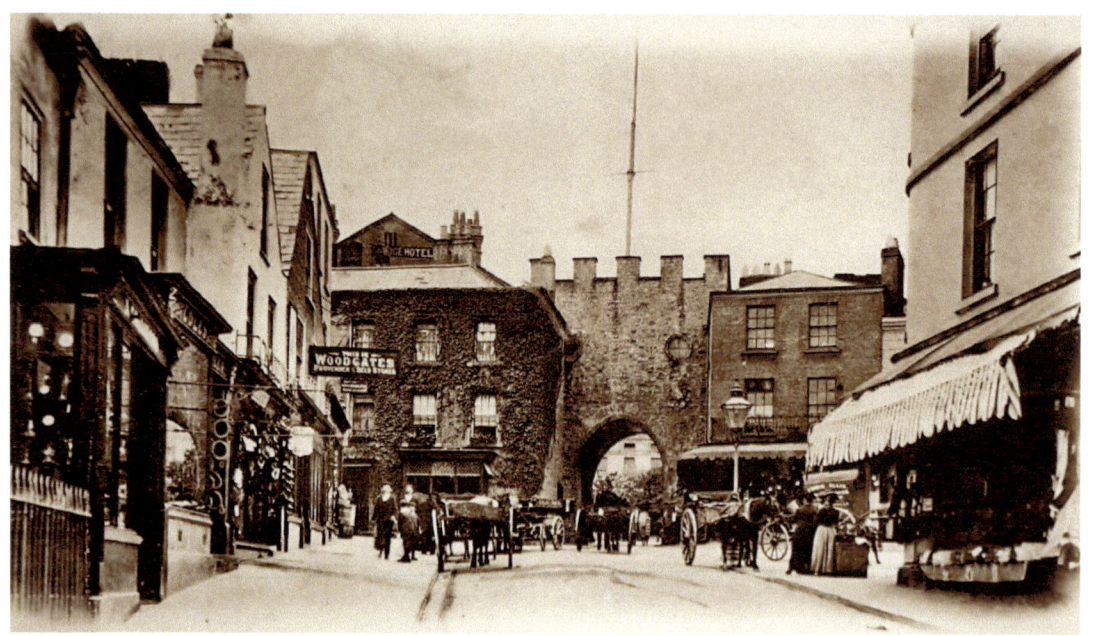

The Town Gate or Gate House

The Town Gate or Gate House, now a single-carriageway road controlled by traffic lights, was once the only point of entry to the town other than the bridge below the castle. It was built by the Normans in 1069 not long after the Great Tower and rebuilt in 1524. The two views on this page were taken of the Gate House (or 'The Arch' as it is entitled on the top 1900s' postcard) looking up High Street to its western extremity. Chepstow Town Council offices occupy the building on the left adjoining the Town Gate.

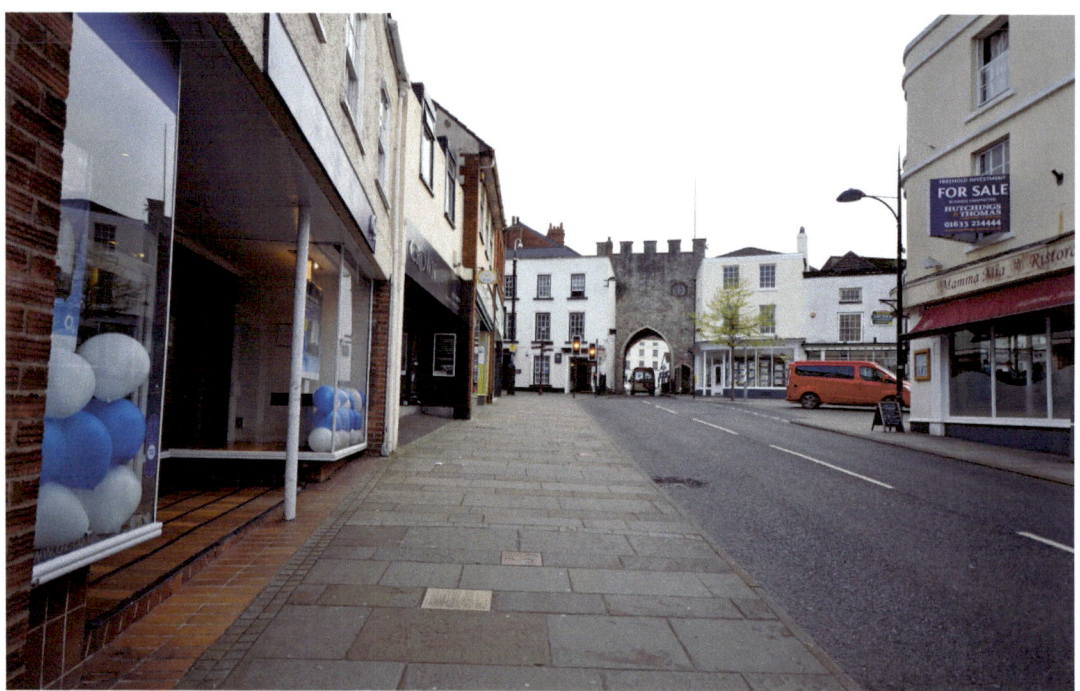

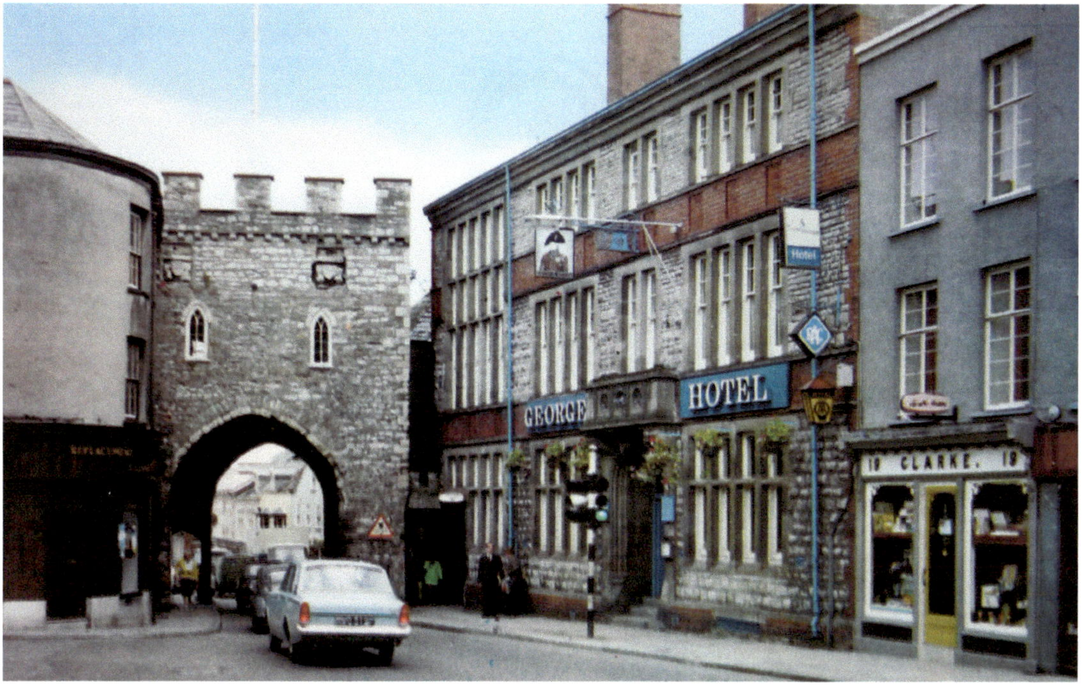

The Town Gate or Gate House

Two further views of the Town Gate, this time from Moor Street 'outside' the town, with the well-established George Hotel on its right-hand side. At one time, Chepstow Museum occupied the room above the archway.

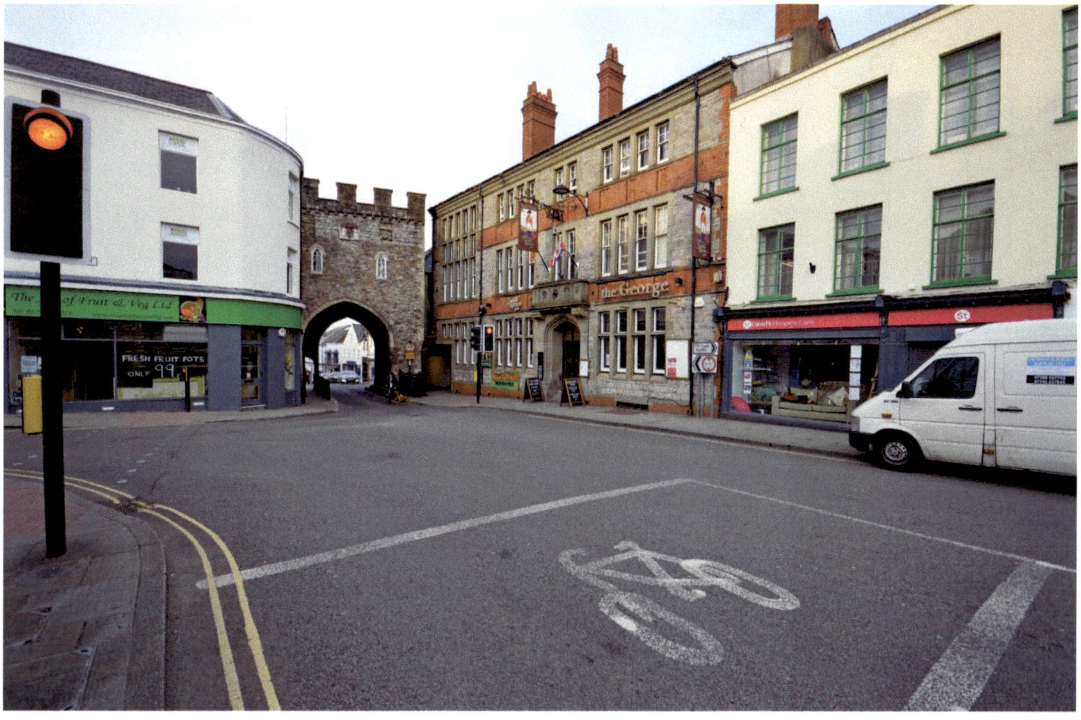

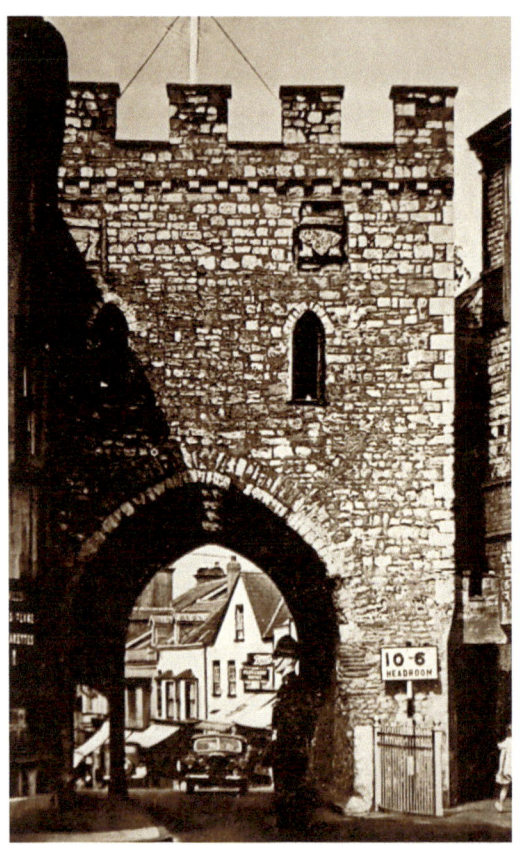

The Town Gate or Gate House
Little appears to have changed since the 1950s when the first of these two close-up views were taken of the Town Gate from the Moor Street side. The coat of arms at the top of the building, where a third has been added in the centre, do however stand out more clearly in the lower photograph, captured in 2016. The Port (Town) Wall extends right and left from the Town Gate.

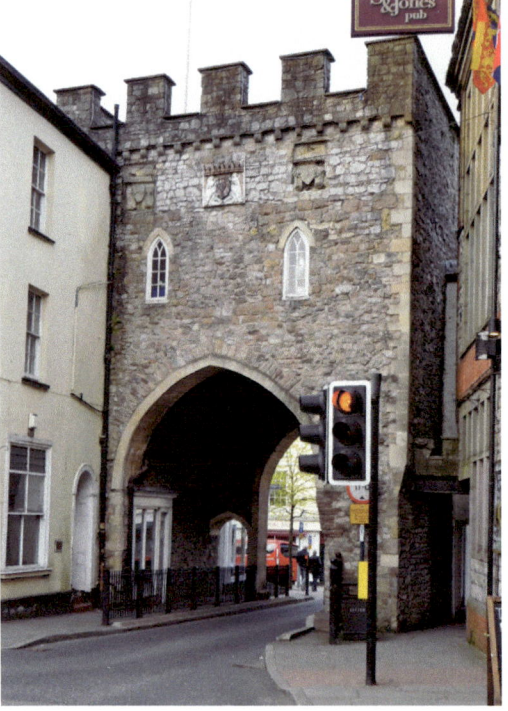

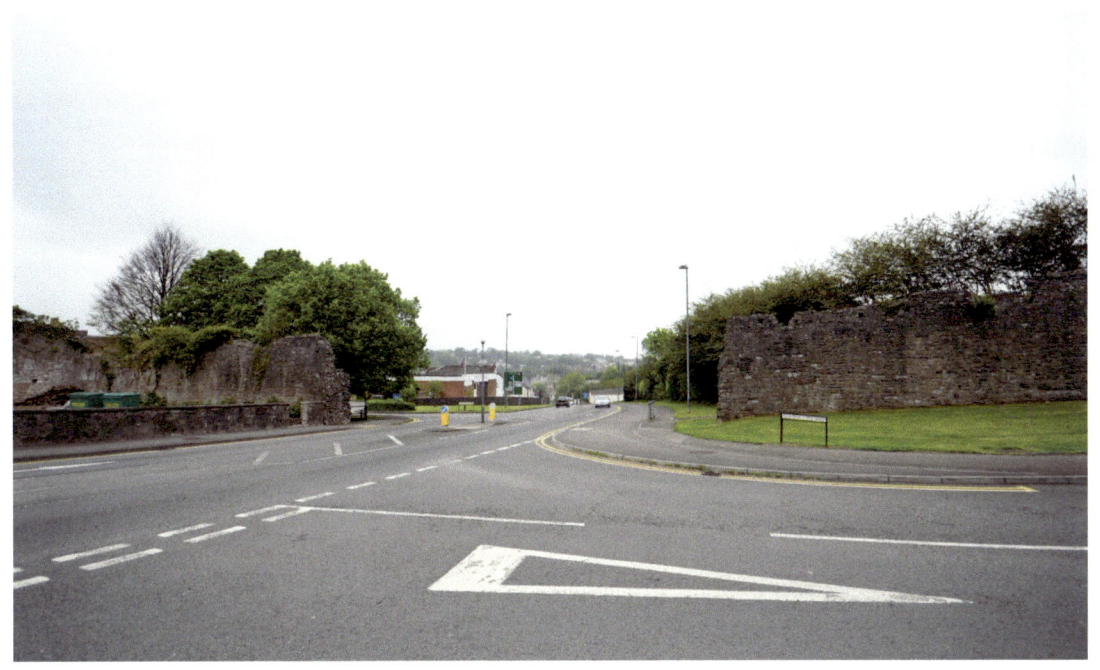

The Town Wall – The Port Wall
Very much of Chepstow's Port Wall remains intact today. The line of the Port Wall is clearly show on the map on page 37 where it runs from the west end of the castle to a point on the bank of the river around three-quarters of a mile below the Chepstow Bridge. The defensive wall was built with eleven integral bastion towers. The wall was breached in 1850 for the railway, part-demolished for the National Shipyard in 1916, and again breached in 1988 for the A48 Inner Relief Road and for access to the main town car park.

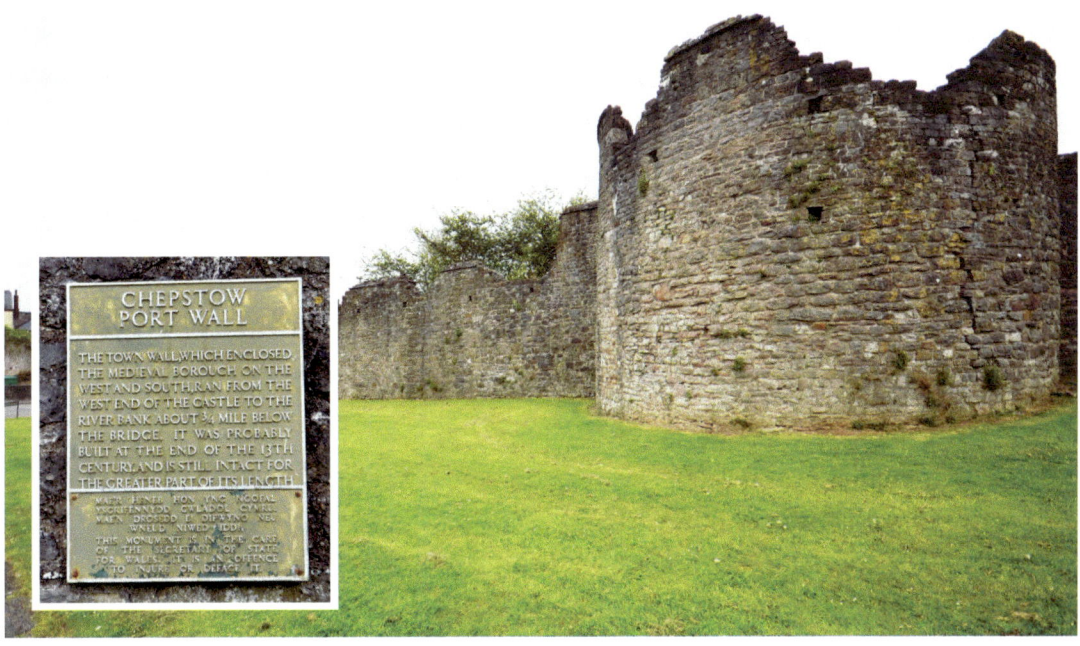

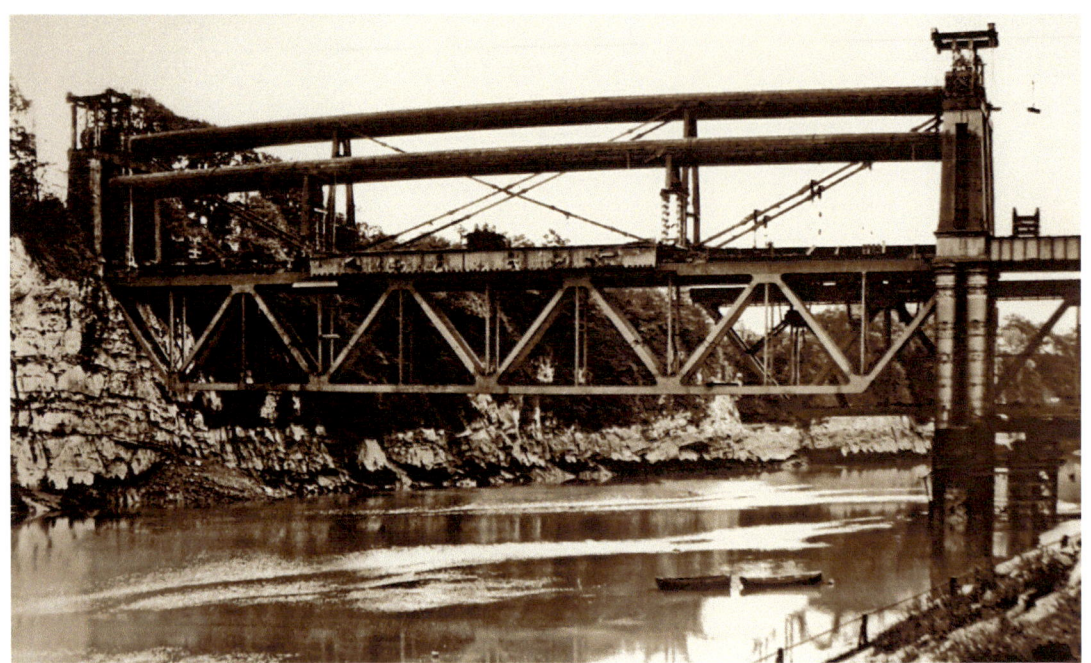

Brunel's Great Tubular Suspension Bridge
To enable the South Wales Railway to pass through Chepstow in 1850, Brunel constructed his famous single span Great Tubular Suspension Bridge across the Wye. This bridge is shown in the top photograph provided by Mabey Bridges Ltd, and illustrates the overhead girder construction of Brunel's bridge. The elaborate superstructure of the rail deck and above, however, was dismantled and replaced by the present span in 1962.

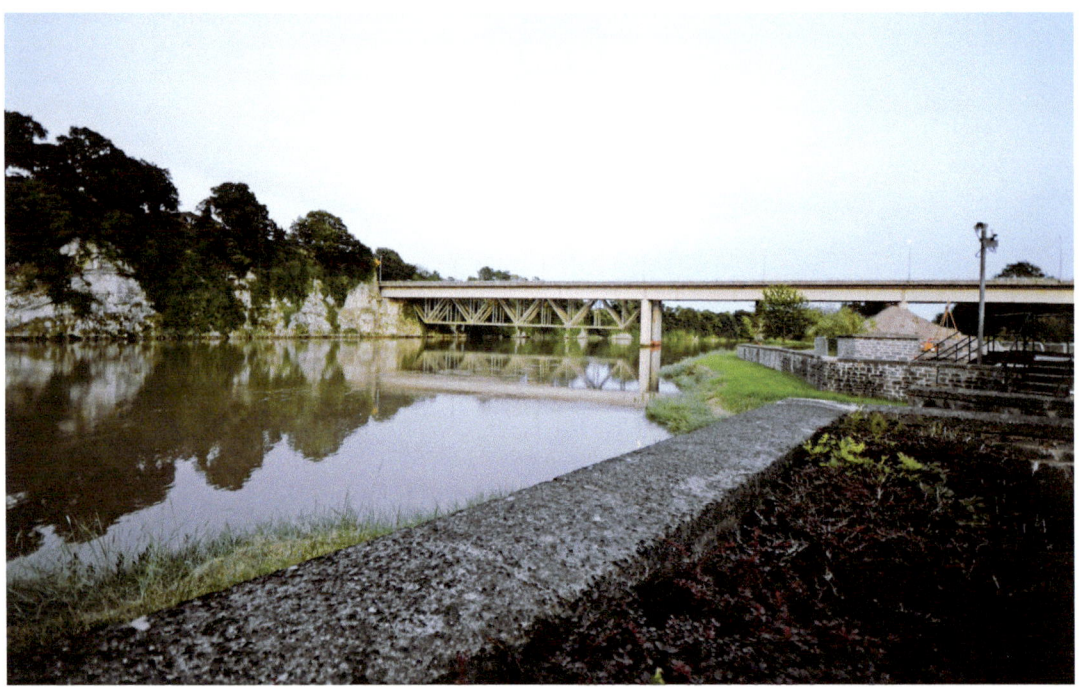

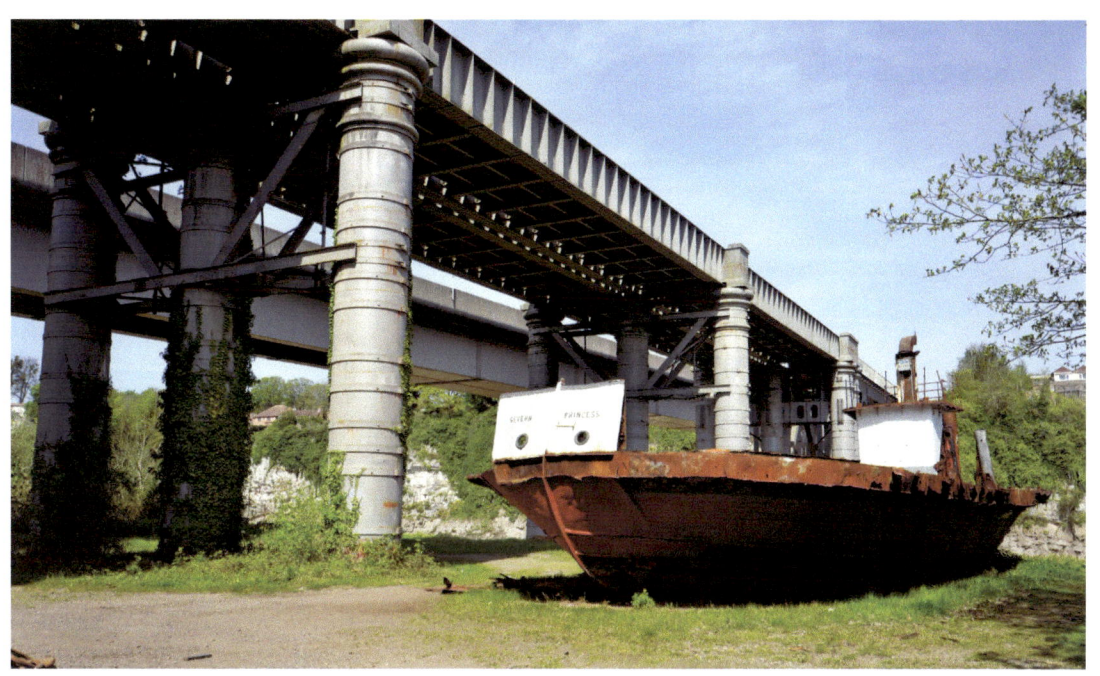

Brunel's Great Tubular Suspension Bridge
Brunel's Great Tubular Suspension Bridge was of an unusual design and was the forerunner of his equally famous Tamar Bridge. Brunel used pioneering techniques in bridge construction and in sinking caissons for the bridge piers. The iron columns of the bridge piers, an important part of the bridge's heritage and illustrated in the two photographs, still support today's railway bridge. Note the remains of the *Severn Princess* under the bridge, an old Beachley–Aust ferry boat.

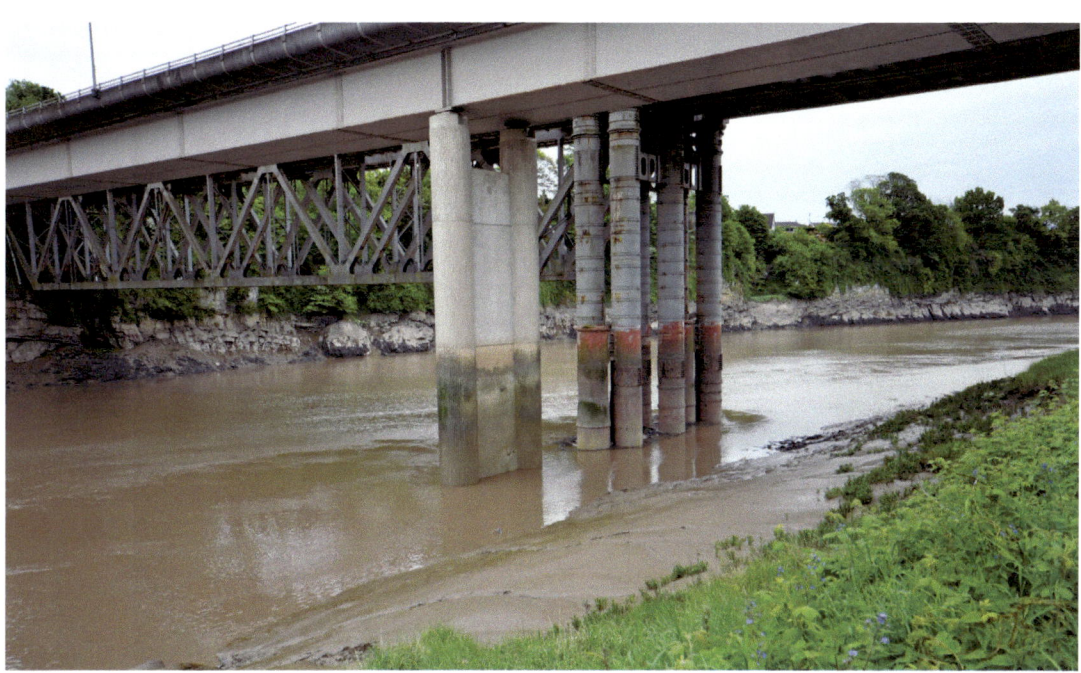

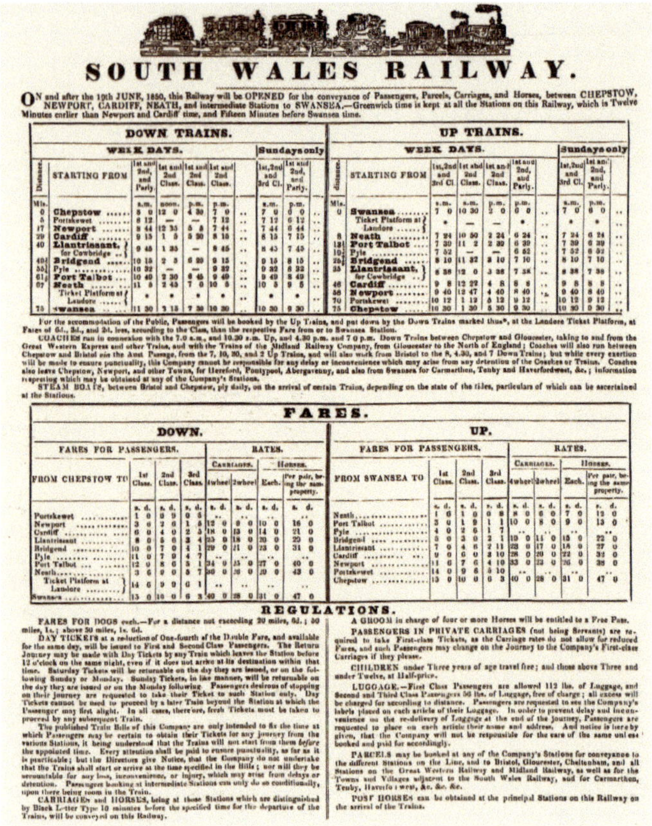

The South Wales Railway

The South Wales Railway between Chepstow and Swansea opened with great ceremony on 18 June 1850. *The Illustrated London News* reported that Chepstow was the starting point where, after receiving an address, the directors left in a train for Swansea, a distance of 75 miles. The train, headed by two engines, stopped at all eight stations en route and reached Swansea just after one o'clock for a further ceremony following its four-hour journey. According to the timetable, the line would be opened for the conveyance of passengers on or after 19 June 1850.

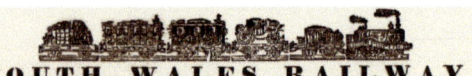

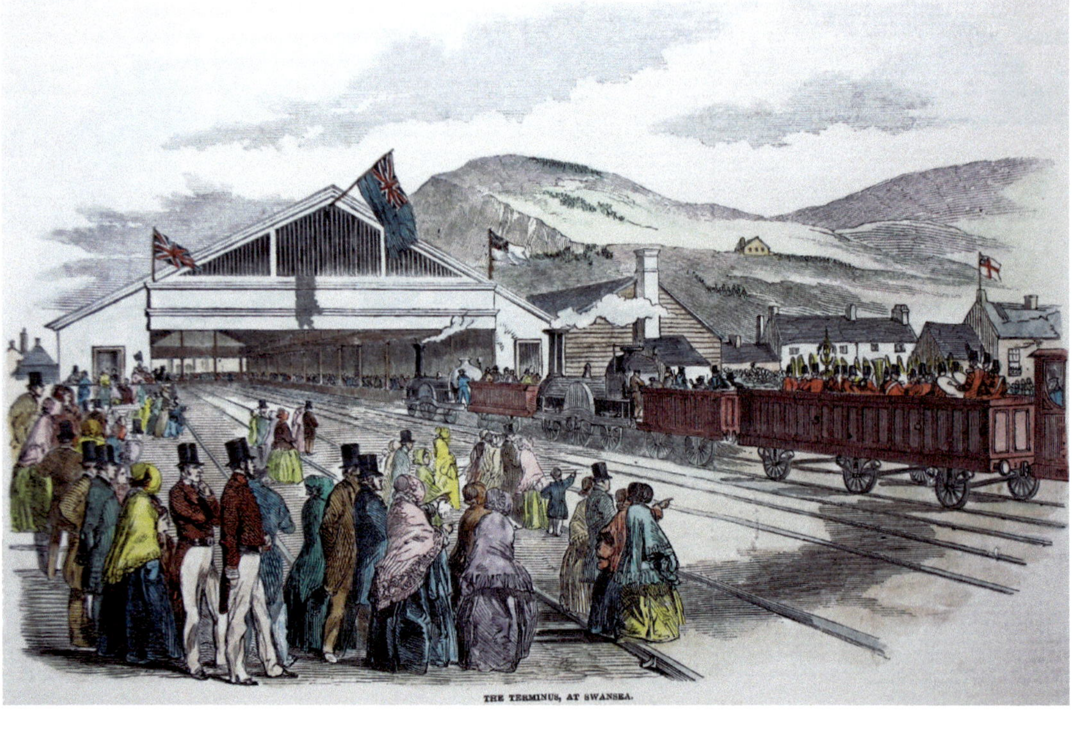

THE TERMINUS, AT SWANSEA.

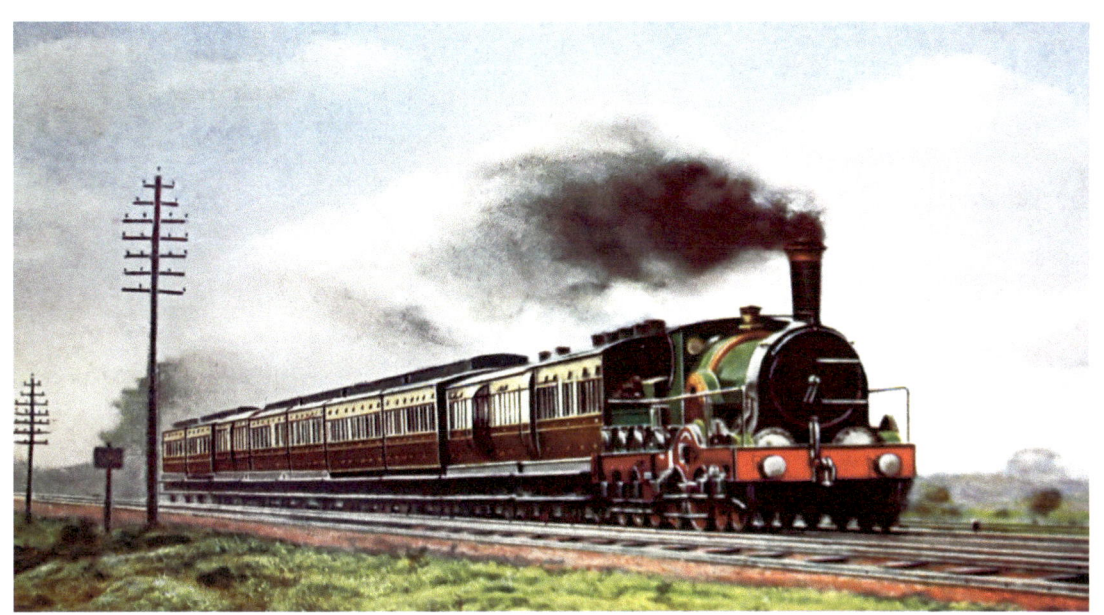

South Wales Railway
One of the engine drivers for the opening run of the South Wales Railway was Daniel Gooch, superintendent of locomotive engines, Great Western Railway. In 1840, he designed the GWR Firefly Class of 2-2-2 express passenger locomotives, the type probably used for the opening. Later in 1846, Gooch designed the 4-2-2 Iron Duke Class of locomotives, the namesake of which is shown in the top postcard; capable of speeds of 70 mph, this type would have seen service at Chepstow. The lower photograph is of GWR Castle Class 2-6-0 locomotive *Chepstow Castle* at Chepstow in July 1926.

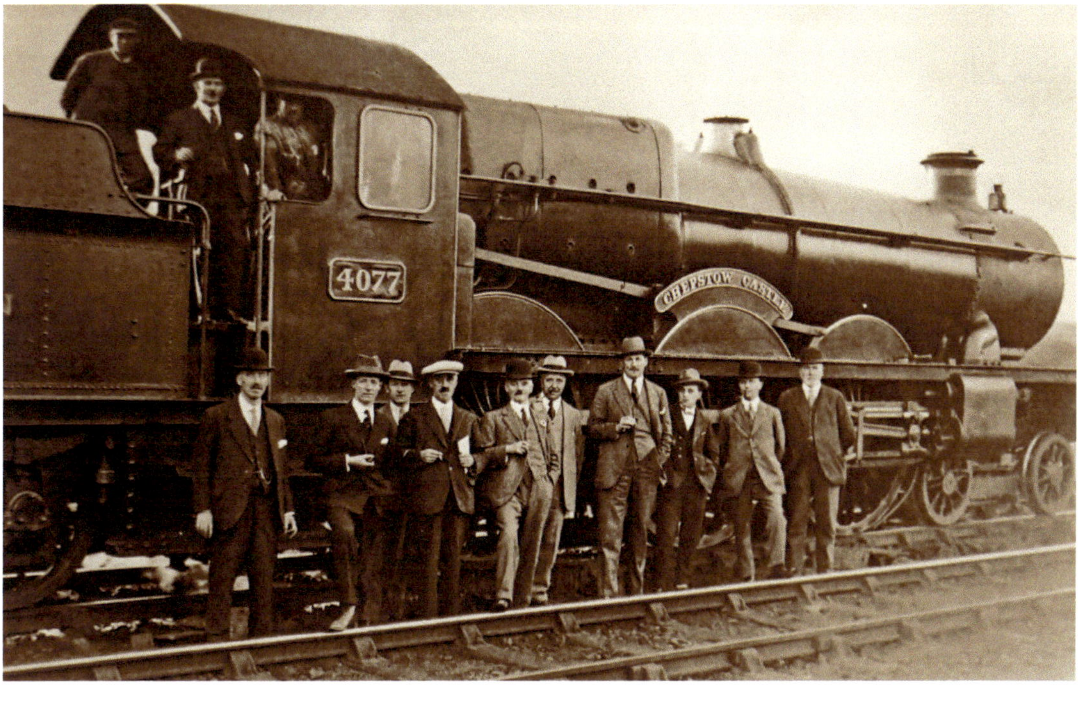

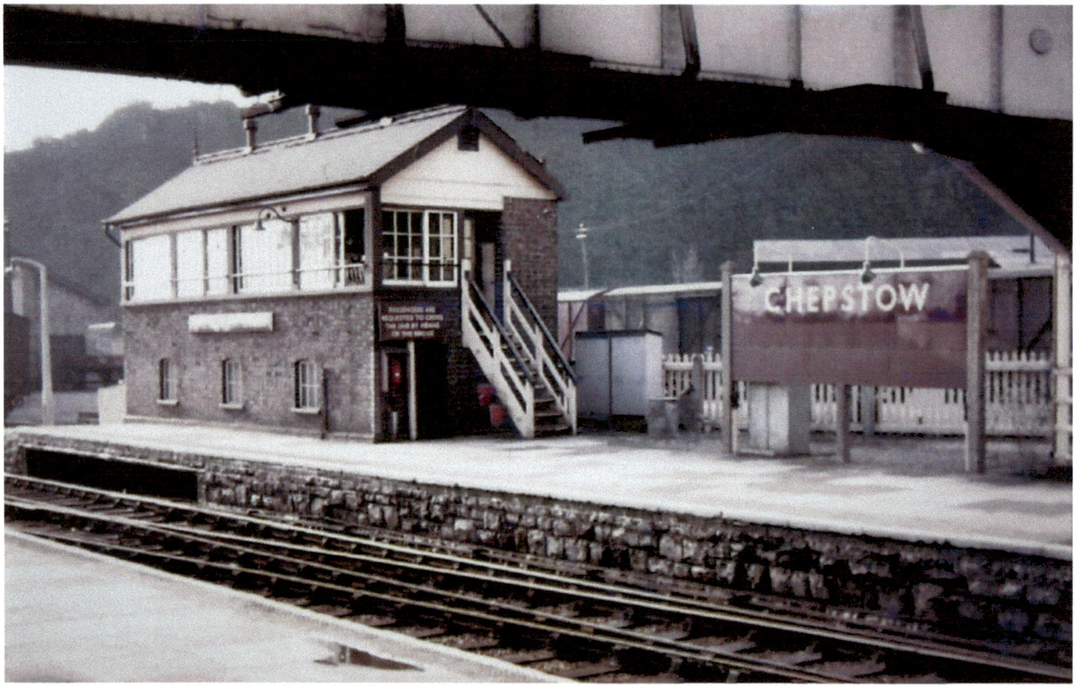

Chepstow Railway Station

Chepstow railway station survived the Beeching Axe of the 1960s and continues to provide an effective rail service today. The old photograph of Chepstow signal box was probably taken around Beeching's time while lower modern picture, taken from the opposite direction, shows today's station. In the inset picture, what was once the main station building now houses a cafeteria and the ticket office is now just a box on the platform.

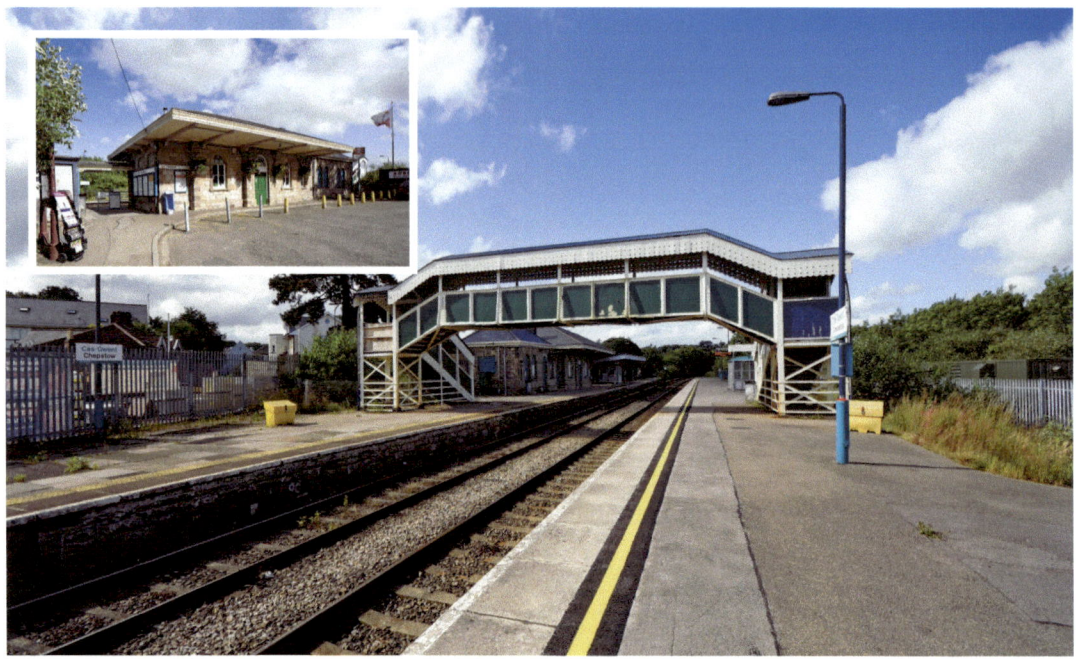

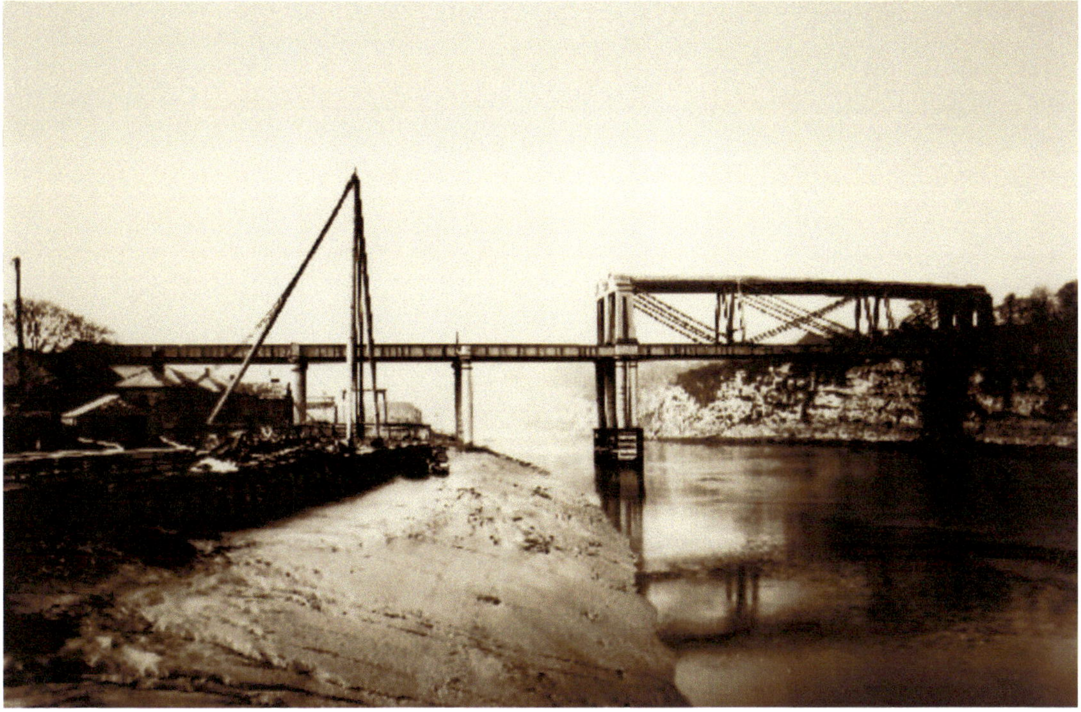

Brunel's Great Tubular Suspension Railway Bridge and Shipyards
The two photographs of Brunel's Great Tubular Suspension Railway Bridge, opened in July 1852, are from the Mabey Bridge Ltd archive and serve to highlight the shipyards that once plied their trade underneath its shadow. The suspension bridge was closed in 1962 and replaced with a new bridge built on the pillars of Brunel's original structure.

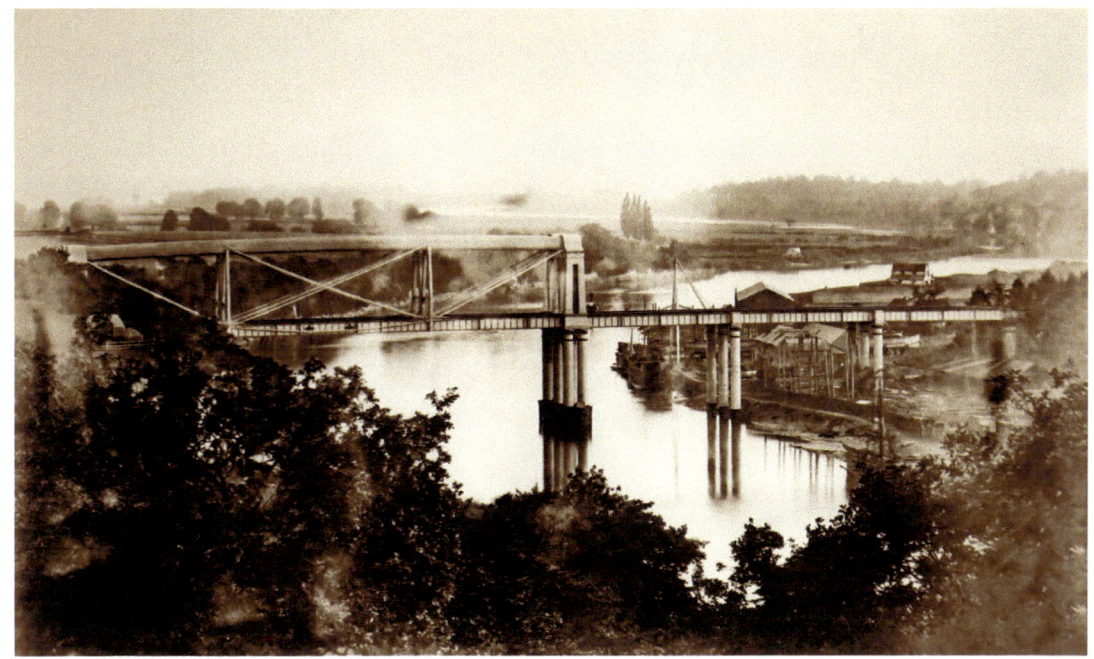

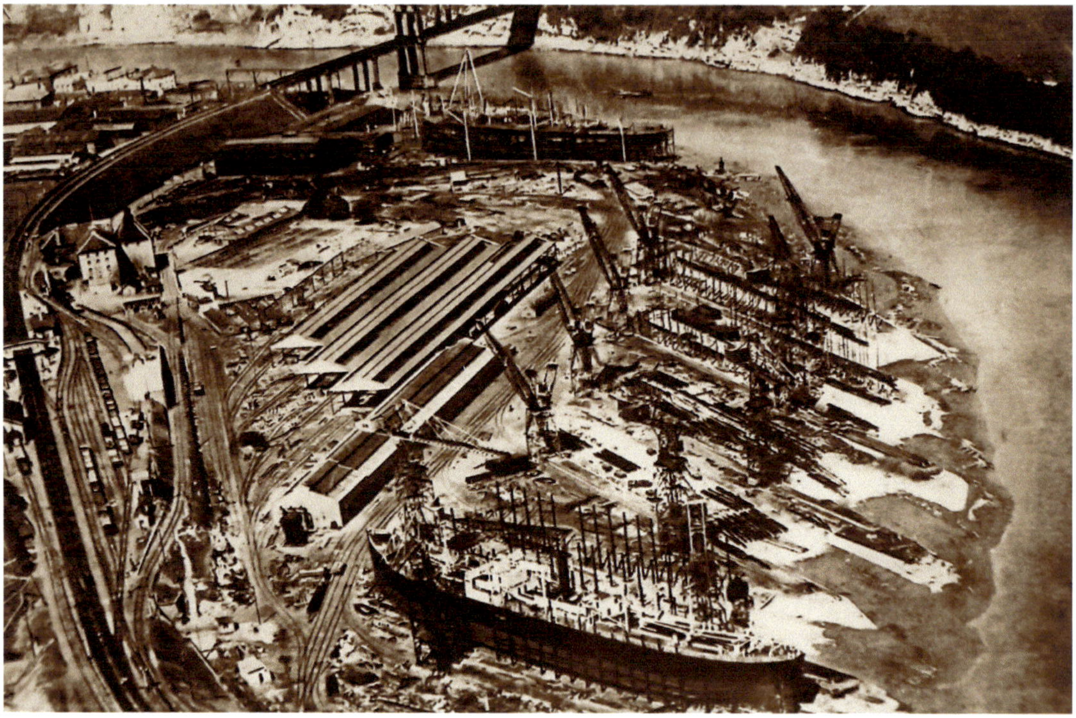

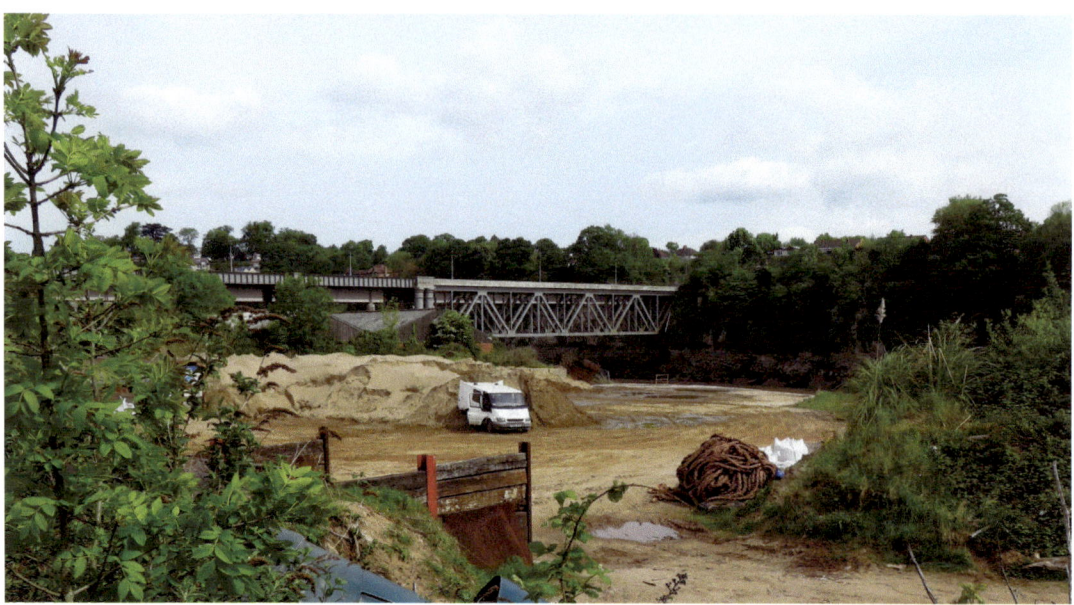

The Shipyards
The two aerial photographs on these two pages (from the Mabey Bridge Ltd archive), show the extent and size of National Shipyard No. 1 in its heyday with many ships in various stages of construction on the slipways. As so many merchant ships were being sunk during the First World War, in 1917 the government established a number of national shipyards. All existing shipyards at Chepstow came under government control to form National Shipyard No. 1. Today the shipyard area nearest the railway bridge is used to store sand.

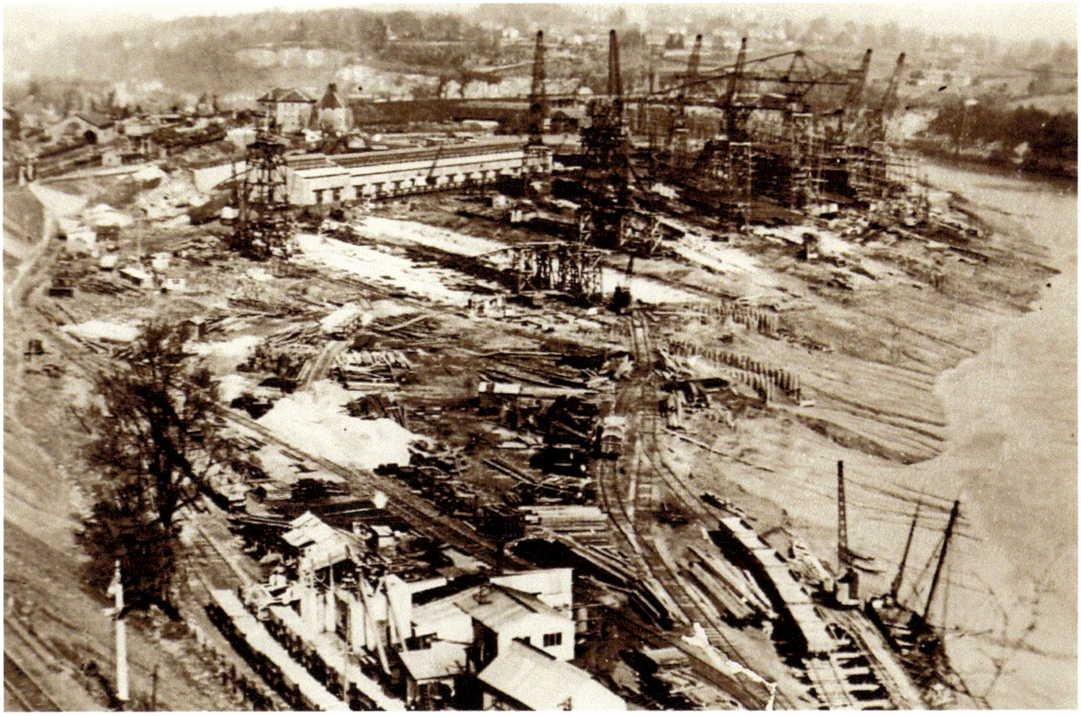

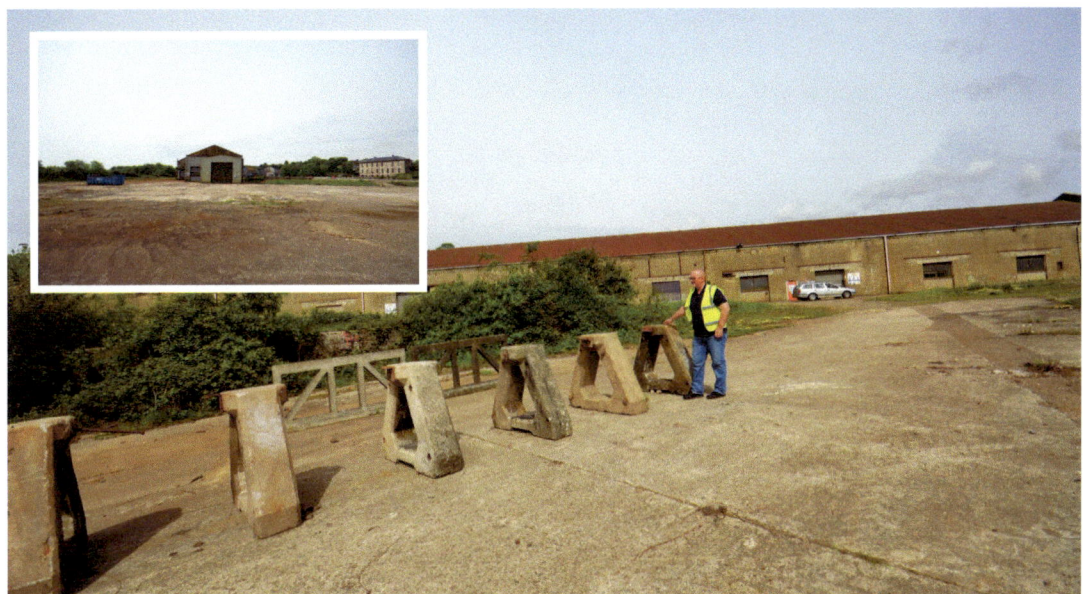

The Shipyards

To accommodate the construction and mass production of 'standard prefabricated' cargo ships as quickly as possible, work started in 1917 to lay down eight slipways at Chepstow, with a further seven planned through taking over the existing adjacent Finch's Yard. The latter took effect in August 1918. The National Shipyard was built by the Royal Engineers and prisoners of war and the ships constructed by civilian labour. Very little evidence is left today of this shipyard except the remains of the slipway blocks recovered by Andrew Leitch of Mabey Bridges Ltd.

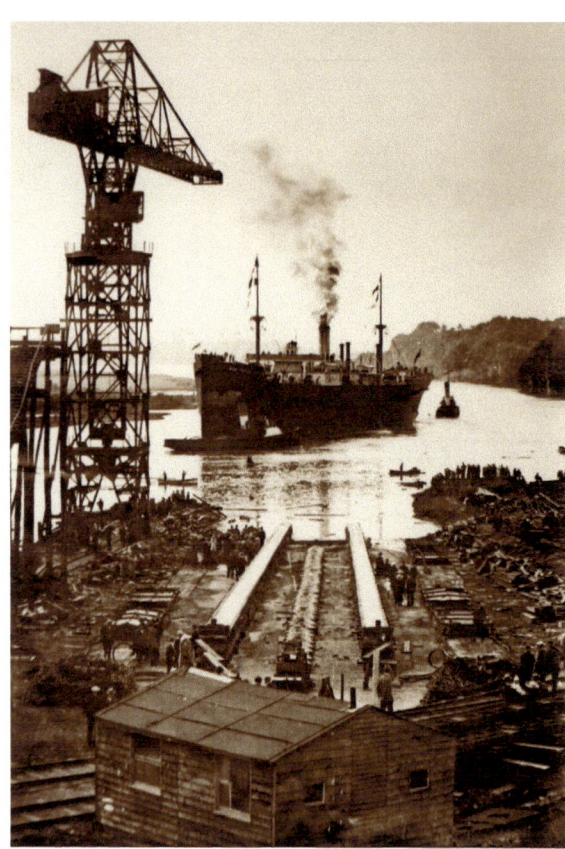

The Shipyards

In September 1918, the first standard ship, the *War Forest*, was launched from Finch's site. However, by the end of the war in November 1918, no prefabricated ships had been completed. After the end of the war, the Chepstow shipyard was taken over briefly by Monmouthshire Shipbuilding Company. Their output peaked in 1920 when eight ships were launched; the largest of these was *War Glory* on 21 April 1920.

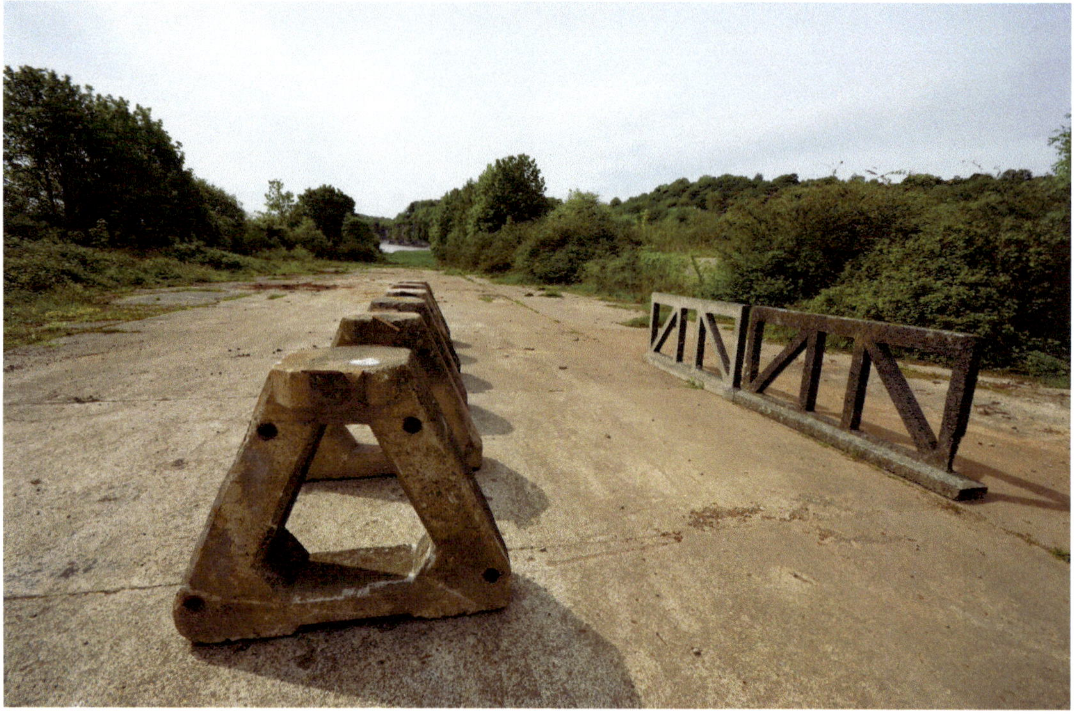

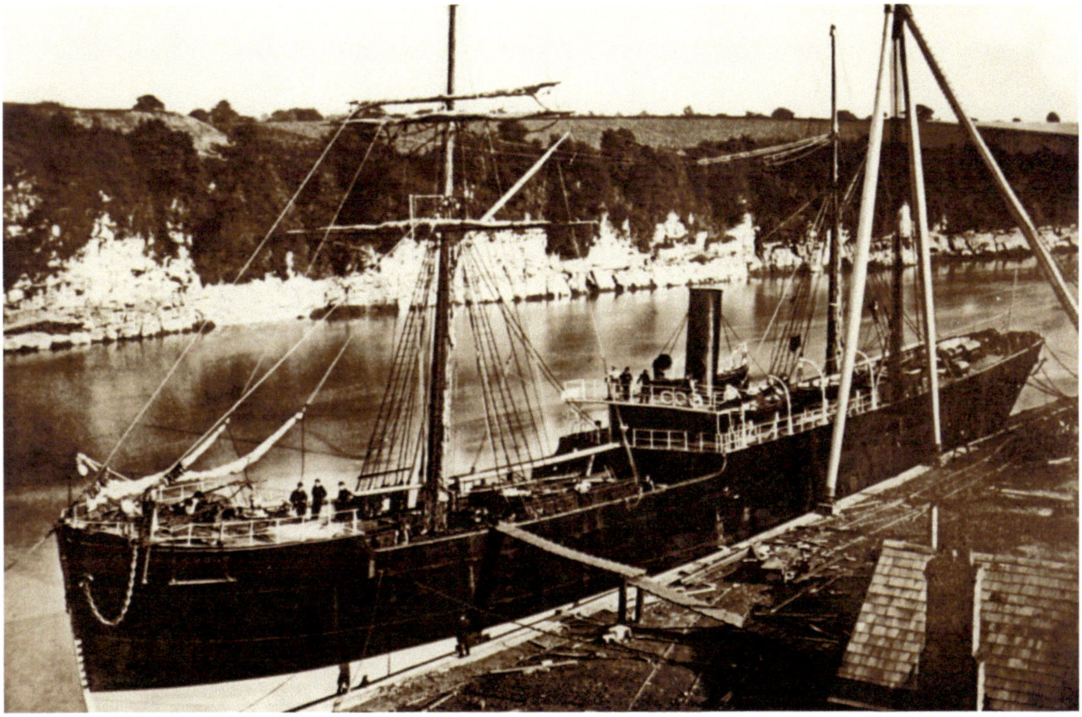

The Shipyards

From medieval times, Chepstow was the largest port in Wales, with ships sailing as far afield as Iceland and Turkey. The port reached its peak during the Napoleonic Wars before losing trade to the major ports that were developing along the South Wales coast. Where the cargo ships used to dock, there is only grass and cracked remains of these berths with the occasional capstan and heaps of old rope to remind one of past glories.

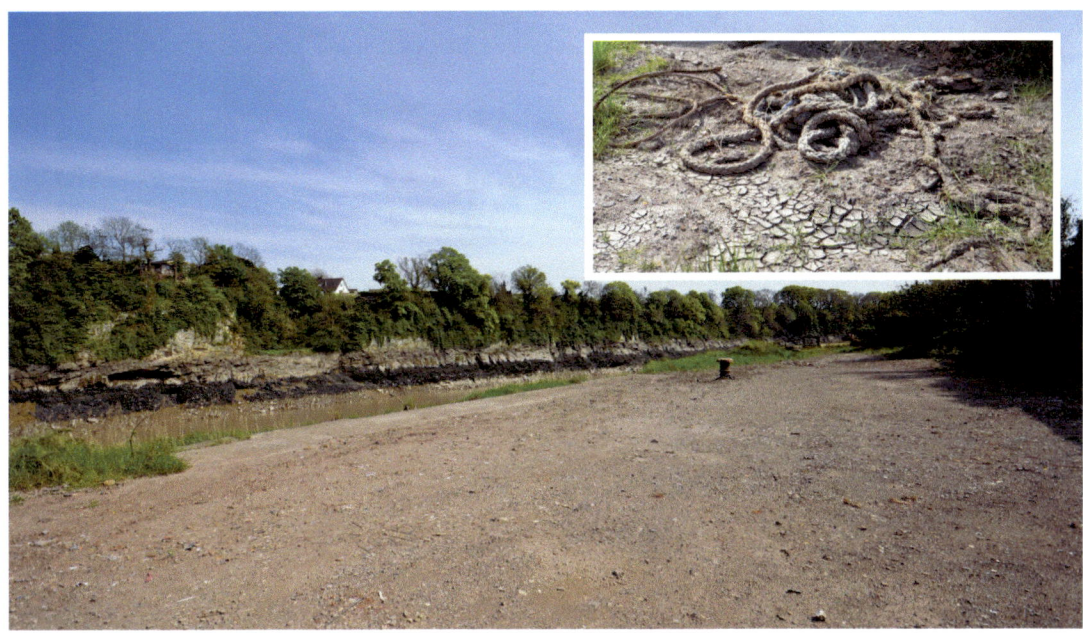

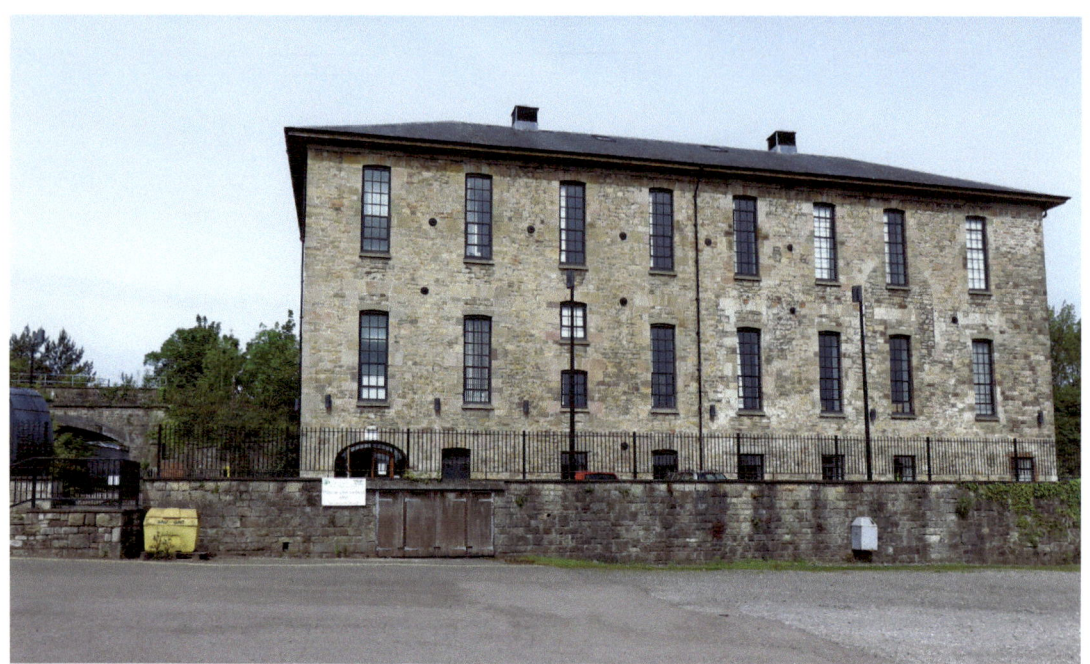

The Shipyards
Mabey Bridge Ltd have owned the old shipyard site since 1966 when the previous occupiers since 1924, Fairfield Shipbuilding, went into liquidation. Mabey Bridge's offices are in the old mill building located just below Chepstow railway station, as shown in the top photograph. Mabey ceased engineering production here some years back and have cleared the shipyard site to the river on two sides for future development, as shown in the lower picture. The inset shows a section of Brunel's Tubular Suspension Bridge that is on display outside the old mill building.

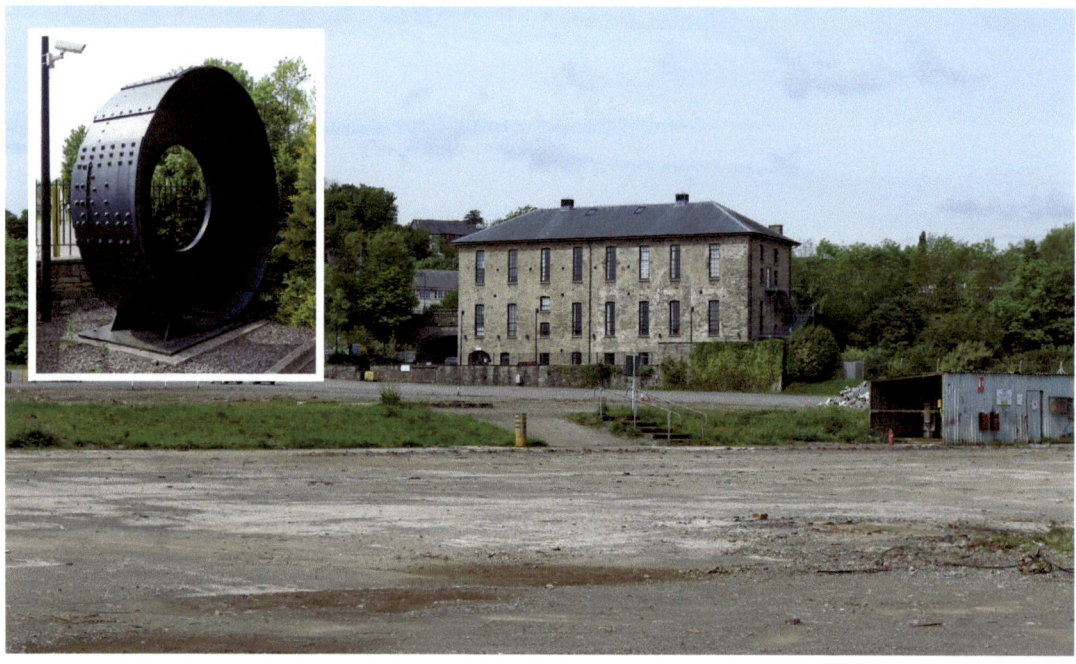

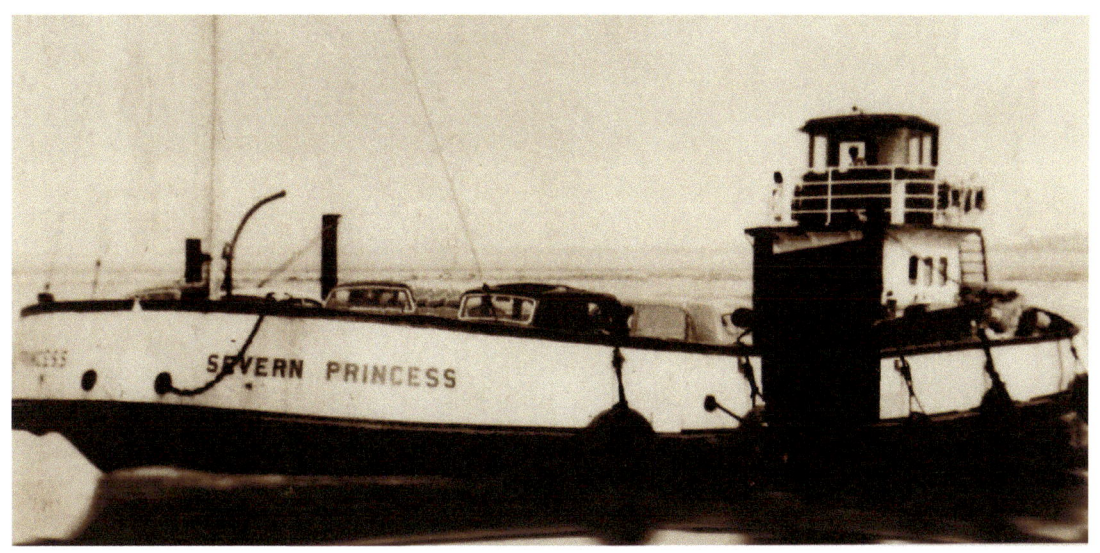

The *Severn Princess*
The *Severn Princess*, launched in 1959, was one of the last boats used on the Beachley–Aust Ferry. It was found wrecked and abandoned in Ireland in 1999 and towed back to Beachley in 2003. After resting for some years alongside the Beachley slipway, it was eventually moved to its present location beneath the railway bridge on the west bank of the Wye where it is undergoing restoration work. Mabey Bridge Ltd have supported the refurbishment as well as the *Severn Princess* Restoration Group, whose long term aim is to have the *Severn Princess* as a permanent heritage display.

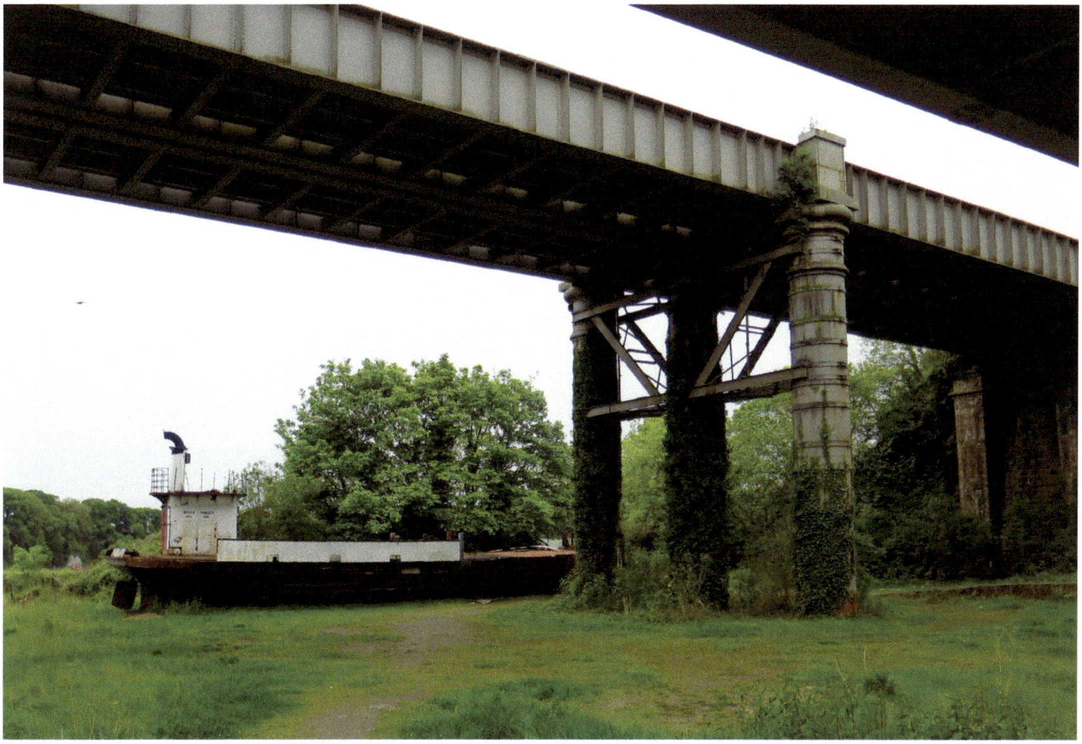

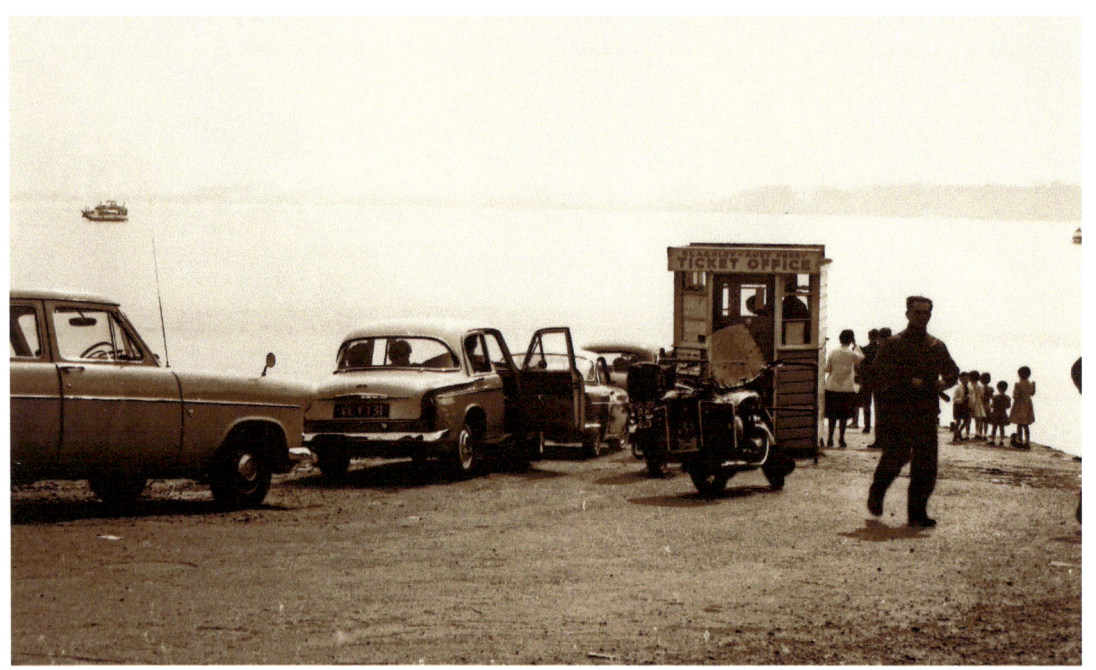

The Beachley–Aust Ferry

Also know as the Old Passage, where crossings of the Severn have been made since Roman times, the Beachley–Aust Ferry was in operation from 1926 until 1966 when the first Severn Suspension Bridge was opened. It provided service across the mile-wide Severn estuary for road traffic crossing between the West Country and South Wales. The nearest fixed crossing was a 60-mile detour via Gloucester. Following its closure, the slipway and ferry buildings were taken over by SARA, the Severn Area Rescue Association, whose Lifeboat No. 1 is shown in action in the lower photograph.

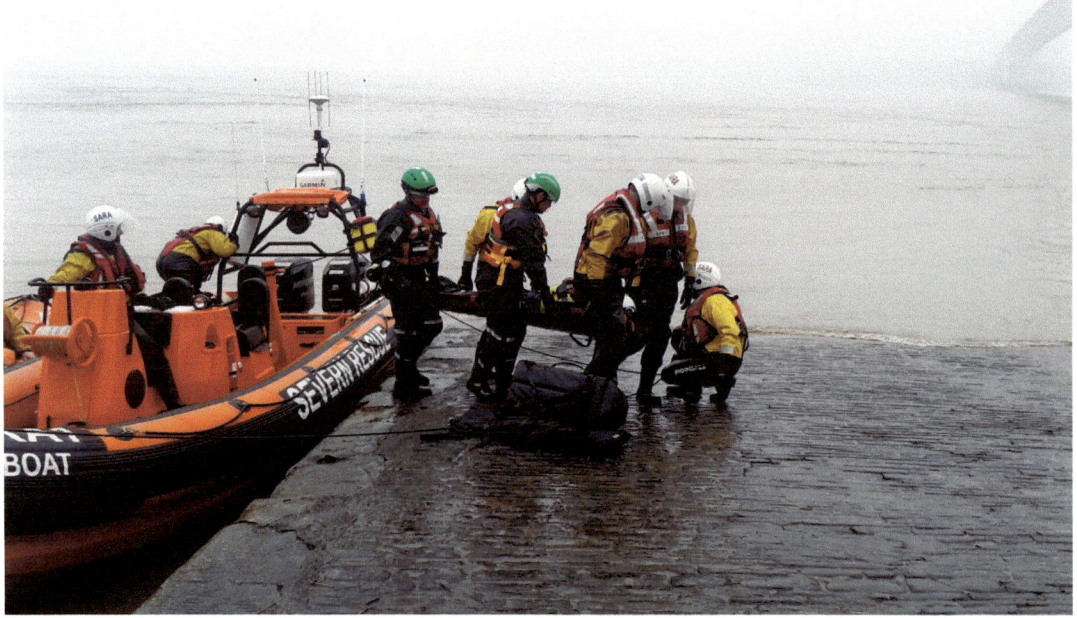

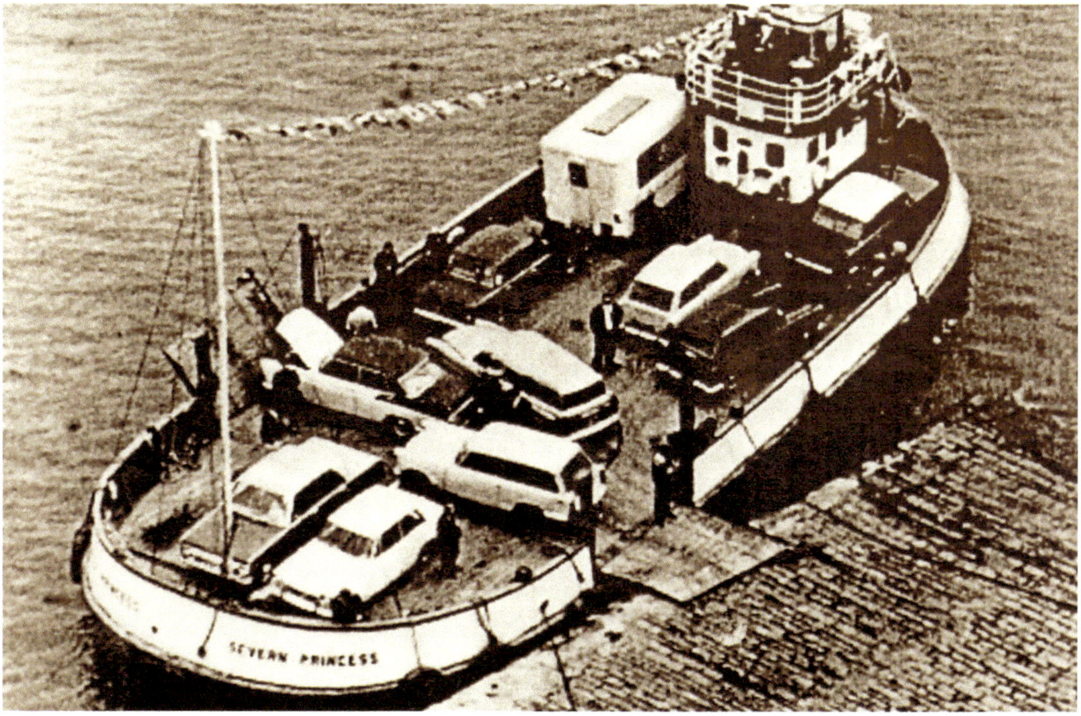

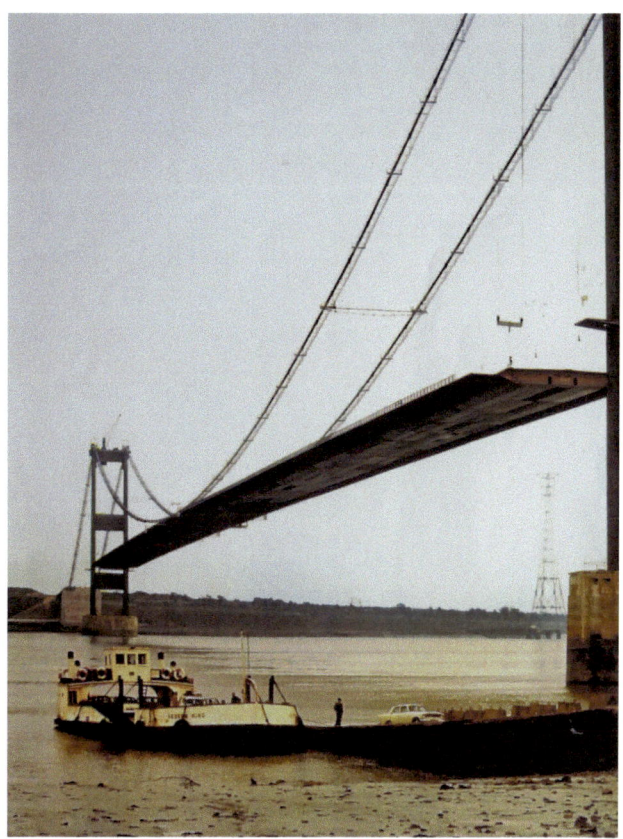

The Beachley–Aust Ferry

In the top photograph, the *Severn Princess* is captured with a full load just prior to setting sail for Aust, while in the lower picture the *Severn King* is under the Severn Bridge whilst the centre span is brought into position. It was quite an experience using the ferry. Often, after waiting hours to board (sometimes you didn't always make it if tidal conditions changed), you drove down an inevitably wet slipway to get to the point where you had to swing sharp to the left and drive across an equally wet boarding ramp to get onto the vessel.

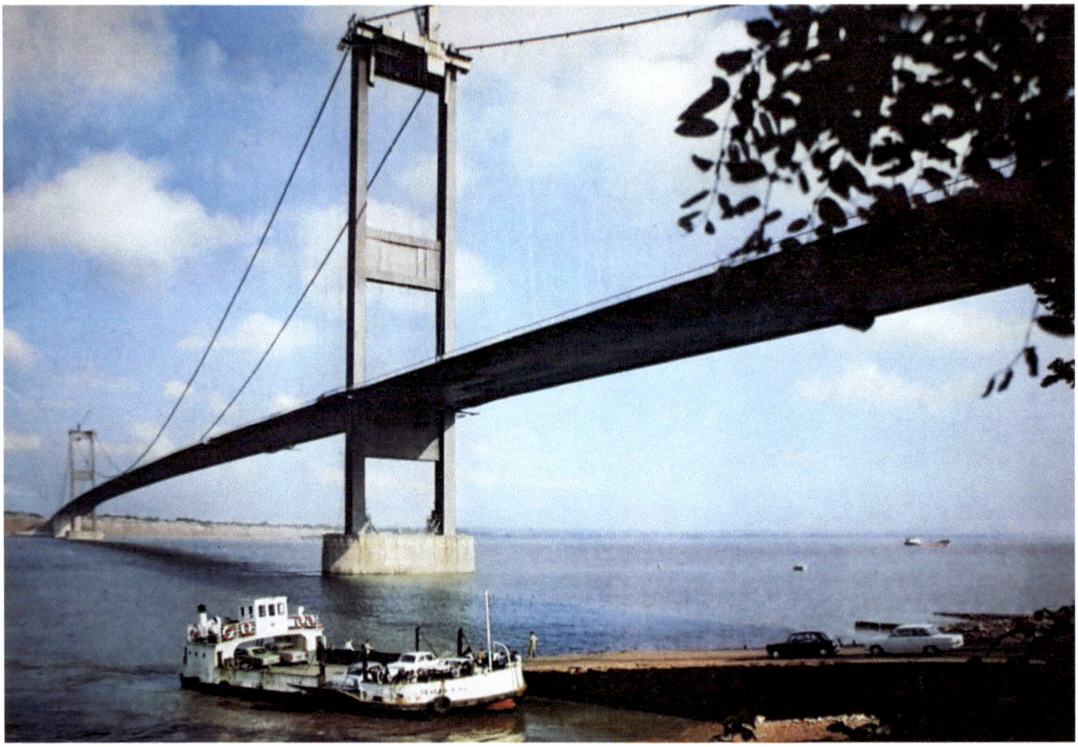

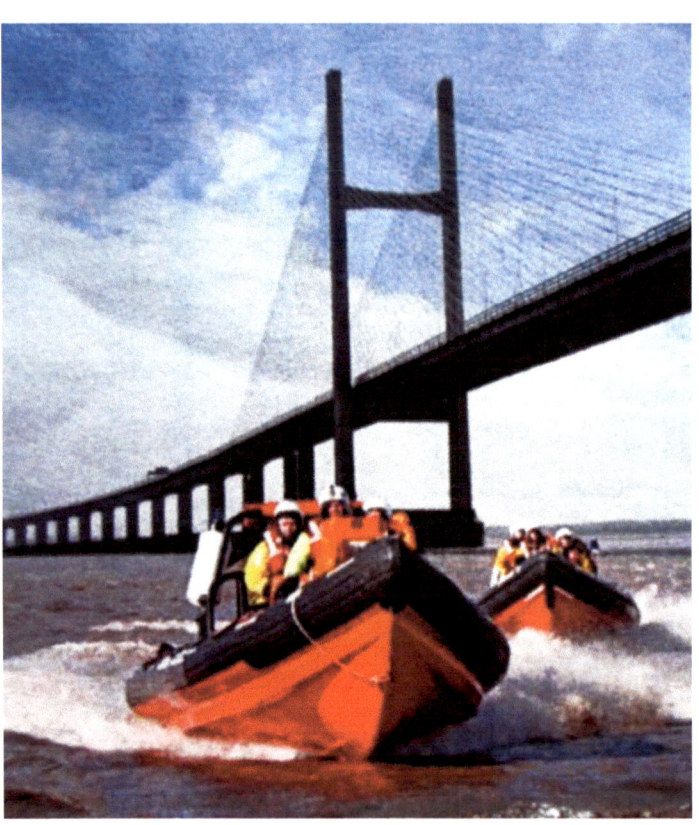

The Beachley–Aust Ferry

Another view of the *Severn Princess*, probably near its swansong, under what appears to be a completed Severn Bridge. Once onboard the boat, unless you were one of the last three vehicles, you drove onto a turntable located on the centre of the deck where you were unceremoniously manhandled around until the crew had you facing in the direction they wanted and you drove into the space allocated. Getting your vehicle off at the Aust end was equally horrendous. The lower photograph shows SARA Lifeboats Nos 1 and 2 in action under the second Severn Bridge.

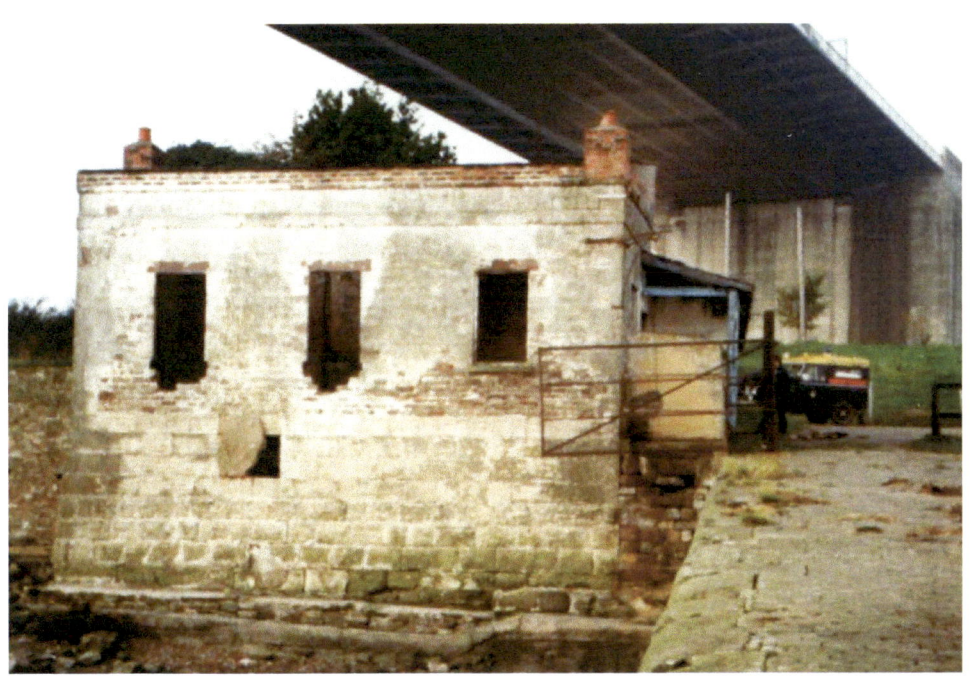

Severn Area Rescue Association

The Severn Area Rescue Association (SARA) was founded in 1973 and became a registered charity in 1976. Run entirely by volunteers, SARA was formed to provide emergency assistance in the treacherous and swift-flowing tidal estuary of the River Severn. It covers an area of seaway from Avonmouth and Newport up to Gloucester that is not served by the RNLI, who do not cover these estuarine waters. SARA took over the old ferry ticket office in 1993 and constructed a new lifeboat station in its place, as shown in the two SARA photographs.

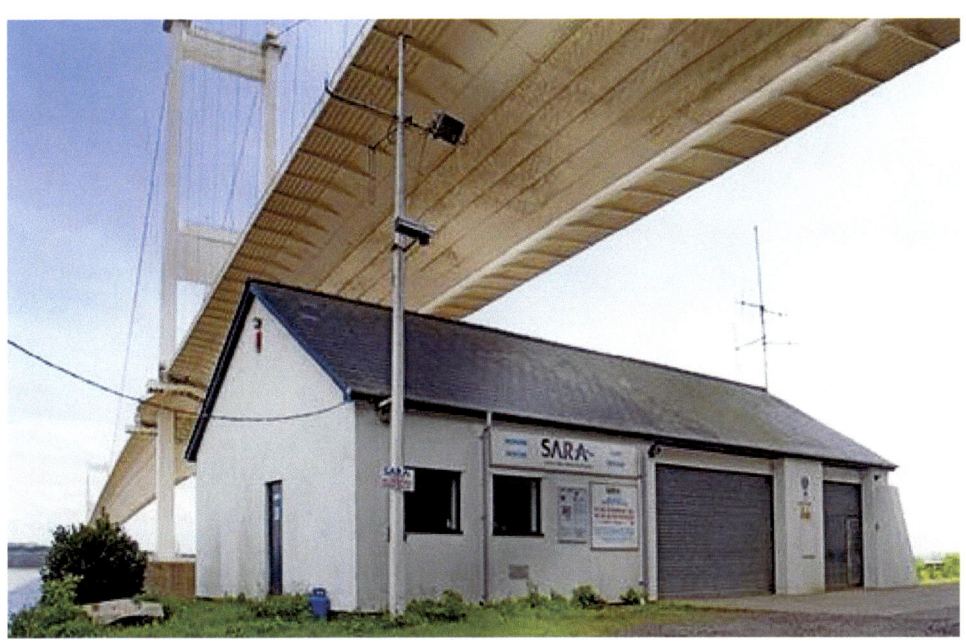

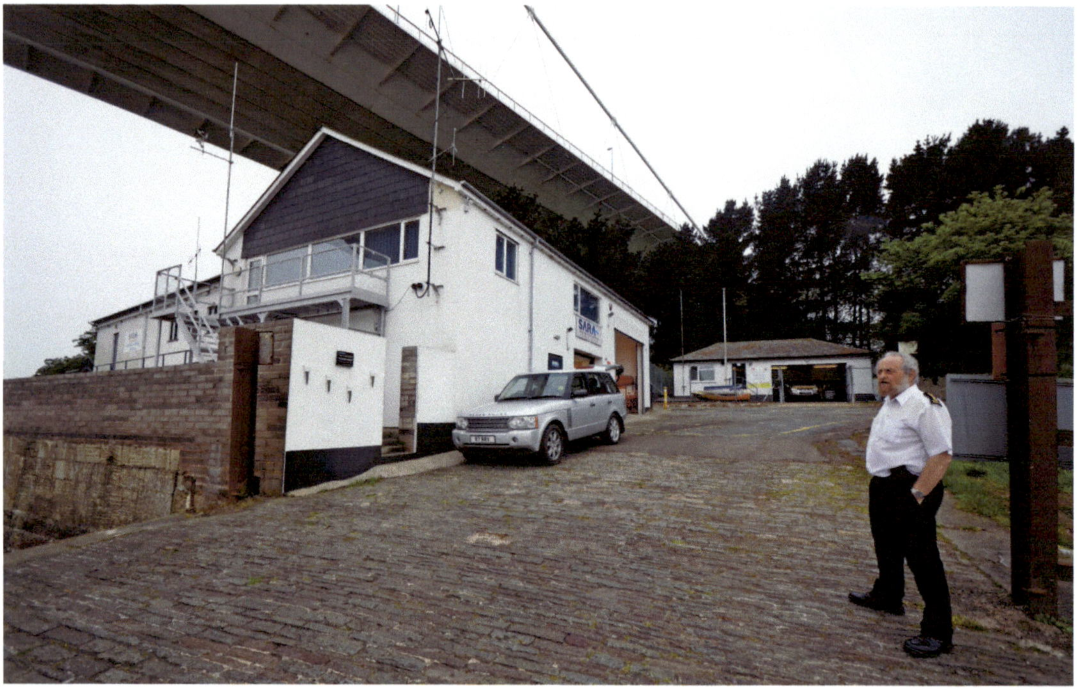

Severn Area Rescue Association
SARA is the largest independent lifeboat service in the UK and is a designated rescue service for the area, being contacted primarily via dialling 999 and asking for the coastguard or the police. The top photograph shows Mervyn P. Fleming, SARA Commander Area West, in front of the extended lifeboat station, which now includes a highly sophisticated command and control centre. The SARA and coastguard teams have come together for the lower group photograph, taken on 19 May 2016.

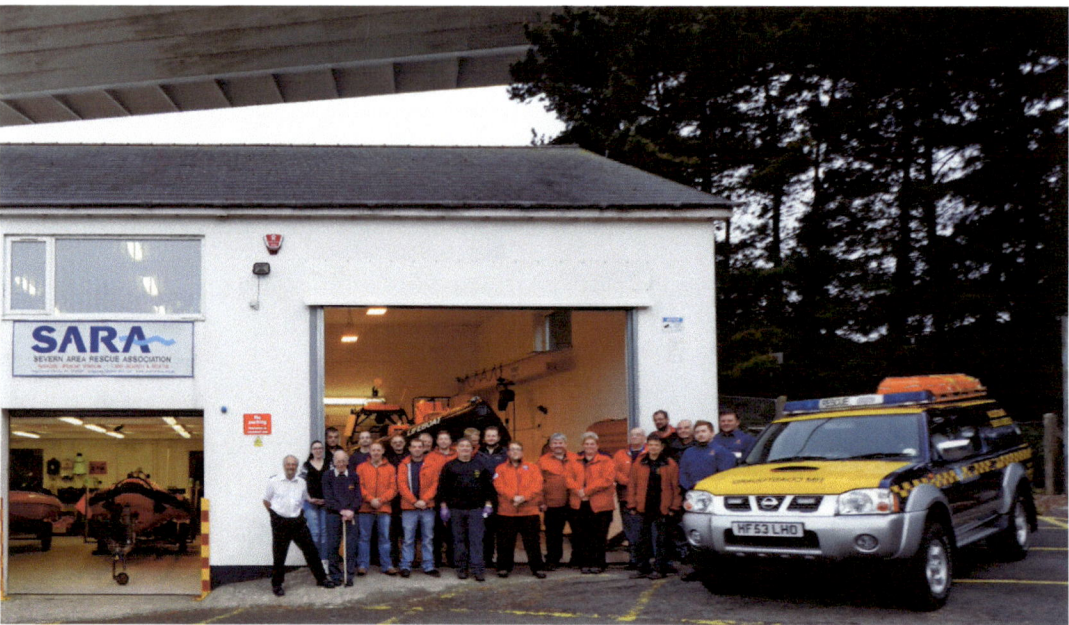

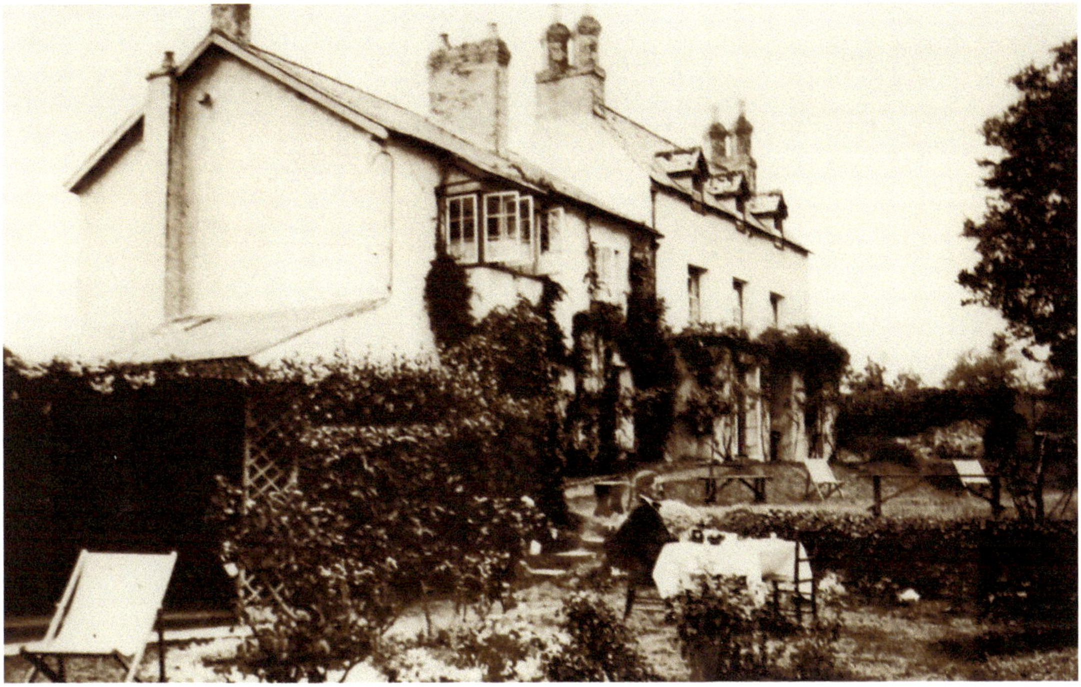

The Old Ferry Inn

Waverley House in the top picture was probably the original name of the now Old Ferry Inn. It then became the Beachley Ferry Hotel, and must have been very busy as at its peak the ferry ran every twenty minutes. The present proprietor and chef of the Old Ferry Inn, Linda Hunt, is shown in the lower photograph in the gardens overlooking both the Severn Estuary and Severn Bridge.

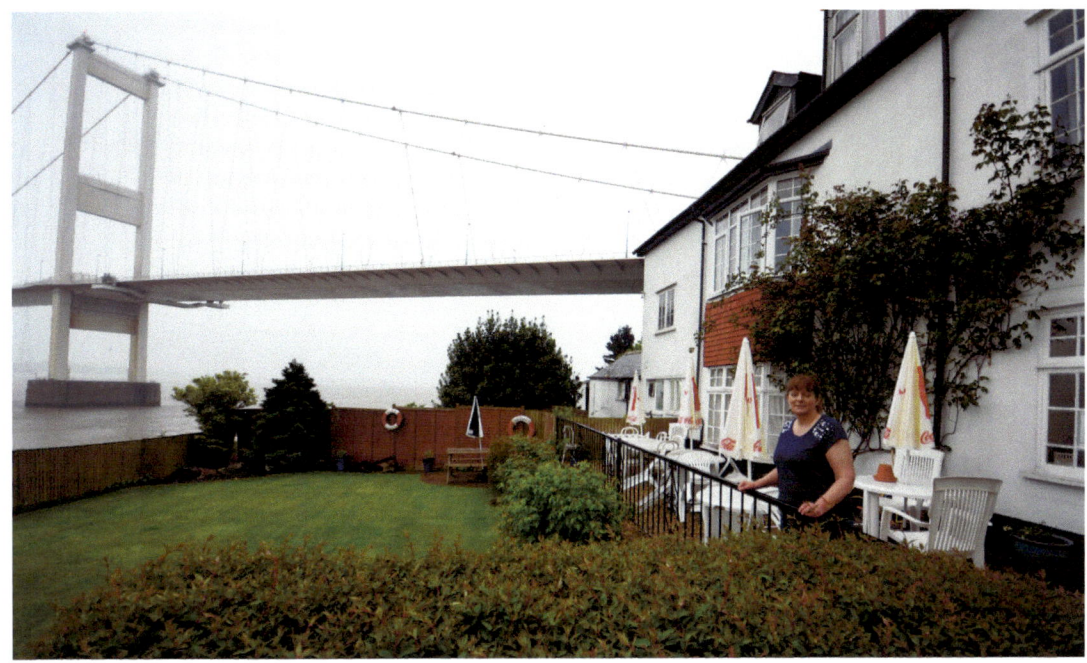

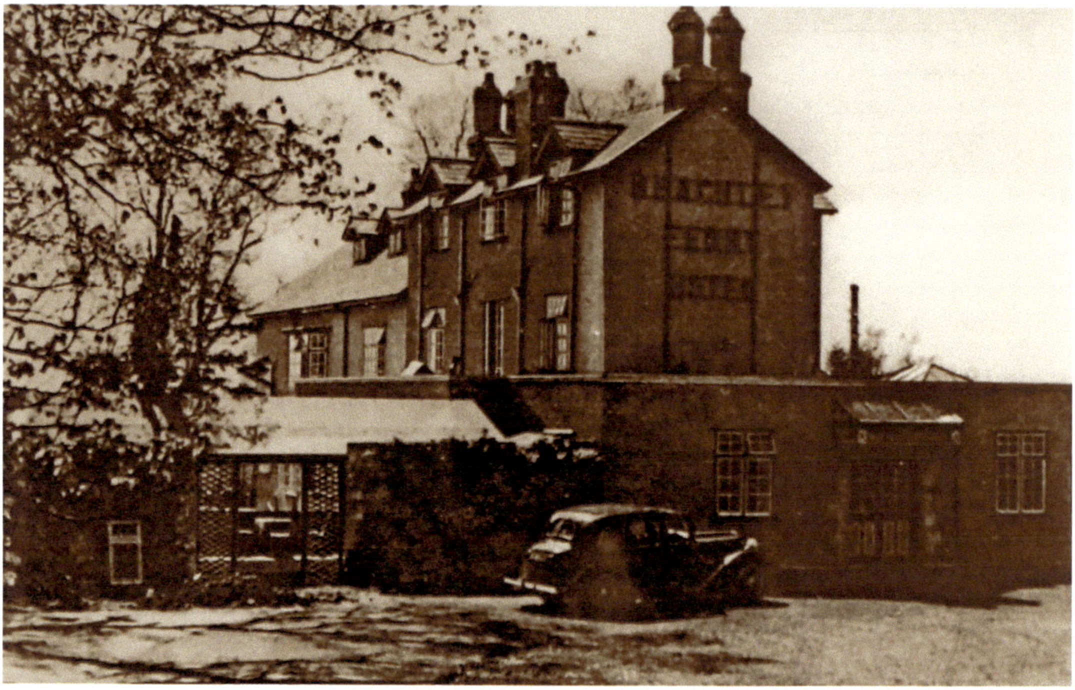

The Old Ferry Inn

The Beachley Ferry Hotel was an establishment where, in the heyday of the Beachley–Aust ferry, you could dine there on freshly caught Severn salmon. This is no longer the case, as today most of the Severn salmon caught are now shipped off to the top-class hotels in London, where they fetch a high price. The lower photograph captures the present Old Ferry Inn at its idyllic best. The inset picture shows one of the once many road signs that directed travellers to the Beachley–Aust ferry.

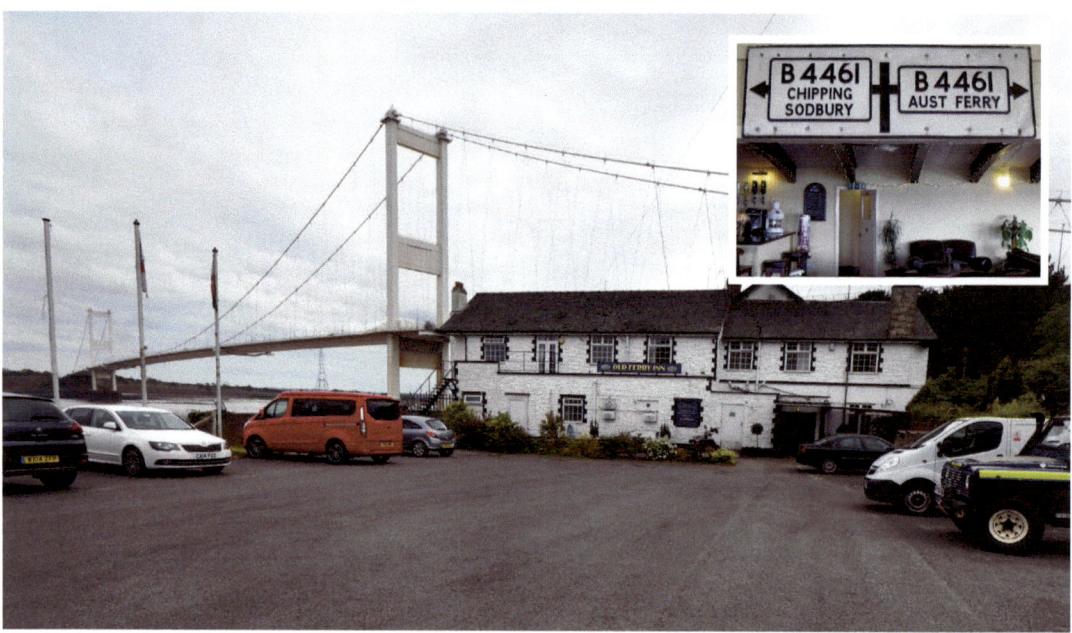

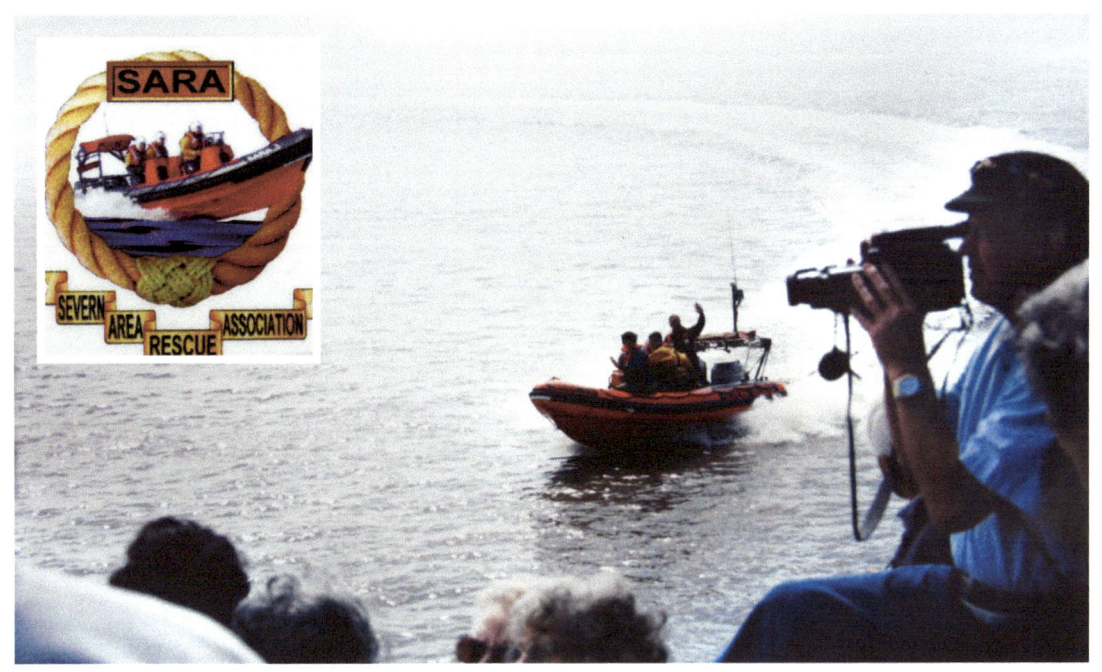

Severn Area Rescue Association
When the second Severn Suspension Road Bridge opened in 1966, the SARA Lifeboat was on hand to ensure the safety of the many pleasure craft there to witness the occasion. The SARA Lifeboat is seen alongside the MV *Balmoral* in the top photograph taken by the author whilst the insert shows the instantly recognisable badge and logo of SARA. Not only does SARA provide a good rescue service, it can also turn its hand to good photography, as exemplified in the lower photograph of the Severn Bridge at night.

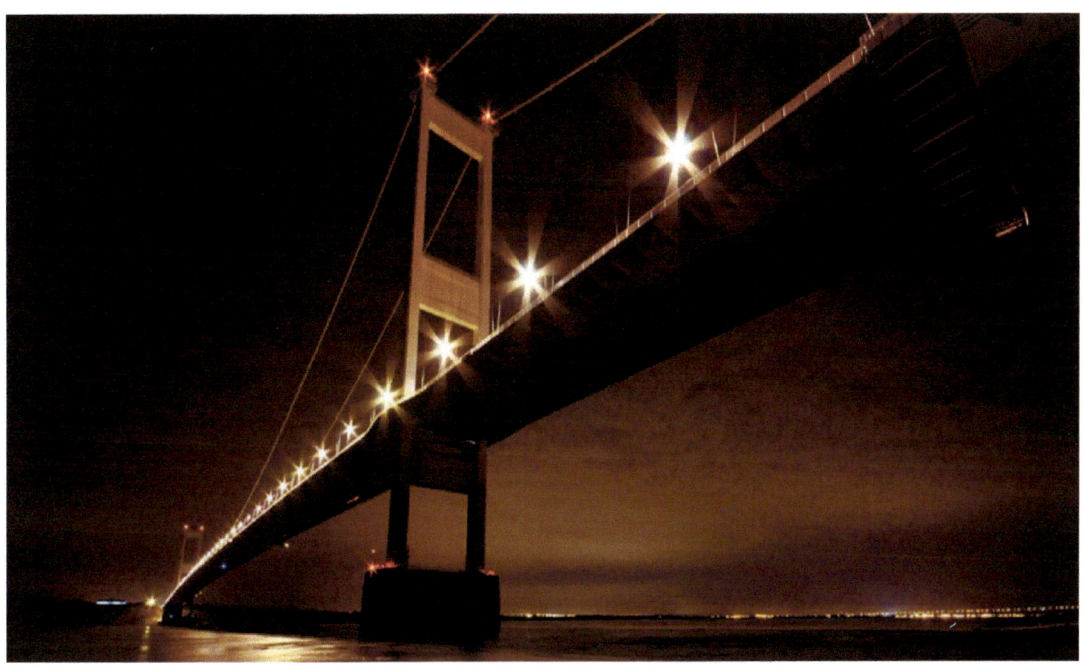

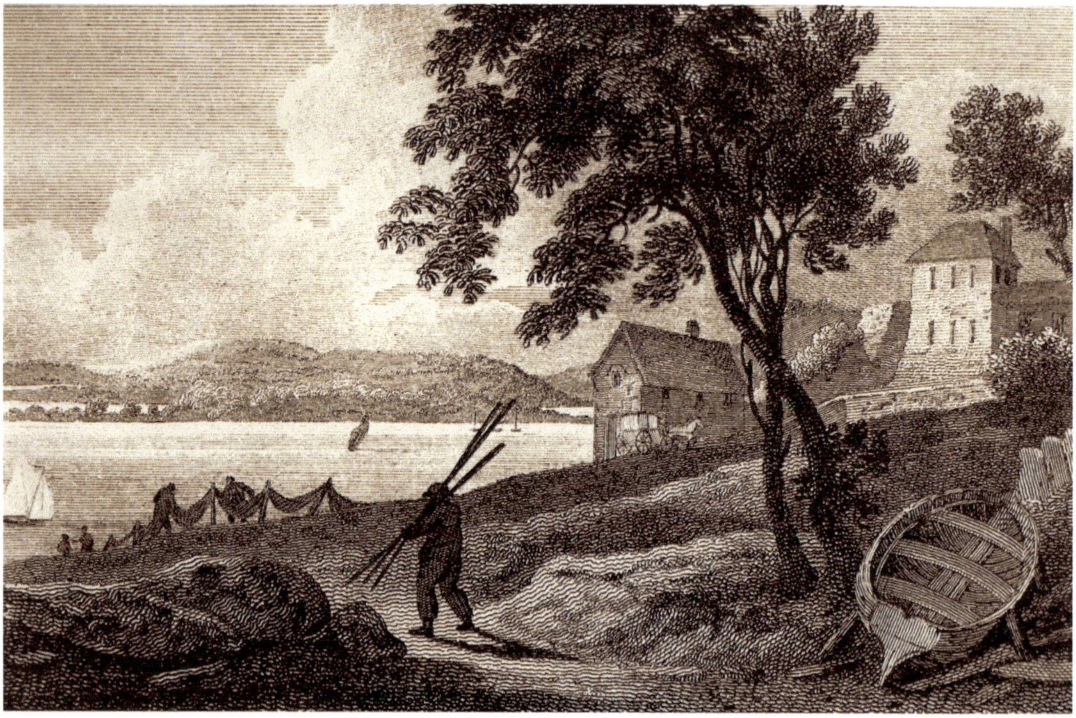

The Severn Crossing

The top etching, the 'AUST PASSAGE', is dated 1 April 1801 and shows the ferry landing on the Aust bank of the Severn. This passage was known to have been used by the Romans to cross the estuary in AD 48. The bottom photograph shows the wood slipway remains of the once-busy Beachley–Aust ferry, again on the Aust side of the Severn. This photograph also highlights the 488 ft (148.75 m) high eastern pylon of the Aust Severn Powerline Crossing (National Grid) with the longest powerline span of 5,380 ft (1,618 m) in the UK.

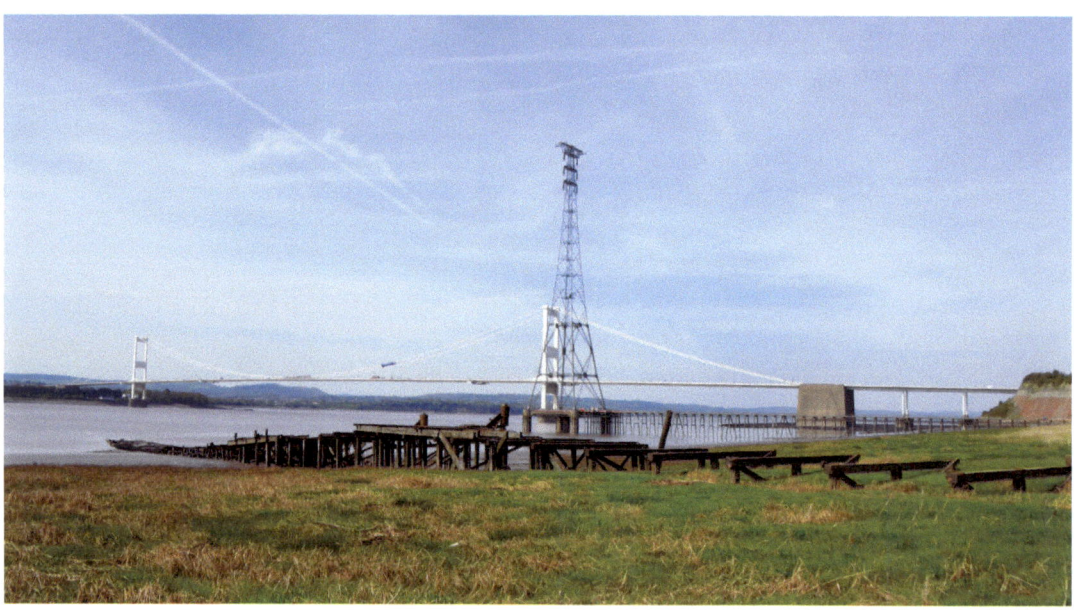

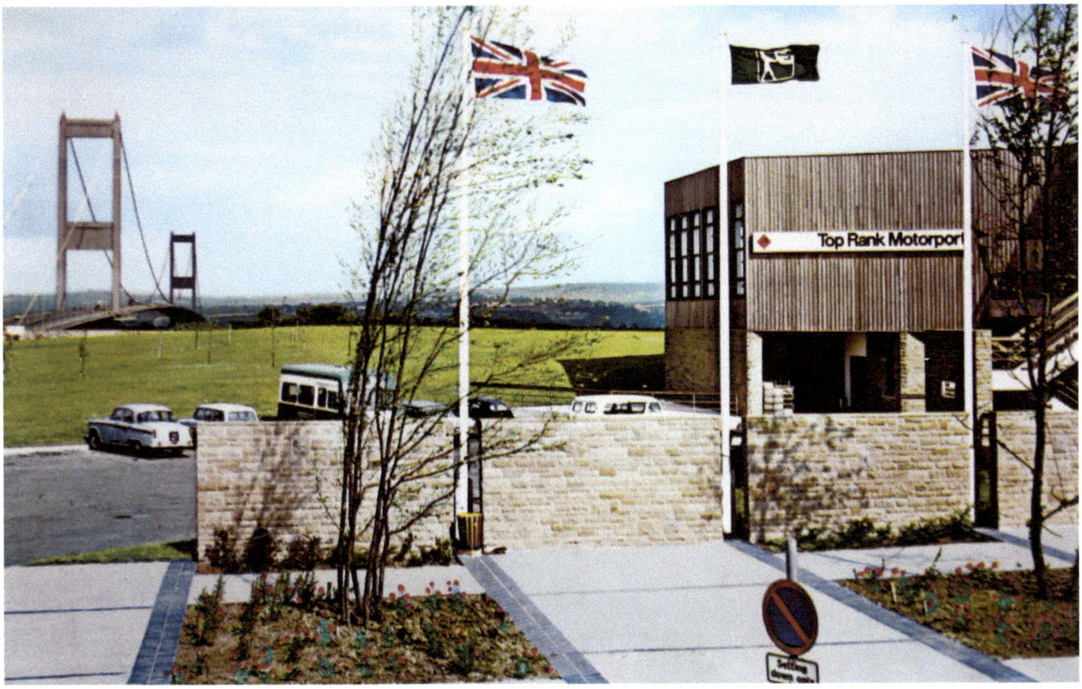

Severn Services

When the first Severn Suspension Road Bridge opened in 1966, Top Rank opened a motorway service station on the clifftop at Aust. It enjoyed an enviable location, which was once a stopping point for those taking in the sight. The Top Rank suite (top photograph) provided magnificent views and an equally magnificent restaurant, which served freshly caught Severn salmon. The novelty of motorway service stations has long faded away and so has the Top Rank suite which is now a large office block.

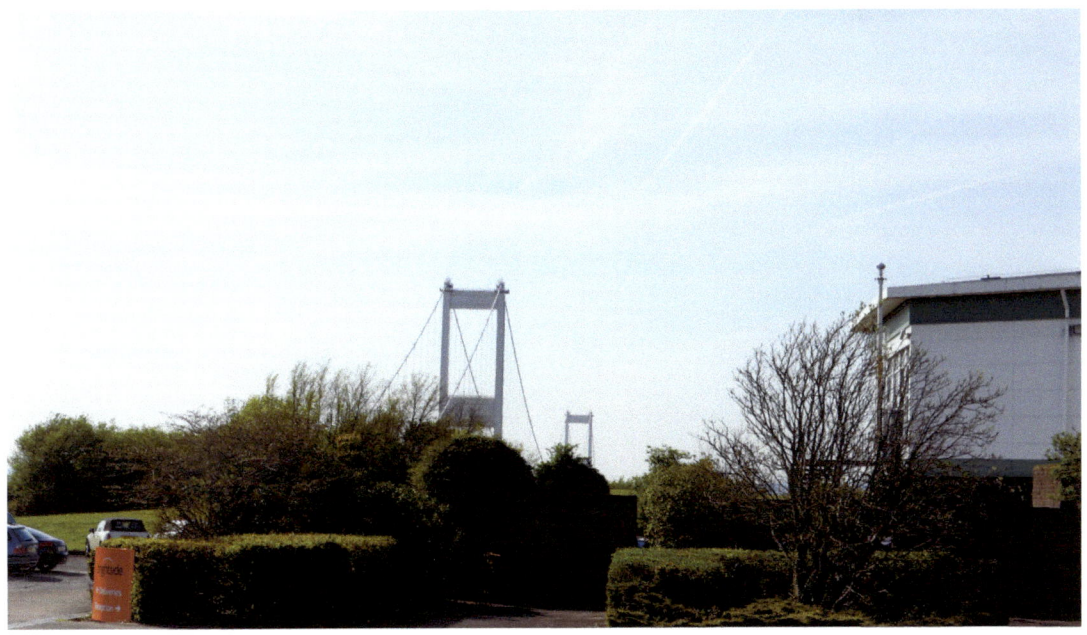

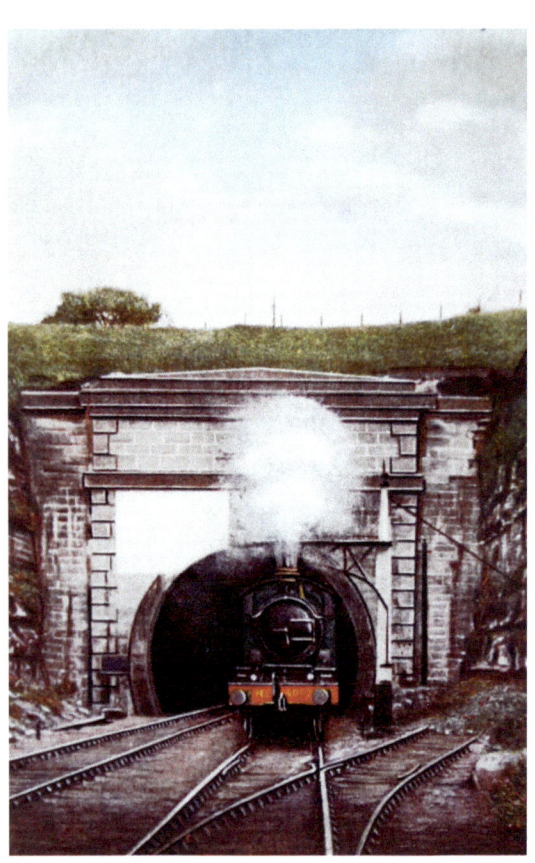

The Severn Railway Tunnel

The top photograph is a pre-1933 postcard showing a GWR express train emerging from the Welsh side of the Severn Tunnel headed by GWR steam locomotive No. 4002 *Evening Star* (1907–33). The same scene is captured in the lower photograph, but on Thursday 5 May 2016, with the Great Western Railway 10.45 a.m. HS 125 London Paddington–Swansea express. Built by the GWR between 1873 and 1886, it takes a train approximately three minutes and forty seconds to travel through the 4.5-mile-long Severn Tunnel, which for over 100 years was the longest main-line tunnel in Britain.

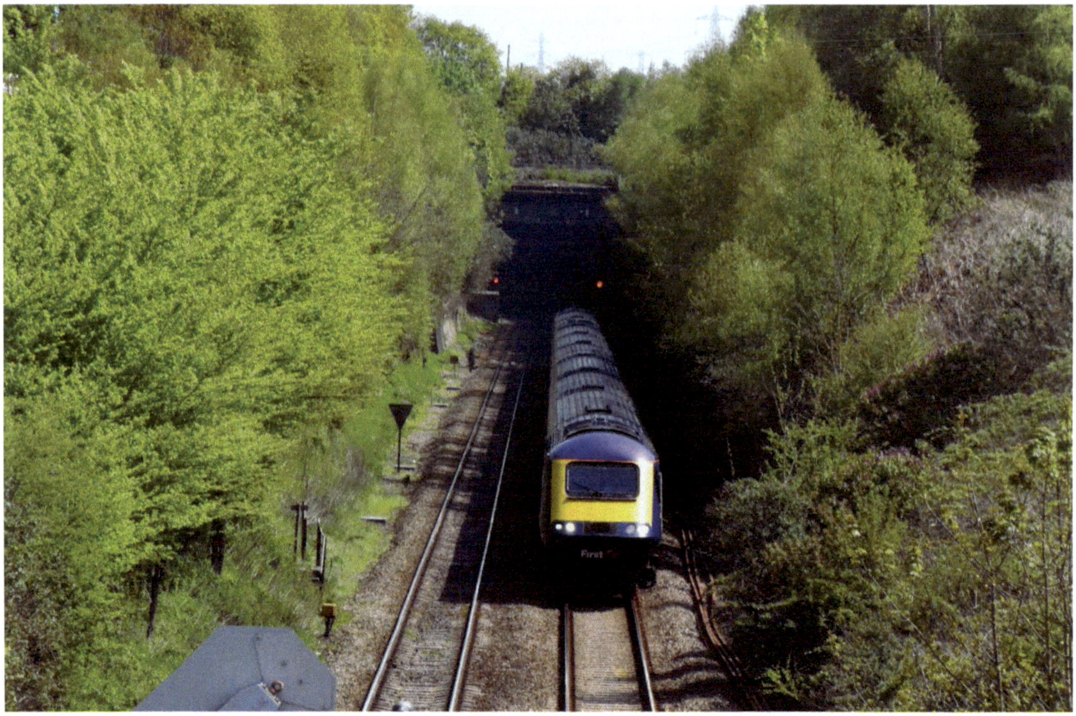

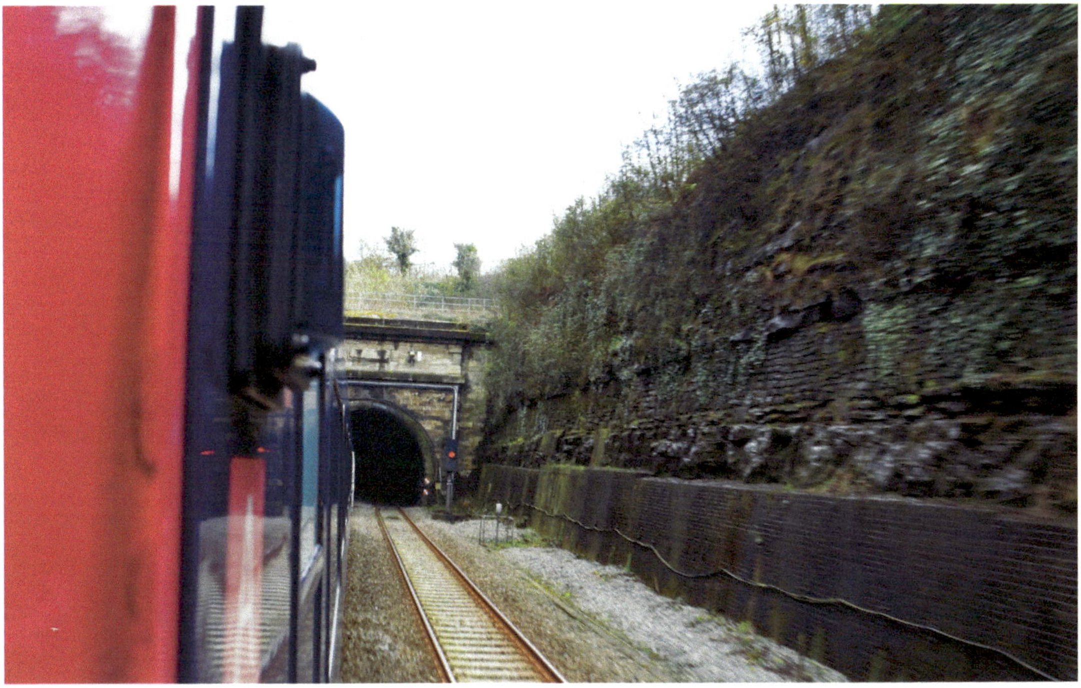

The Severn Railway Tunnel

The top photograph was taken on 12 March 2016 on the GWR 9.28 a.m. of the HS 125 Swansea to Paddington express as it prepared to disappear into the blackness of the Severn Tunnel. The bottom picture is of the Sudbrook Pumping Station, which has to cope with pumping 14 million gallons of water out of the Severn Tunnel every day. The tunnel will be the 'first' to use a new customised electrified roof track as part of the ongoing electrification of the South Wales main line, due to be completed in September 2016.

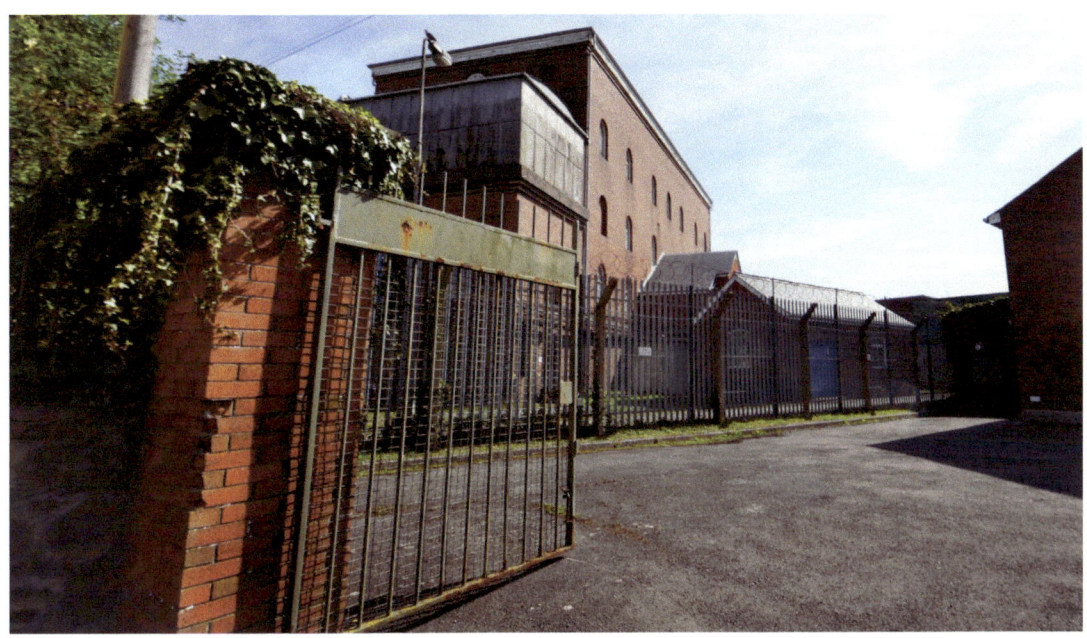

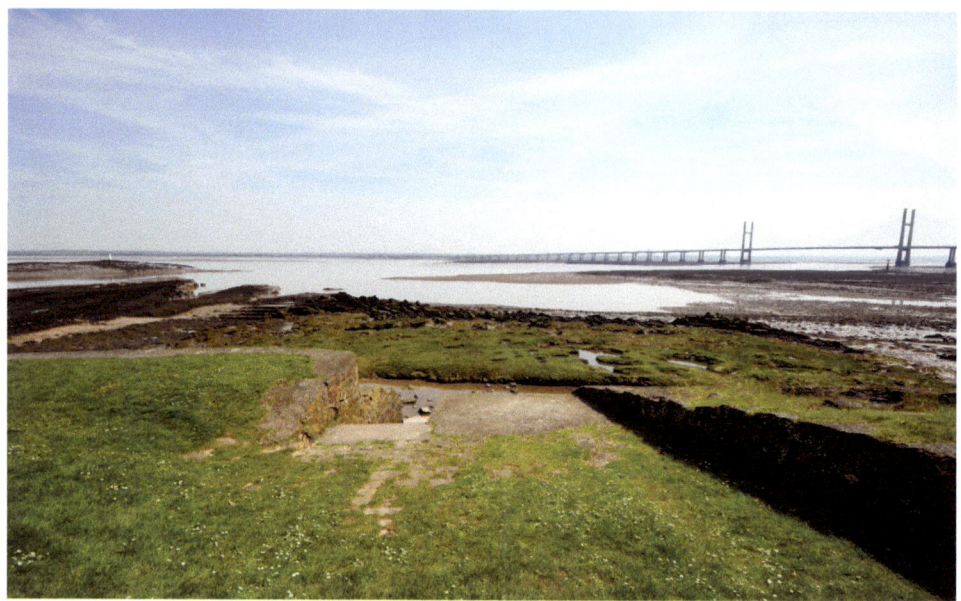

The New Passage

The idyllic scene captured in the top photograph was taken from the old ferry and rail terminal at Black Rock looking across the Severn to New Passage. The lower map shows the narrow estuary at this point – New Passage has, since Roman times, long been the location for a ferry crossing. By the end of the seventeenth century, ferry crossings between Black Rock and New Passage rivalled the Beachley–Aust ferry 2 miles (3 km) upstream known as the 'Old Passage'. The New Passage ferry became redundant when the Severn Tunnel opened in 1886 virtually 'under its feet'.

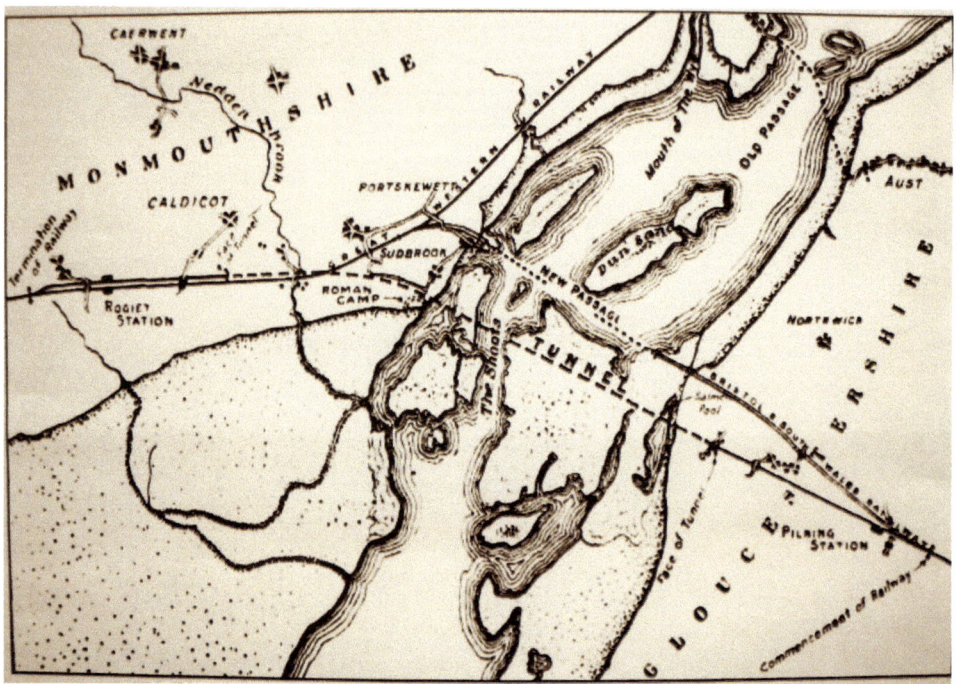

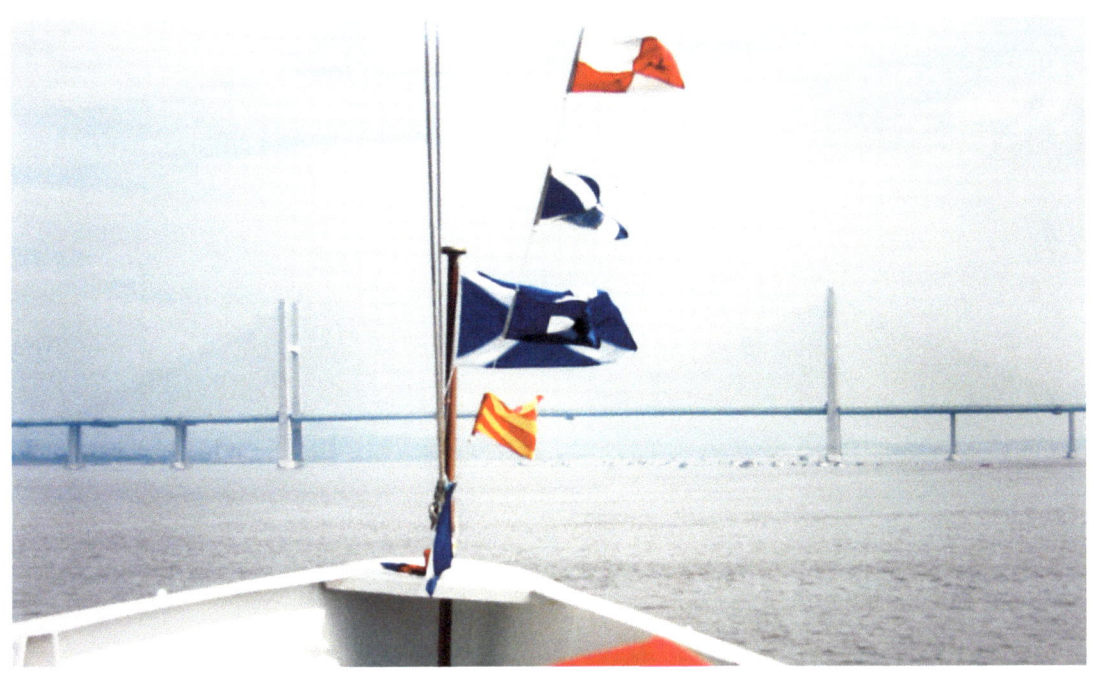

The Second Severn Suspension Bridge
The two photographs on this page were taken from the deck of the MV *Balmoral* as it sailed up the River Severn towards the second Severn Suspension Bridge as part of the opening celebrations on 5 June 1996. The inset image highlights the fly-past by the RAF to mark the occasion. The bridge, the longest in the UK, was completed virtually along the same line as the Severn Tunnel and carries M4 motorway traffic.

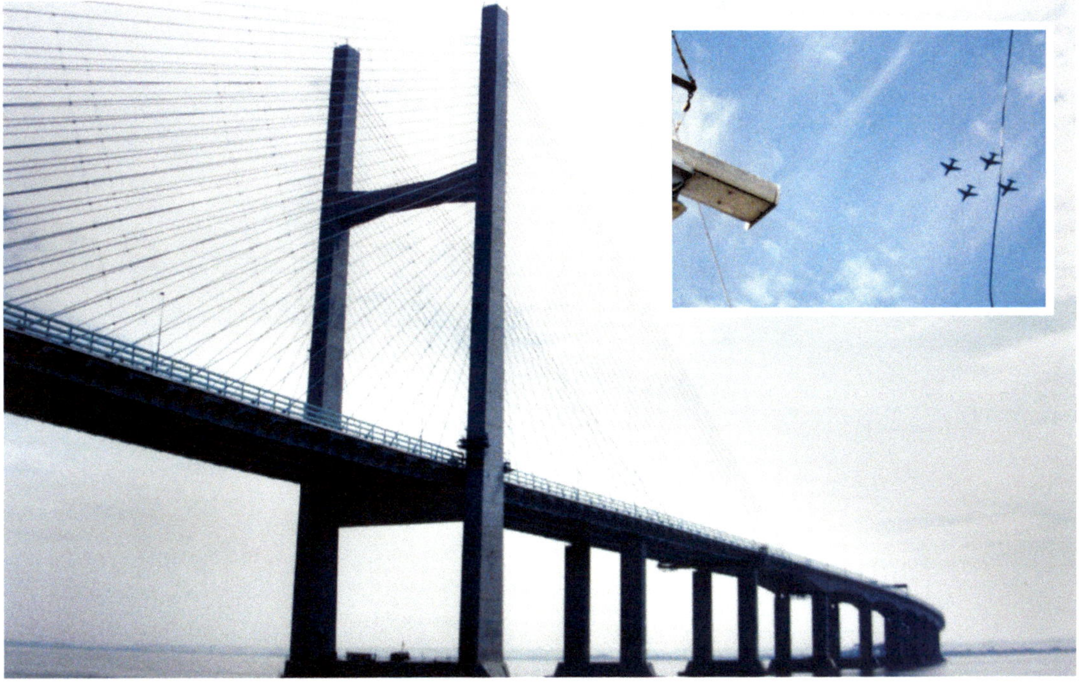

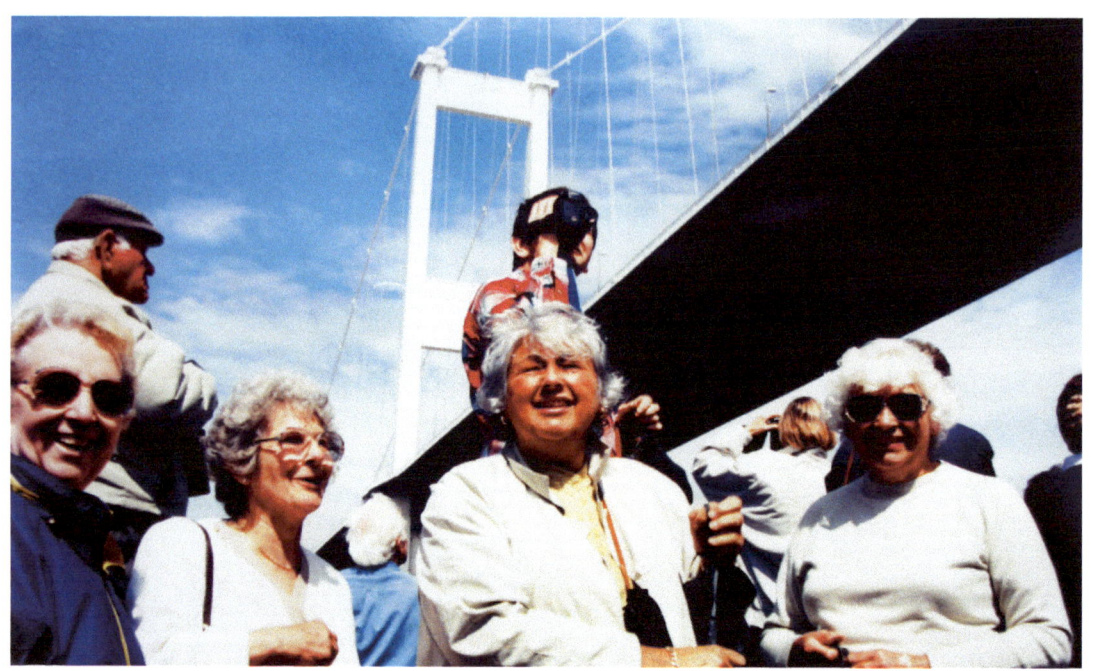

The Second Severn Suspension Bridge
On board the MV *Balmoral* on the right of the top picture, sisters Jacqueline and Malvina wait expectantly for a wave from HRH Prince Charles on the new bridge above, while in the lower photograph *Balmoral*'s sister ship, the paddle steamer *Waverley*, steams gracefully under the central span of the new Severn Bridge. The MV *Balmoral* had sailed from Porthcawl harbour early in the morning to arrive at the bridge for the opening ceremony.

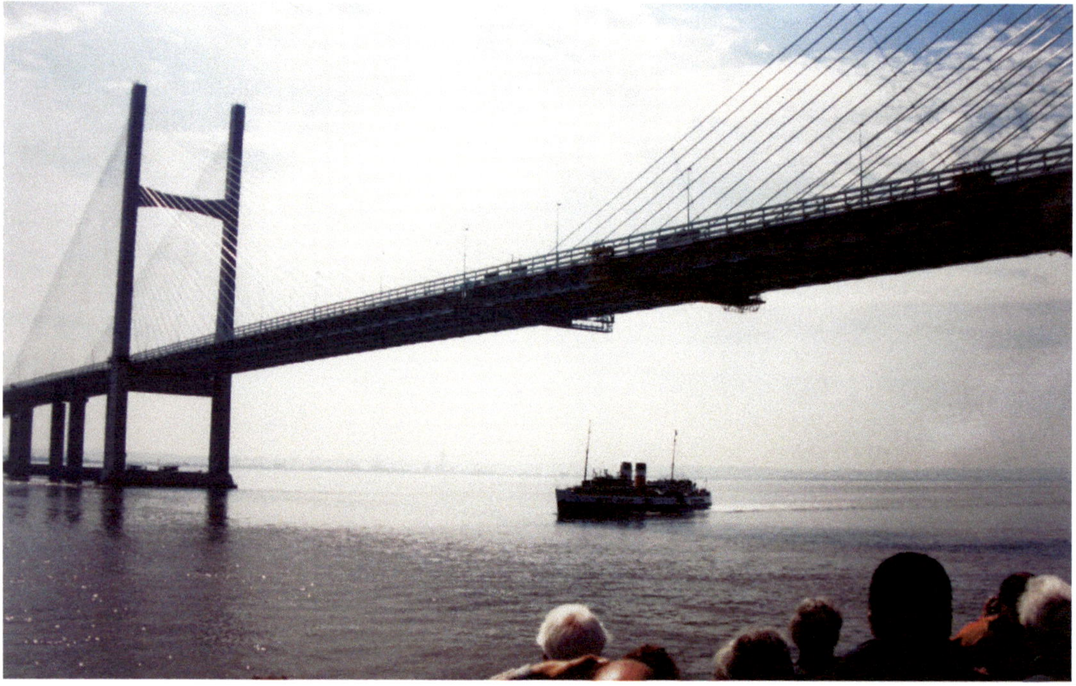

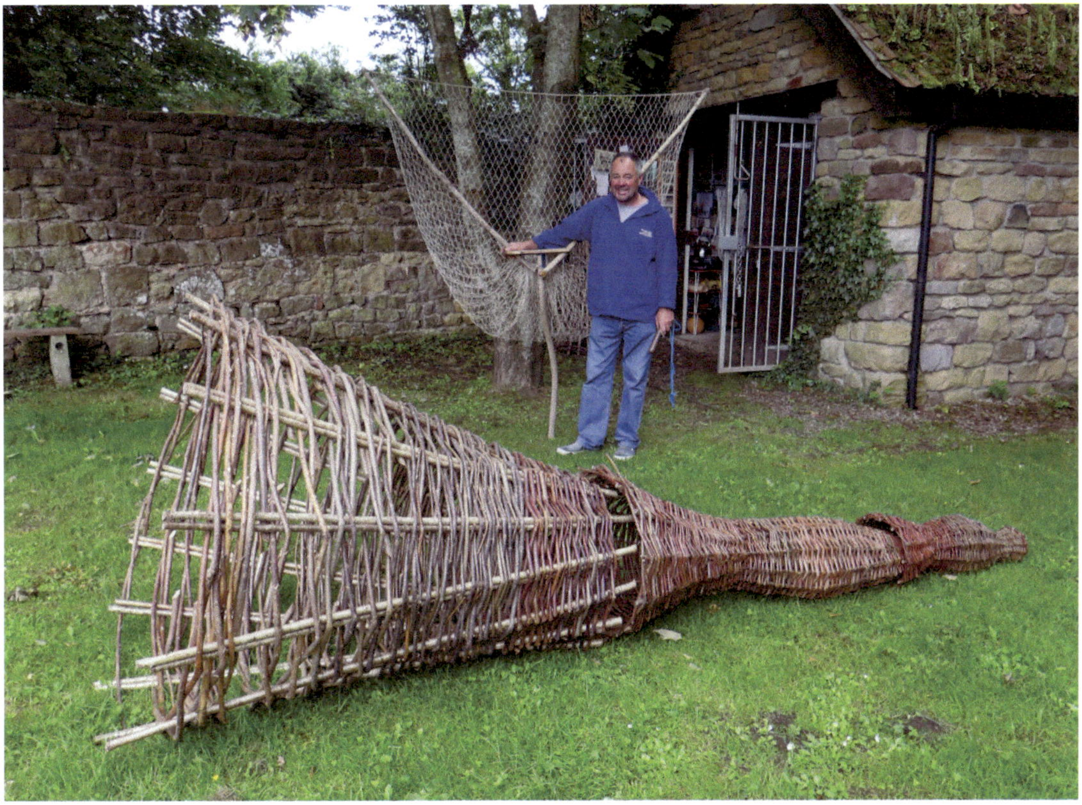

Lave Net Fishing

In these two photographs, Martin Morgan of the Black Rock Lave Net Fishermen Association is demonstrating a traditional method of salmon fishing on the River Severn at Black Rock. The net Martin is holding is called a lave net, whilst the basket at his feet is called a 'putcher' and belongs to another traditional form of salmon fishing. The triangular net is supported by a vertical ash rock/hand staff with two arms of willow called rims (or reams), which support and hold the net using a horizontal headline and are all connected together by a pine yoke/headboard.

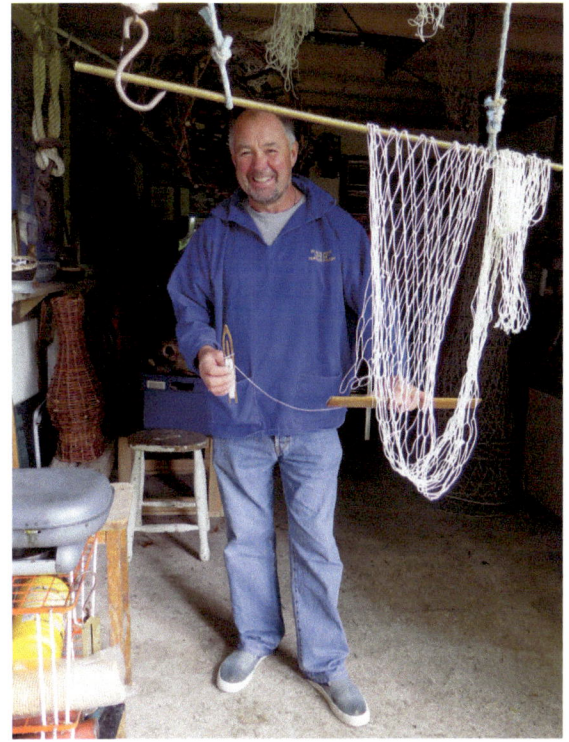

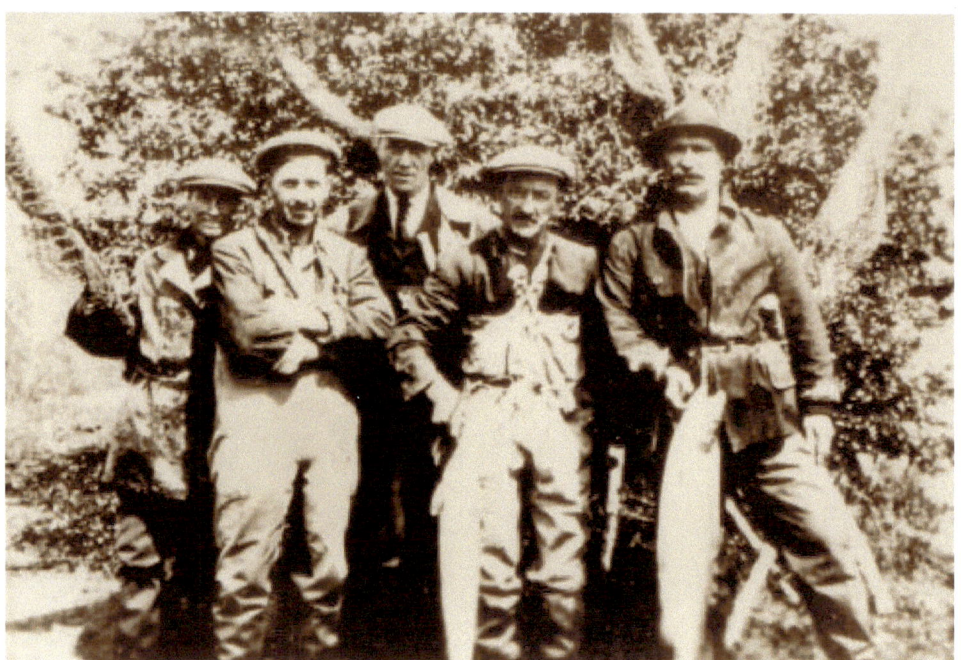

Lave Net Fishing

Captured in the top photograph are Black Rock Lave Net fishermen with their catch of salmon in 1920. The lower picture is of the present members of the Black Rock Lave Net Fishermen Association outside their headquarters building at Black Rock preparing to go fishing in June 2016. Note the way the lave nets can be folded for carrying and moving to different locations when fishing and the way that they can be supported to stand upright and rest upon.

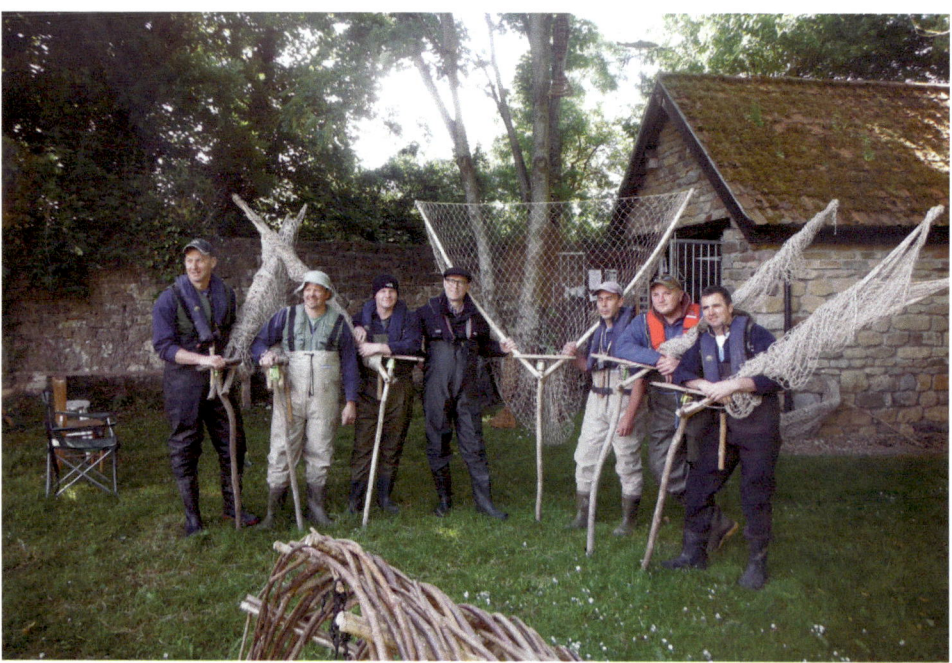

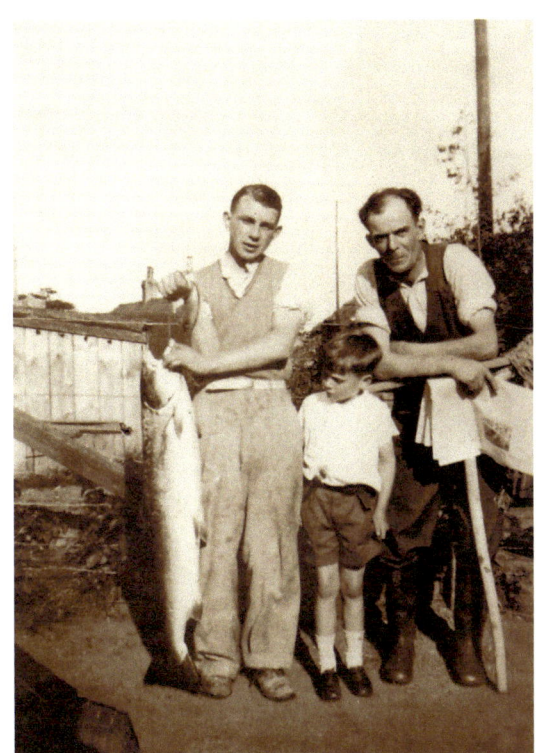

Lave Net Fishing
The top picture is of Doug Brown showing off his catch of salmon to a youngster in 1930. An equally proud lave net fisherman is doing the same to two appreciative children during the 2010 season.

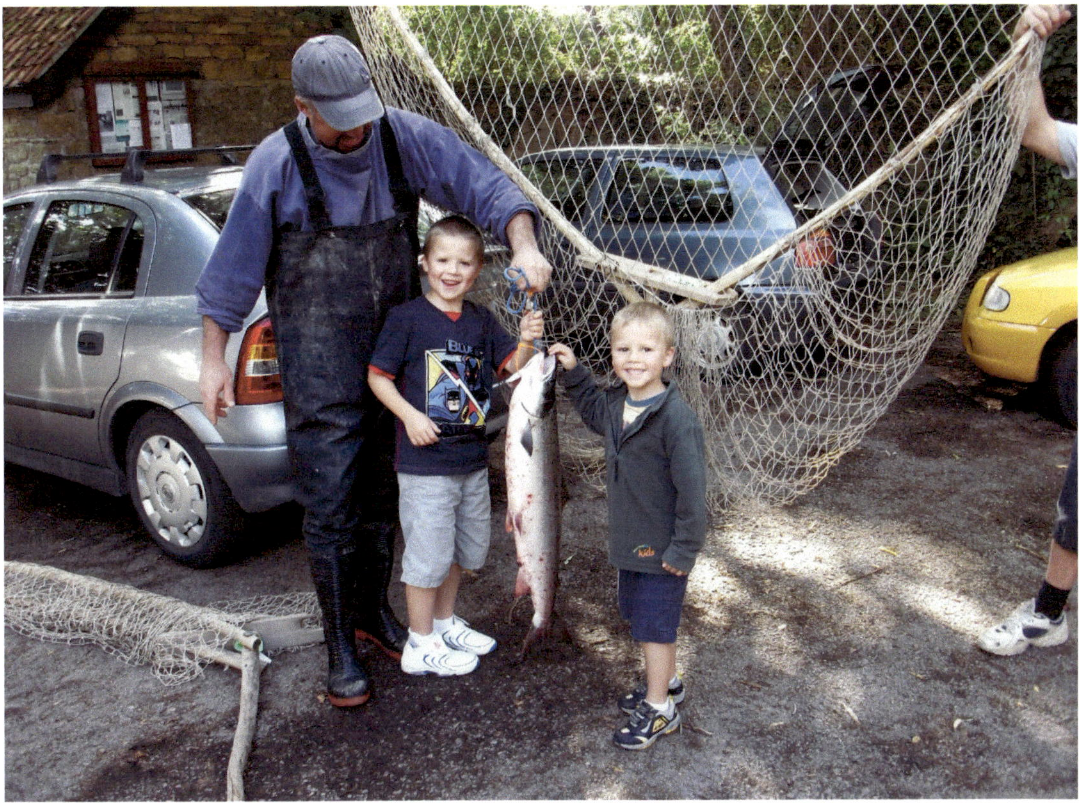

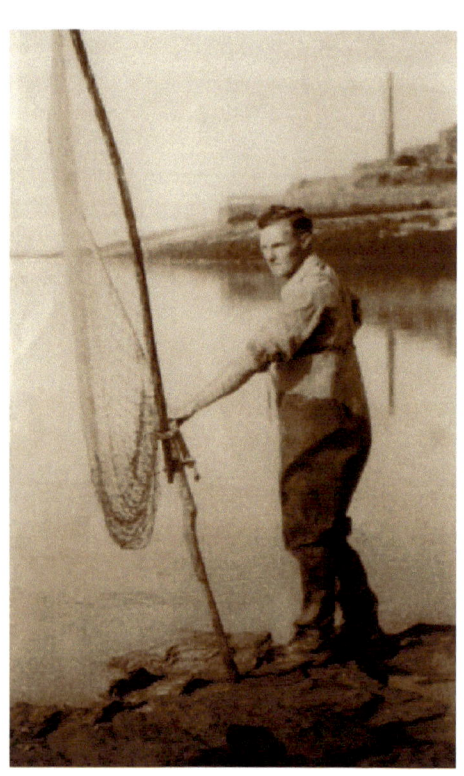

Lave Net Fishing

In the top photograph from 1940, Ron Evans demonstrates how the lave net, completely made out of natural local wood, can be stood upright on its rock/hand staff whilst selecting an area for fishing. In the lower photograph, Martin Morgan is ready to fish in 'The Gut' and is preparing his lave net for that purpose. The lave net fishing season lasts from 1 June to 31 August. During this period, only five salmon per month over three months are allowed. The fishing grounds are only accessible during low water spring tides, which occur every other week for a maximum of two hours.

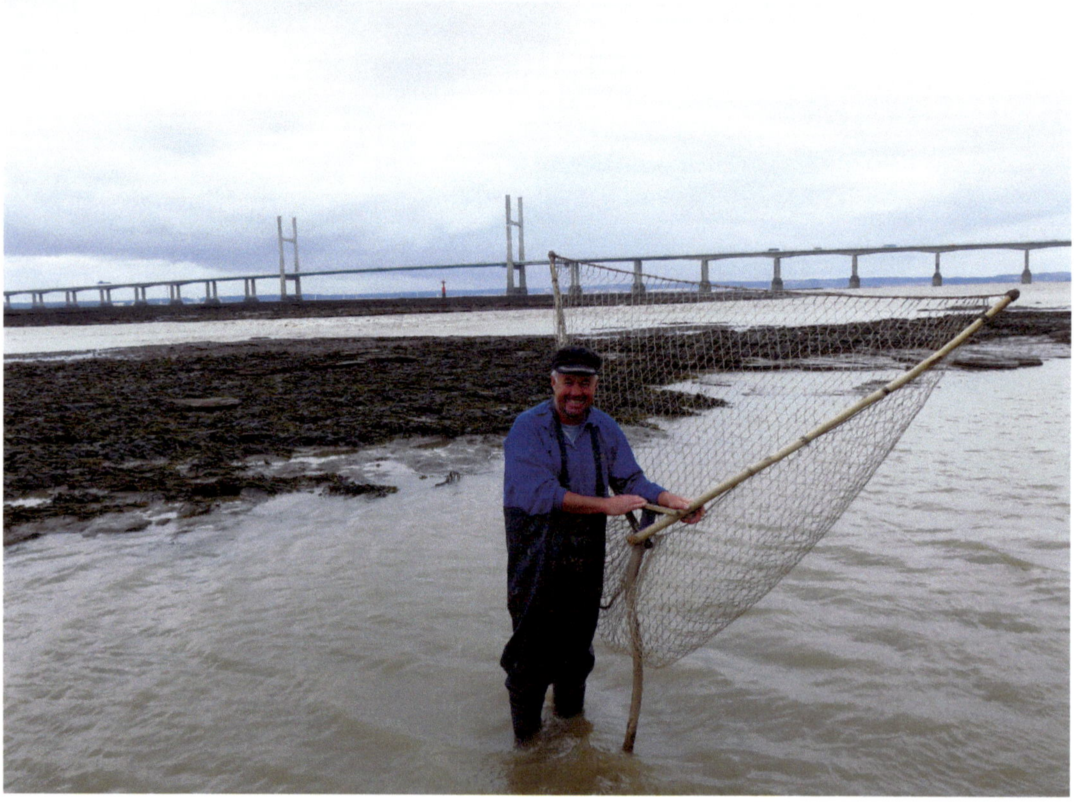

Lave Net Fishing

Billow Thomas is shown in the top picture with his record 1958 salmon catch, while the serenity and peace of a lave net fisherman plying his trade at sunset has been captured in the bottom photograph. All of the fishing grounds are near to the Welsh side of the Second Severn Bridge and each has a unique name such as 'The Gut', 'Grandstand', 'The Hole', 'Gruggy', 'Nester's Rock', 'The Marl', 'Lighthouse Vear' and 'The Lubey'.

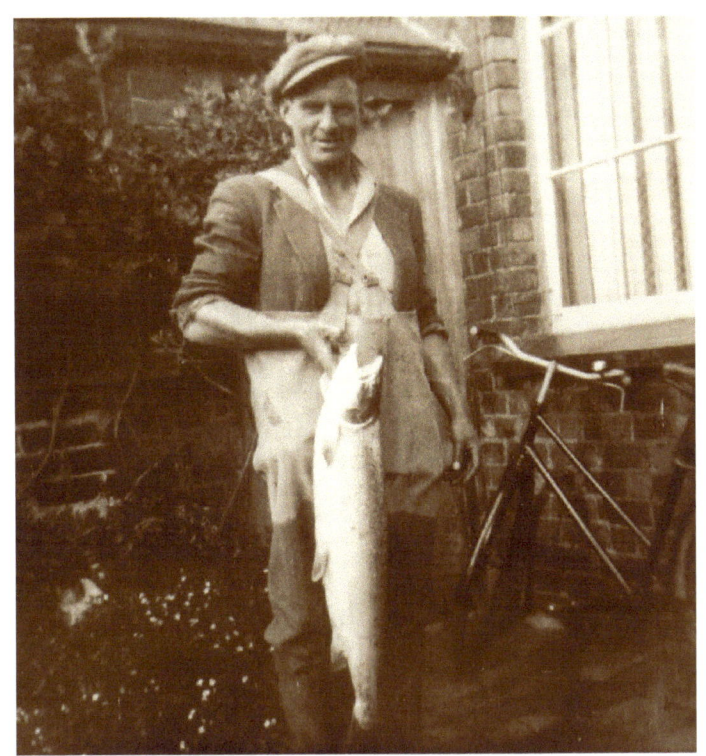

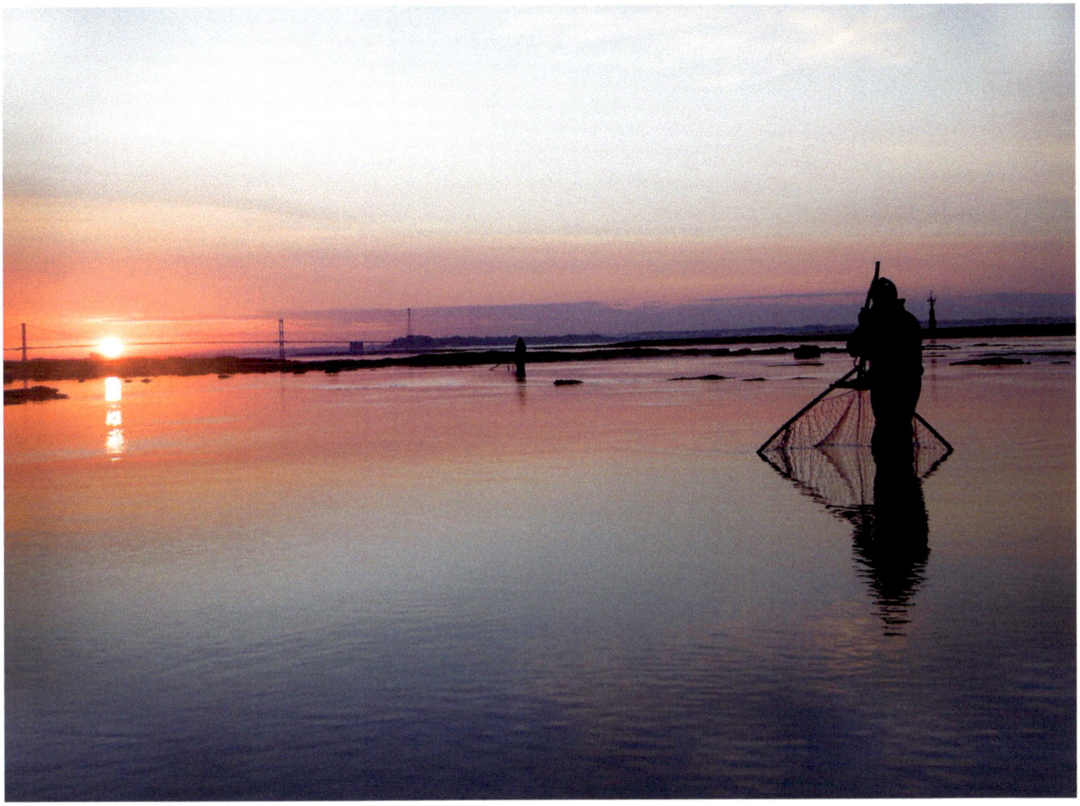

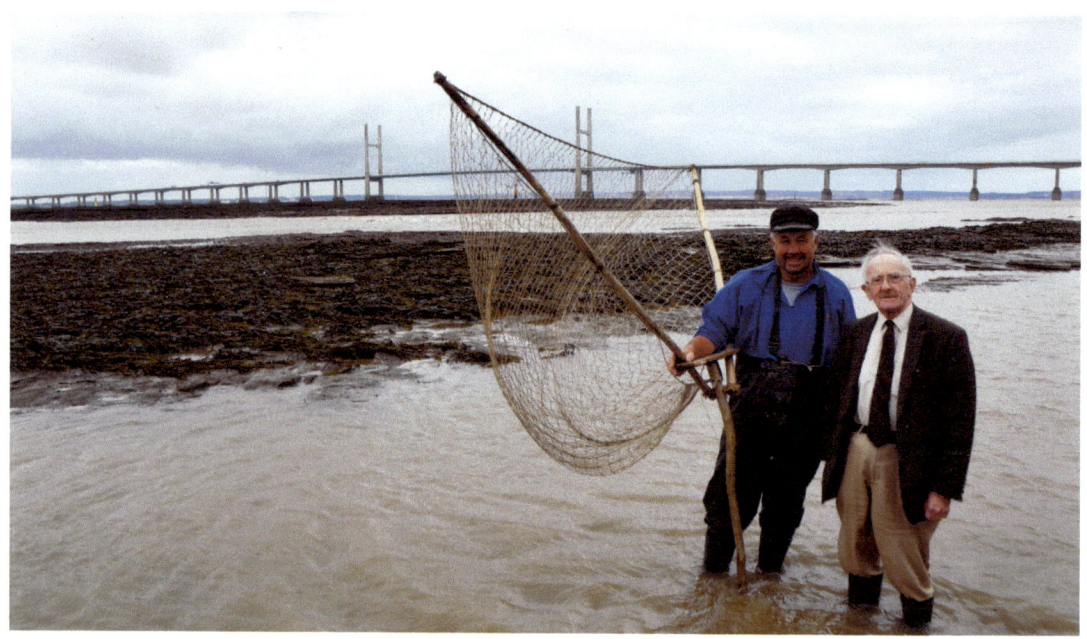

Lave Net Fishing
Some people will do anything to get their picture in a book. This photograph shows the author with lave net fisherman Martin Morgan in 'The Gut' fishing ground of the River Severn at low tide, having gone through knee-deep mud to get to the water.

Acknowledgements

In compiling this book, I am grateful for all the assistance and support that I have been given by the following organisations and individuals, for which I offer my sincere thanks and gratitude.

Andrew Leitch Esq., project manager and cultural consultant, Mabey Bridges Ltd; Linda Hunt, landlady, Old Ferry Boat Inn; Mervyn P. Fleming Esq., SARA Commander Area West; photographer Patrick Hogan; Martin Morgan and Rob Evans of the Black Rock Lave Net Fishermen Association; staff of the Dell Primary School, Chepstow; CADW Custodians of Chepstow Castle; and Richard Dutson, Wye boatman, whom I had the privilege of interviewing from the Wye Bridge while he casually paddled his way downstream.

Please accept my apologies if I have inadvertently missed anyone from the above list.

Reference has been made to the works of William Coxe, *An Historical Tour in Monmouthshire Illustrated with Views by Sir R. C. Hoare Bart; A New Map of the County and Other Engravings* (1801) and Mr and Mrs S. C. Hall's *The Book of South Wales: The Wye and the Coast* (1861).